Hooded Knights on the Niagara

HOODED KNIGHTS ON THE NIAGARA

The Ku Klux Klan in Buffalo, New York

Shawn Lay

NEW YORK UNIVERSITY PRESS
New York and London

NEW YORK UNIVERSITY PRESS
New York and London

Library of Congress Cataloging-in-Publication Data
Lay, Shawn
Hooded knights on the Niagara : the Ku Klux Klan in Buffalo, New
York / Shawn Lay.
p.   cm.
Includes bibliographical references (p.   ) and index.
ISBN 0-8147-5101-6 (cloth); ISBN 0-8147-5102-4 (pbk.)
1. Ku Klux Klan (1915-   )—New York (State)—Buffalo—History.
I. Title.
HS2330.K63L33   1995
322.4'2'0974797—dc20   95-4285
                                        CIP

New York University Press books are printed on acid-free paper,
and their binding materials are chosen for strength and durability.

Manufactured in the United States of America

10   9   8   7   6   5   4   3   2   1

For Ginnie Lay and Thorne Lay

Contents

Tables

Figures

Acknowledgments

Many people have assisted me in the research and writing of this book. My largest scholarly debt is owed to Dewey W. Grantham, of Vanderbilt University, who guided the study through its dissertation stage; without Professor Grantham's steadfast support and wise counsel, all would have been lost long ago. The dissertation's second reader, Samuel T. McSeveney, also provided invaluable help at critical junctures, challenging me to hone both my prose and the quality of my analysis. Through the years I have additionally benefited from the advice, support, and professional example of Lewis C. Perry, Jimmie L. Franklin, Daniel B. Cornfield, Don H. Doyle, Jonathan Dewald, David A. Gerber, Robert G. Pope, and Kenneth K. Bailey.

Others have rendered crucial assistance. The archival staffs of the Buffalo and Erie County Historical Society, the State University of New York at Buffalo, and the Roman Catholic Diocese of Buffalo fulfilled all my requests for materials in a cheerful and professional manner. Several Buffalonians consented to personal interviews, helping me fill in major gaps in the book's narrative; I am particularly grateful for the cooperation of Francis X. Schwab IV and Cathy Desmond Hughes, whose families played a prominent role in fighting the Klan. Special thanks are likewise due to my research assistants, Lynn Brunner, Alan Nothnagle, and Isabella Mark, and to the eighteen senior history majors who helped conduct a telephone survey to determine the religious affiliation of Buffalo Klansmen.

As always, the love and support of my family have sustained me through the years of research and writing. I would like to express my deepest appreciation to my wife, Imelda; my four children, Alexander, Lawrence, James, and Katerina; my sister-in-law Susan; and my nephew Griffin. I am also exceedingly grateful for the help and encouragement of my mother and brother, two extraordinarily gifted and generous people. To both of them, this volume is dedicated.

Hooded Knights on the Niagara

Introduction

They came in the dead of night, marking the homes and businesses of their enemies with crude symbols and dire warnings. They plotted against those of other religious faiths and circulated secret lists of alleged "traitors" to the nation and community. They mailed anonymous threats to local residents who refused to be intimidated into silence, all the while claiming that they were the true champions of American justice and freedom. They were strongly implicated in the bombing of a private residence; an undercover operative in their employ killed one man and seriously wounded another. Indeed, by the late summer of 1924, their activities had brought the city of Buffalo to the brink of open religious warfare, a local newspaper editor lamenting that "In a community where people have lived peaceably and harmoniously for many decades, worshipping as they have seen fit and with the highest respect for one another's beliefs and convictions, this issue of religion is hauled into the political arena by persons with no more principles than a 'snake has hips,' with bigotry and dissension taking the place of peace and goodwill."[1]

These unsettling and dangerous developments in Buffalo resulted from the recent arrival of a racist and religiously exclusive secret society—the Knights of the Ku Klux Klan. Arguably the

1

largest and most influential manifestation of organized intolerance in United States history, the second Klan pursued a program
that often promoted hatred, fear, and divisiveness; in many American communities, citizens lived in complete dread of the organization. In the case of Buffalo, however, it is intriguing, and significant, that the activities alluded to above were engaged in not
by Klansmen but by the hooded order's local opponents; in fact,
the newspaper editor who desperately invoked "respect for one
another's beliefs and convictions" was an active member of the
KKK. While the Klan may have proceeded with relative impunity
in certain other locales, it clearly encountered a very different
situation in Buffalo, where opponents enjoyed access to government power and refused to countenance the Klan as a legitimate
force in civic affairs. In New York's second largest city, the knights
of the Invisible Empire soon discovered the powerful constraints
that limited Klan growth and influence in the urban Northeast.

At the time of its founding in Georgia in 1915, it appeared highly
unlikely that the second Klan would ever develop a following in
places as far away as Buffalo. Headed by "Imperial Wizard" William J. Simmons, an impractical and chronically inebriated former Methodist circuit rider, the organization posed as the reincar-
nation of the Ku Klux Klan of Reconstruction but offered recruits
little beyond mystic fraternalism and group-rate insurance. Although the KKK's advocacy of white supremacy, Protestant solidarity, and strict law enforcement seemed to offer the basis for
some type of social or political action, Imperial Wizard Simmons's lack of direction and obsession with arcane ritualism hindered the development of an effective program. During its first
years, the Klan was just one of many bizarre men's societies in the
United States, a small and obscure fraternal group that lacked
any meaningful degree of social relevance.[2]

All of this suddenly changed in 1920, when Simmons, in a
desperate attempt to breathe new life into the Klan, acquired the
services of the Southern Publicity Association. The owners of this
small advertising firm, Edward Young Clarke and Elizabeth Tyler,
recognized that the hapless Imperial Wizard had barely begun to
exploit the Klan's potential, and they took decisive measures to

improve the order's finances and solicitation procedures. Clarke and Tyler's most important innovation was the hiring of hundreds of KKK recruiters (kleagles) who worked on a commission basis. This application of modern sales techniques reaped almost instant rewards, as throughout the South thousands of new members entered the fold in 1920 and 1921.[3]

Much of the kleagles' success was the result of the adaptable manner in which they approached potential recruits. Although hostile journalists routinely characterized KKK representatives as unscrupulous "salesmen of hate" who exploited the unusually virulent strains of racism, bigotry, and nativism that prevailed after World War I, a variety of other appeals was also utilized. Depending on whom they were soliciting, Klan recruiters might stress the "character building" aspects of membership, the KKK's rich fraternal life, the opportunity for business contacts, or the group's potential for improving community conditions—any type of sales pitch that might secure a commission. The hooded order's practice of absolute secrecy also assisted expansion, many men joining simply out of curiosity or because they did not want to be left out of what appeared to be an up-and-coming organization. An individual's decision to join the Invisible Empire, therefore, could not always be solely credited to racial and religious intolerance.[4]

By mid-1921 the Klan's multifaceted appeal had resulted in the establishment of scores of local chapters (klaverns) across the South, and Imperial officials had begun dispatching recruiters to other parts of the country. In many locales the hooded order succeeded in attracting prominent and influential citizens; the charter members of the klavern in Houston, Texas, for example, "represented literally a glossary of Houston's *who's who*," including "silk-stocking men from the banks, business houses, and professions."[5] In other communities, such as the west Texas city of El Paso, the Klan failed to acquire the support of local elites yet remained largely peaceable and law-abiding. Other chapters, however, soon demonstrated the profound danger posed by the existence of an unregulated secret society whose group image was strongly linked to a tradition of extralegal vigilantism. Throughout 1921 hundreds of Klansmen—almost all of them residents of the South—participated in appalling acts of violence, using guns, whips, and a variety of other weapons to terrorize African Americans and white opponents in certain communities.[6]

The violence accompanying Klan expansion naturally alarmed law-abiding citizens and soon attracted the attention of the national press. Prominent publications such as *Literary Digest*, the *Nation, Outlook*, and *Independent* detailed Klan outrages, and William Randolph Hearst's newspaper chain presented a sensational exposé in the late summer of 1921. By far the most influential assessment of the KKK was that prepared by the Pulitzer-owned *New York World*. Widely syndicated and presented in installments over a three-week period in September, the *World's* investigation characterized the Klan as an inherently lawless and violent movement that exploited the fears of gullible Americans. Because the Invisible Empire's "evil and vicious possibilities" were "boundless," the paper demanded that Congress move quickly to suppress the organization.[7]

Federal action was not long in coming. For one week beginning on October 11, 1921, the House Rules Committee conducted public hearings to determine if there was a need for anti-Klan legislation, focusing upon charges that the KKK was violent and financially corrupt. Despite the repeated efforts of committee members to impugn the Klan, surprisingly little solid evidence came to light. The highlight of the hearings was the extended personal testimony of Imperial Wizard Simmons, who stressed his order's lofty intentions and fraternal orientation; the recent outbreak of violence, he claimed, was the work of impostors with no link to the Klan. Simmons concluded his appearance with a theatrical flourish, avowing that the congressmen were as "ignorant of our principles as were those who were ignorant of the character and work of Christ," then collapsing from his chair onto the floor.[8]

The national attention directed toward the Klan in the late summer and fall of 1921, rather than discrediting the hooded order, greatly assisted expansion. The threat of federal anti-Klan legislation evaporated, and millions of Americans learned about the order for the first time. Ever hungry for new recruits and klectokens (initiation fees), Imperial officials wasted little time in exploiting this abundance of free publicity, ordering kleagles to intensify their efforts across the nation. The response was remarkable: within a matter of months, dozens of thriving klaverns had been established in California and the Pacific Northwest, Colorado was well on its way to becoming a Klan stronghold, and tens of thousands were donning hoods and robes in the Midwest; even in New York and New England the Invisible Empire seemed to be making considerable gains.[9]

Several important factors assisted the Klan's growth outside of the South. First, and most importantly, the KKK's claim that the values of native-born white Protestants should predominate in the United States found a ready audience from Maine to California. Strong strains of racism, nativism, anti-Catholicism, and anti-Semitism had longed influenced American national life, and they were particularly influential during the early 1920s, a time of growing concern over race relations, the impact of foreign immigration, and the influence of religion in politics. The Klan also benefitted from the romantic image of the original KKK that had been planted in the public's mind by David Wark Griffith's immensely popular film, *The Birth of a Nation*. Shown repeatedly across the country after its premiere in 1915, Griffith's epic portrayed the first Klan as a manifestly noble group that had saved white civilization during a dangerous period.[10] Now, non-Southerners (if they were willing to pay the Invisible Empire's ten-dollar initiation fee) could for the first time personally partake of the mystery and excitement of the Klan movement.

The appeal of the second Klan, however, extended beyond its militant ethnocentrism and its manipulation of romantic imagery. By 1922 it was clear that the Invisible Empire intended to involve itself in political affairs, and many citizens joined with the hope that the Klan could address specific problems in their communities. Recognizing this, Imperial Wizard Hiram W. Evans (who replaced William J. Simmons in 1922) advised Klan leaders not to "put into effect any set program, for there are different needs in the various localities. Your program must embrace the needs of the people it must serve."[11] As a result, the Klan in many communities evolved into a medium of corrective civic action that spent more time addressing local issues such as public education and zoning laws than it did in advancing the KKK's warped ideology.

Indeed, almost all major case studies of the second Klan outside of the South have discovered that the secret order, sans its hoods and mysterious rituals, bore a remarkable resemblance to other locally oriented political and social movements in American history.[12]

Sustained by its grass-roots popularity, the Invisible Empire became a major force in the nation's political life during the period 1922–1924. The state governments of Oregon, Colorado, and Indiana fell under the control of the Klan for a period, and in many other parts of the country the hooded order scored major victories in municipal elections. By 1924 the perceived power of the Klan was such that neither of the major political parties was willing formally to denounce the organization; it appeared very likely, in fact, that the Klan would be a fixture on the electoral landscape for years to come.[13] At this very moment of triumph, however, the Invisible Empire entered a period of steep decline that would eventually render it powerless. The causes of this collapse are still not fully clear, but the fading of the group's romantic image, internecine feuding, scandals involving high-ranking Klan officials, and increased activism by the order's opponents all seem to have played a role. The KKK may also have been a victim of its own success: having effectively served notice to established leaders that millions of white Protestants were dissatisfied with the course of public affairs, the organization had possibly fulfilled its chief purpose; thus, like other forms of organized mass protest that have emerged from time to time, it had little reason to continue and simply faded away.[14]

Considering that the second Klan recruited from three to six million Americans and profoundly influenced the nation's political and social life for a period, one might assume that the hooded order would have immediately been the subject of intensive scholarly investigation. Yet, with the exception of a few tracts prepared by sociologists in the 1920s and one historical case study presented in 1936, the KKK for decades evaded serious scrutiny. One major reason for this was that the organization left behind very few records, but probably even more important was the general conviction among scholars that the nature and appeal of the Klan movement did not merit further investigation. Clearly, a hate-mongering organization such as the KKK could only thrive among fanatics and low-status individuals, particularly those residing in the declining villages and small towns of rural America.[15] This was not an assessment that need to be documented or verified; it was self-evident to any reasonable and enlightened member of the academy.

Over the past thirty years, historians have finally begun to assay this traditional view of the Klan and have found it sorely lacking. Major regional and national studies produced in the 1960s revealed that the KKK was as popular in urban areas as in the rural hinterland and that Klansmen were motivated by a complex variety of concerns, not just racial and religious hatred.[16] In more recent years a growing collection of case studies has employed the techniques of the new social history to further revise traditional thinking about the Klan, arguing that the secret order drew its membership from a broad cross section of the white male Protestant population and generally functioned in the manner of a typical civic action group. This recent body of work suggests that the KKK was much more of a mainstream organization than was once believed and that Klansmen, although assuredly racist and bigoted, were average citizens in the context of the times; indeed, a major theme of this new scholarship is that the intolerance that characterized the KKK pervaded all levels of white American society during the 1920s.[17]

Work produced by Klan revisionists over the past fifteen years has focused upon communities across the nation, with scholars examining some twenty klaverns in California, Oregon, Utah, Colorado, Texas, Indiana, Ohio, and Georgia. Yet the Klan experiences of communities in an important part of the country, the urban Northeast, have remained completely unassessed. This is unfortunate if only because of the large number of Klansmen in the region. In New York and Pennsylvania alone there were half a million members, with tens of thousands more in New Jersey and New England; a single rally on Long Island could attract a hooded throng of over eight thousand knights.[18] Who were these men? What combination of impulses, influences, and motivations had brought them into the Klan? Why, in this most cosmopolitan and culturally diverse section of the nation, did they embrace an organization that virtually ensured them the enmity of fellow residents?

As a first step toward redressing the shortage of work on the second Klan in the Northeast, this study will present a detailed examination of the experiences of the hooded order in the large industrial city of Buffalo, New York. The focus here, as in most other case studies of the KKK, shall be upon Klansmen themselves—the problems they confronted, their social characteristics, and the actions that they took; less emphasis shall be placed upon the national Klan's ideology and rhetoric, for these often proved to be poor indicators of what transpired at the local level. As is true of much recent social history, this study has been guided by the conviction that scholars are obligated to treat the people they write about with a certain degree of restraint and respect—even those with whom they vehemently disagree. Frankly, this has proven very difficult for this author, a devout Roman Catholic who is married to a woman of color and committed to a variety of progressive causes. The presentation of a prolonged and emotional denunciation of the Klan, however, would have been both self-indulgent and counterproductive. Although the flaunting of one's liberal sensibilities might be emotionally gratifying (as well as politically expedient), it will only be through careful research and neutral reasoning that the complex sources of racial and religious intolerance in American society will be adequately assessed.

While a commitment to scholarly objectivity is important, it means little if research materials are not available. Fortunately, this study has benefitted from an unusual abundance of primary sources on the Buffalo Klan, including a comprehensive membership list, undercover reports on the klavern's secret meetings, and a rare KKK business directory. In addition, newspaper reports of Klan-related developments have proved particularly valuable. Although all of Buffalo's six major papers covered aspects of the local Klan episode, the most extensive coverage was that of the *Buffalo Daily Courier*, which established contacts within the klavern shortly after the chapter's founding. Accordingly, the *Courier* has served as a core source for much of the basic narrative here, despite the paper's overt anti-Klan bias and intensely pro-Democratic orientation. In an attempt to mitigate any distortion that might result from this reliance, *Courier* reports have been checked against accounts appearing in the pro-Republican *Buffalo Morning Express*, which also, although in a less hostile fashion, displayed an abiding interest in the KKK; at certain points, material from other newspapers has also been extensively utilized.

This book has been composed in as straightforward a fashion as possible. Chapter 1 discusses the social and political factors that contributed to the rise of the KKK in Buffalo and chapter 2 describes the founding and early development of the klavern. Chapters 3 and 4 present an extended evaluation of the Buffalo Klan's activities and membership and chapter 5 analyzes the ruthless fashion in which the local chapter was destroyed. The conclusion evaluates the study's findings in the context of Klan historiography. The overall result, the author hopes, is a work that will advance scholarship, enlighten readers, and help ensure that what occurred in Buffalo during the first half of the 1920s never occurs again.

One

A Troubled Community

Buffalo, the self-proclaimed Queen City of the Great Lakes, entered the 1920s well-established as a major urban center. Scores of churches, a progressive public school system, three colleges, a university, a fine arts academy, museums, libraries, and concert halls attested to the city's rich spiritual, educational, and cultural life; dozens of charitable, social, and professional organizations and a municipal government that employed nearly eight thousand workers likewise indicated an advanced stage of urban development, as did the modern office buildings and hotels that dominated the downtown skyline.[1] The federal census for 1920 placed the local population at 506,775, certifying Buffalo as the eleventh largest municipality in the United States, and by 1925 the number had increased to just over 538,000. When the rapidly expanding populations of nearby communities (see figure 1) such as Lackawanna, Tonawanda, Lancaster, Cheektowaga, West Seneca, and Amherst are considered, the number of residents in the greater Buffalo area was approximately 580,000 at the beginning of the decade and more than 640,000 five years later. In few previous periods had future growth and prosperity seemed more assured, city planners confidently predicting that the metropolitan population would exceed two million by 1950.[2]

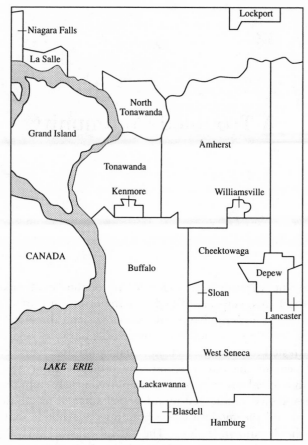

Figure 1
Buffalo and Nearby Communities circa 1920

This optimism rested in large part on a recent and remarkable upsurge in local industrial production. In 1919, the total value of manufactured goods produced in Buffalo was $634,409,733, an increase of 256 percent over the total for 1914. Benefitting from electrification, modernized facilities, and better management, almost all of the city's chief industries were achieving unprecedented output by 1920: within a five-year period, flour milling production had increased by 137 percent, meat packing 115 percent, foundry and machine products 184 percent, and automobile bodies and parts 414 percent; similarly impressive gains took place in the steel, chemical, furniture, and tanning industries and in many smaller sectors of the economy, with the result that the Commerce Department ranked Buffalo as the eighth largest manufacturing center in the country.[3]

Industry and manufacturing, conducted in a vast ring of factories and plants that circled within and just beyond the city limits, constituted the chief source of Buffalo's growth and prosperity, but other forms of economic activity were also important. The city was second only to Chicago as a commercial shipping center in the 1920s; over five hundred freight trains arrived and departed daily, and each year millions of tons of bulk commodities passed through the port. Local trade with Canada steadily increased throughout the decade, and the wholesale marketing of coal, lumber, machinery, food products, and automobiles experienced unprecedented expansion. Commercial banking also grew rapidly, more than sixty branch banks being opened between 1916 and 1926. The profits of industry and commerce—distributed in the form of more jobs and higher wages—in turn sustained a burgeoning retail economy that employed over thirty thousand workers by 1929.[4]

Economic advancement depended, of course, upon people. In 1920, Buffalo's working population—proprietors, self-employed professionals, salaried employees, and wage-earners—numbered 215,323. More than three-quarters were white males, but the percentage of women and blacks was gradually increasing. Just under 46 percent of all workers were engaged in manufacturing and industry; 26.1 percent held clerical positions or were involved in trade, and 17.1 percent held jobs in public, professional, personal, and domestic service; most of the remainder worked in transportation. Over the course of the decade, this distribution changed somewhat, but industry and manufacturing remained the largest sources of employment.[5]

The prejudices and social customs of the period inevitably influenced the occupational status of certain groups within the working population. African Americans were more likely to hold low-status jobs than whites and females were more concentrated in low-manual, semiskilled, and service employment than males. Among white workers, those who were native-born and of native parentage enjoyed the highest overall status, approximately half holding nonmanual positions in 1920; in contrast, only 22.8 percent of foreign-born workers filled nonmanual roles.[6]

Socioeconomic disparities among the work force were well reflected by Buffalo's residential development. West of Main Street, within the boundaries of the Twenty-Fifth Ward (see figure 2), resided many of the city's most prominent business and professional people; here, along beautiful tree-lined boulevards such as Delaware Avenue, the wealthy and near-wealthy lived in homes as elegant as any in the United States. To the north, near the Chapin, Bidwell, and Lincoln parkways in the Twenty-Third Ward, were other affluent neighborhoods. These elite districts were located in wards with the highest percentage of native whites of native parentage in the city. Less exclusive, middle-class residential areas—the eastern sections of the Twenty-Second and Twenty-Fourth Wards on the west side; the North Park, Central Park, and Kensington districts in northeast Buffalo; new housing developments near the Humboldt Parkway on the upper east side; and south-side neighborhoods along South Park Avenue—were also characterized by large native-white-of-native-parentage populations, although residents were more likely to be of German and Irish ancestry that was the case in the most prestigious wards.[7]

While middle-class Buffalonians tended to reside in outlying areas, those of lesser means were concentrated in the more central and congested parts of the city. As in previous decades, the poorest wards were on the lower west and east sides, where, amid the noise and pollution from nearby railroads, factories, and stockyards, residents endured substandard housing and the other problems typical of low-income neighborhoods. The populations of these inner-city districts contained the highest ward-level percentages of foreign-born whites in Buffalo, matched only by the heavily industrialized Twenty-First Ward in the northwestern part of the city.[8]

Two important facts concerning the foreign born in the 1920s should be stressed. First, as a group, they were a declining element

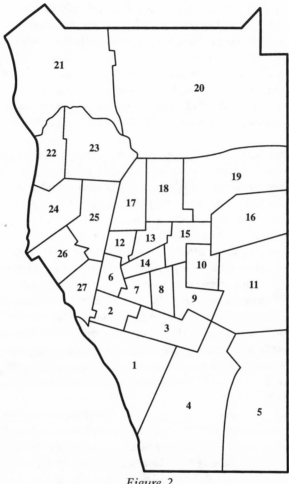

Figure 2
Location of Buffalo Wards

in the city; in fact, as immigration restriction went into effect, their numbers shrank for the first time in decades, from 121,530 (23.9 percent of the total population) in 1920 to 118,941 (20.7 percent) in 1930. Second, the foreign born had attained an unprecedented degree of national and ethnic diversity. Poles (6.2 percent

of the city population), Germans (4.1 percent), Italians (3.2 percent), Canadians (3.1 percent), Irish (1.4 percent), and English (1.3
percent) composed the largest local groups in 1920, but there were
sizable contingents from many other countries. Over the course of
the decade, most of the non-English-speaking nationalities experienced a decline in numbers, with the exception of Italians, who
increased by 19 percent. At the same time, the combined number
of immigrants from Canada and Britain rose by nearly 27
percent.[9]

Residing with, among, and near the foreign born were many
native-born ethnics of foreign, mixed, and native parentage.
Wards in the heavily Polish, Italian, German, and Irish parts of
the city included the highest percentages of second-generation
ethnics, but even in the elite districts nearly a third of the native-
born white residents had at least one foreign-born parent. Published federal census data do not reveal the precise ethnic composition of ward populations in 1920, but reliable estimates for several major ethnic groups can be culled from manuscript census
returns. These percentages indicate that Buffalo can be viewed as
being roughly divided into six ethnic zones: a heavily Irish south
side, a Polish lower east side, a German upper east side, an Italian
lower west side, a large Anglo-American district encompassing the
upper west side and the northeastern part of the city, and an
ethnically diverse—Polish, Anglo, and German—sector to the
northwest.[10]

Race also divided the community. By 1920, there were nearly
five thousand blacks in Buffalo, most of whom lived in the Sixth
and Seventh Wards on the lower east side, one of the most impov-
erished parts of the city. As elsewhere in the United States, local
African Americans confronted racist attitudes that severely limited socioeconomic mobility. In a study conducted in 1927, University of Buffalo sociologist Niles Carpenter discovered that
many city employers considered blacks to be "slow thinkers" who
were "not able to assume any responsibility"; most of those inter-
viewed agreed that blacks "should always have a white man as
foreman."[11] With such sentiments prevailing, it is not surprising
that the large majority of black workers were confined to low-paid

unskilled and semiskilled jobs and that their status improved only marginally during the 1920s. Buffalo's African-American population did include, however, a number of talented business and professional people who spearheaded efforts on behalf of racial improvement and expanded civil rights; voicing their opinions in the black-owned *Buffalo American* and working through such organizations as the National Association for the Advancement of Colored People, these leaders kept a close watch on developments that might threaten their community.[12]

Religion supplemented race as a source of potential conflict in Buffalo in the 1920s. According to federal census data, just under 64 percent of all city church members in 1926 were Roman Catholic; Protestants, in contrast, composed only 27.8 percent of those affiliated with a particular church, while Jews constituted less than 6 percent. These figures probably exaggerate the extent of Catholic dominance somewhat, because many Protestants did not belong to a specific denomination; but—just on the basis of the large number of residents of Irish, Polish, Italian, and German ancestry—it seems virtually certain that a majority of Buffalonians were Roman Catholic.[13]

As an institution, the Catholic Church was one of the largest, wealthiest, and best established organizations in Buffalo. It maintained eighty-four churches and sixty-two parochial schools, published its own newspaper, and owned hundreds of acres of valuable real estate throughout the city. Under the leadership of a series of politically astute bishops, the Buffalo Diocese had forged a close relationship with local political and business leaders, earning gratitude for its strong stand against socialism and other forms of "radicalism." The church remained a force for social conservatism throughout the 1920s, its clergymen regularly denouncing divorce, marital infidelity, birth control ("race suicide," one priest termed it), the erosion of traditional family life, and a perceived abandonment of Christian ideals.[14] Catholics, therefore, occupied common ground with Protestants on many social issues. Differences over controversial matters such as prohibition, however, kept traditional suspicions and animosities fully activated.

Local politics in the 1920s reflected the generally conservative orientation of most Buffalonians. Throughout the decade, despite rising ethnic tensions, the large majority of voters enrolled as Republicans; even in 1924, when controversy over the Ku Klux Klan threatened to explode into open religious warfare, over 64 percent of the potential electorate affiliated with the party of Lincoln. As had long been the case, partisanship demonstrated a close relationship with ethnicity in Buffalo. Average Republican-enrollment percentages for the period 1922–1924 (the time when the local KKK was most active) show that Republican strength was below 50 percent in only eight wards—all located in the heavily Irish and Polish parts of the city—while Italian, German, and old-stock wards had sizable Republican majorities. The large Republican following in wards on the upper east side is of particular interest because it strongly suggests that significant numbers of German Catholics had abandoned their longtime support of the Democratic party.[15]

Not surprisingly, given enrollment figures, the Republican party won presidential elections in Buffalo throughout the 1920s. Warren G. Harding carried the city with a landslide 63.4 percent of the vote in 1920, and four years later Calvin Coolidge received 57.2 percent in a three-way race; in 1928, Herbert Hoover narrowly prevailed over New York Governor Alfred E. Smith.[16] In state and local races, however, the electorate was far more unpredictable. The fortunes of Al Smith provide a good case in point. In his successful 1918 race for governor, Smith failed to carry Buffalo, and in 1920 he was handily defeated in the city by Nathan L. Miller. Two years later, emphasizing his opposition to prohibition, Smith trounced Miller locally, only to be soundly defeated in 1924 by Theodore Roosevelt, Jr.; in 1926, Smith narrowly carried the city in a contest with Ogden L. Mills.[17] As the governor's ups and downs in local polling well demonstrated, the intermingled and ever shifting influence of religion, ethnicity, party, and class resulted in a very complex and volatile political situation. This was even truer at the municipal level, where diverse interests converged with particular intensity. Because the events that were taking place in city politics played such a crucial role in shaping the local Klan experience, they should be examined in some detail.

.　.　.

The aspirations and attitudes of Buffalo's large population of recent immigrant stock were well represented by the controversial
individual who would dominate city government for most of the
1920s. Born on Buffalo's east side in 1874, the son of poor immigrant parents from Austria and Bavaria, Francis Xavier Schwab
scarcely seemed destined for civic prominence. Shortly before
completing his elementary education, Schwab went to work as a
tinsmith's apprentice, later claiming that his real education had
come in the "school of experience and in the university of hard
knocks." Over the next decade, Schwab worked for a number of
local industrial firms, then changed careers and became a salesman for the Germania Brewing Company. Hardworking and naturally gregarious, Schwab soon established himself as a popular
figure among local tavern keepers and restaurateurs, many of
whom were fellow German-Americans; he also was active in the
Knights of St. John, a German-dominated Catholic men's group
similar to the Knights of Columbus. Several years later, Schwab
utilized his contacts and expertise to secure a position as manager
of the Buffalo Brewing Company, which later became the Mohawk
Products Company, one of Buffalo's most prominent breweries. In
the interim, he assumed the joint position of president and general
manager, thereby completing an impressive rise in the world of
business.[18]

By this time, Frank Schwab had developed a personal style that
delighted his friends and infuriated his enemies. A tall, lean man
with a dark moustache, always dapperly attired with his silk tie
adjusted in a distinctive "submarine" fashion beneath his collar,
he delighted in being the center of attention; noontime would
typically find him in a local saloon or cafe, surrounded by cronies
and holding forth on a variety of topics in his heavily accented
English. Ever ready with an encouraging word, a friendly smile,
or a small cash handout for the less fortunate, he considered
himself to be a special friend and representative of the common
people. Such populistic sentiments, however, were largely unre-
lated to any type of coherent political philosophy or partisan
orientation. Although nominally a Republican, Schwab was in
actuality an independent who remained free of links to profes-

sional politicians, being motivated more by cultural issues and the pursuit of personal power than any desire to ingratiate himself with the political establishment.[19] He constituted a wild card on the local political scene, one who only came to power because of the unusual opportunities created, ironically, by prohibition.

From the time of its implementation in 1920, prohibition had generated tremendous resentment in Buffalo. The electorate had never been consulted on the issue, giving rise to the impression that a relatively small group of zealots, headed by the Anti-Saloon League, had managed to impose unrealistic restrictions. There was also the sense that prohibition did not represent a sincere attempt to improve society but was, rather, a heavy-handed effort to dictate arbitrary standards of personal behavior to those whose cultural traditions included the consumption of alcoholic beverages. The prominent role assumed by evangelical Protestants, particularly Methodists, in the dry crusade additionally bred resentment, the editor of the Buffalo *Catholic Union & Times* eventually concluding that the noble experiment constituted "a tyranny that was foisted upon us by Methodist fanaticism."[20] Despite such attitudes, however, federal, state, and local authorities pressed ahead with enforcement efforts throughout 1920 and 1921, further outraging the proponents of "personal liberty."

The widespread hostility to prohibition in Buffalo offered a ready-made campaign issue for aspiring politicians. Recognizing this, members of the Knights of St. John circulated a petition in behalf of the mayoral candidacy of Frank Schwab in the summer of 1921, and he subsequently announced his intention to stand for office. At first, it seemed very unlikely that Schwab could survive the nonpartisan city primary in October 1921. Although well-known for his charity work and his success in the brewing industry, he had never run for elective office and was opposed by four veteran politicians, including incumbent Mayor George S. Buck; Schwab's campaign was staffed largely by inexperienced volunteers and his Catholicism, occupation, ethnic origins, and brash personality—while assets in certain quarters—alienated many voters. Moreover, Schwab was currently under federal indictment for violating the Volstead Act; the two-count charge stemmed from a raid on one of his breweries early in 1920, during which federal agents discovered that real beer, rather than legal "near beer," was being manufactured and distributed.[21] Even for many of those who opposed prohibition, the prospect of voting for a man who had violated federal law was far from attractive.

In contrast to his opponents, all of whom steered clear of the prohibition issue, Frank Schwab made repudiation of the Eighteenth Amendment the centerpiece of his campaign. Proclaiming a desire to restore "sane liberty" to Buffalo through the legalization of light wines and beer, he charged that the dry laws had resulted in a proliferation of unregulated "soft drink" shops that sold dangerous concoctions, and that a recent surge in illicit home brewing threatened the morals and health of the city's children. While Schwab admitted that it was beyond the mayor's ability to end prohibition, he promised to reduce the level of enforcement by assigning the police "dry squad" to other duties, claiming that the fourteen federal prohibition agents stationed in Buffalo could manage the situation in "splendid fashion." He also assured the voters that the indictment currently pending against him would not prove to be a problem, indicating that he was "content to let that matter rest with the district attorney and the proper authorities."[22]

To the astonishment of local party professionals, Schwab's grass-roots campaign gained momentum right up to polling day on October 18. The final tallies revealed that Mayor Buck had received 24,478 votes and Schwab 19,273, while the other contenders, including those backed by Buffalo's Republican and Democratic machines, trailed badly. This meant that Buck and Schwab, both independent Republicans, would face each other in a runoff in the general election in November. As the editor of the *Buffalo Courier* observed, the returns demonstrated that "the people vote as they will, not as political machines and bosses dictate."[23]

Throughout the following three weeks, Buffalo experienced one of the most bitterly divisive mayoral campaigns in the city's history. This was, perhaps, inevitable given the stark contrasts between the two candidates. The scion of a wealthy and prominent local family, George Sturges Buck was a graduate of Yale University and the University of Buffalo Law School. He resided in one of the community's most prestigious neighborhoods, served as an elder of the First Presbyterian Church, and had long been a leading progressive figure in county and city government. Frank Schwab, on the other hand, was a second-generation German-American, a working-class Roman Catholic with no previous experience in politics but plenty of familiarity with the liquor industry.[24] Given these particular differences, sharp divisions in the electorate along ethnic, religious, and class lines could be anticipated.

Schwab and his supporters stayed on the offensive throughout the campaign, concentrating their efforts on neighborhoods in central, east, and south Buffalo. Schwab continually stressed his opposition to prohibition and pledged to lobby in Washington, D.C., for the legalization of light wines and beer: "I want to tell you that prohibition is a curse to the country and to the children, and the mayor can at least protest against it. That is what I propose to do if elected." He also emphasized his intention to establish a city administration that would be sensitive to the needs of all local residents, regardless of their ethnicity. "When I am elected I want you to drop in and see me anytime," he advised a group of Italian-Americans. "Just say, 'Hello, Frank,' and I'll take care of you." He extended this invitation to other immigrant groups as well, speaking before the Polish Singing Circle, the Hungarian Brotherhood, the Ukrainian Men's League, and many other ethnic clubs and societies. At one gathering of Irish-Americans held at a Catholic high school, Schwab informed his coreligionists that "The time has come when they must say the Irish and the Dutch [Germans] amount to much. We are all people of one type and just as good as there are on God's earth. . . . I appeal to the Irish of the first, second, and third wards to put me over on election day."[25]

Schwab's strong appeal within certain ethnic communities distressed Mayor Buck, who accused the brewer of pandering to "all of the racial prejudices [and] to all of the discontented elements in our city, promising everything that he thinks is necessary to win a vote here and there." The mayor particularly decried Schwab's promise to reduce prohibition enforcement, stressing that "Respect for the law is the basis of security in a democracy.

Defiance of law propagates anarchy."[26] In Buck's view, the central issue was not the advisability of prohibition per se, but the broader matter of maintaining the integrity and authority of established institutions. Elect Schwab mayor, he warned, and the "forces of evil which are repressed by constant exertion from the police force will flaunt themselves in the face of decency."[27]

As the campaign heated up, religious and ethnic tensions became more apparent. Not surprisingly, the Protestant-dominated Anti-Saloon League vehemently opposed Schwab's bid for the mayoralty; William H. Anderson, the group's New York state superintendent, commented during a special trip to Buffalo that the brewer was a "political faker" and that "any city which will elect to enforce the law a man who does not deny that he has violated the law deserves exactly what it will get."[28] The Reverend Dr. Charles H. Stewart of the North Presbyterian Church also openly opposed Schwab, arguing that his election would tear the community apart: "Does Buffalo want sectional, racial, and sectarian issues to determine her policy? Never! We want no east side against west side, no issue as to one's religious convictions, whether Catholic, Protestant or Jewish, and no distinction as to nationality whether German, Italian or Pole. We must all be first and always American." Having made this lofty appeal for civic unity, Stewart went on to urge members of his congregation to vote for their fellow Presbyterian, George Buck.[29]

In the end, Protestant solidarity fell short. On November 8, Frank Schwab scored a narrow victory, out-polling Buck 62,747 to 59,986. A number of factors had contributed to this win, but probably the major reason was that the recent implementation of prohibition, in association with the contrasting backgrounds of the two candidates, had strongly polarized the electorate, imparting unusual saliency to preexisting ethnic, religious, and class divisions. The election totals revealed that Schwab had handily carried Buffalo's older wards where the bulk of the community's foreign born and native-born ethnics resided, while the strongest support for Buck was in the northern districts and in the wealthy west-side neighborhoods (see figure 3). Statistical analysis of the vote for Schwab indicates a very strong and negative correlation with ward-level population percentages of native-born whites of

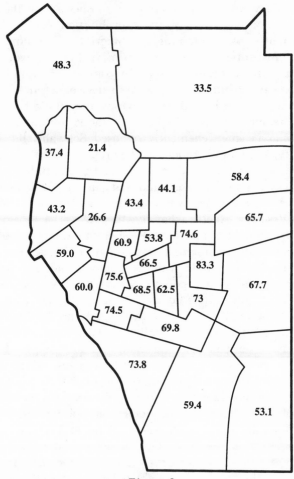

Figure 3
Percentage Voting for Schwab in 1921
Buffalo Mayoral Election, by Ward

native parentage (-.829) and strong and positive correlations with the percentage of foreign-born whites (.617) and native-born whites of foreign or mixed parentage (.649), all correlations being statistically significant at .001, one-tailed test. Schwab did particularly well in the Irish and Polish parts of the city, but he also garnered decisive majorities in the Italian wards and in Wards Six and Seven, where many African Americans and Russian Jews lived. Intriguingly, however, the brewer did less well in the German districts, a possible reflection of Protestant-Catholic divisions within the local German community.[30]

Quite naturally, Schwab partisans exulted in their triumph; to many, it seemed that the common people—particularly those of non-Anglo-Saxon stock—had truly triumphed, unseating a politically experienced member of the civic elite and replacing him with one of their own, a second-generation ethnic who would be the first Roman Catholic mayor of Buffalo. The election results also appeared to constitute a firm rebuff to the advocates of strict prohibition enforcement, particularly the widely despised Anti-Saloon League. In an action hardly calculated to cultivate good will, Schwab backers sent a gloating telegram to State Superintendent William Anderson as soon as victory was assured: "We have just elected the leading brewer of Buffalo mayor of the city. We have canned the dry out of dry. Please notify President Harding, [Anti-Saloon League General Counsel] Wayne B. Wheeler, and John D. Rockefeller. You made 15,000 votes for Schwab by your speech [in Buffalo during the campaign]. In the future, please stay home."[31] What was possibly forgotten, however, was that 59,986 voters, fully 48.9 percent of those participating in the election, had not voted for Schwab, and that many in this group did not intend suddenly to abandon the principles and values that they believed should guide community life. As Frank Schwab would soon discover, his education in the "school of experience and the university of hard knocks" was far from over.

From the time that he assumed office at the beginning of 1922, Mayor Schwab was determined to fulfill his campaign pledge to be accessible to average citizens. He answered his own phone, opened all of his own mail, and moved his desk at city hall to an outer office so that he could personally receive callers. He also remained in close touch with residents through his continued active participation in twenty-seven fraternal societies and numerous organized charity efforts. This open style, complemented by the mayor's natural gregariousness, helped solidify his following in Buffalo's ethnic neighborhoods, reassuring his supporters that he would remain committed to their concerns.[32]

A significant number of Buffalonians, however, were not impressed by the changes in the mayor's office, seeing them as being both undignified and part of a shameless attempt to pander among gullible elements. Other actions taken by Schwab—his energetic lobbying on behalf of "home rule" legislation for New York cities, his efforts to reduce the power of the city hospital commission, his support for $1.5 million in bonuses for municipal workers, and his proposal that he be given a seat on the Buffalo school board—also seemed to be part of a coordinated campaign to expand his power and political base.[33] So, too, did a proposed ordinance that the mayor sponsored in regard to the regulation of the city's thousands of "soft drink" shops. Under the provisions of the suggested law, owners of such establishments would be required to secure an annual license, but the mayor could refuse to grant a license to any applicant whom he deemed to be of poor moral character. Because much of the "soft drink business" served as a front for the illegal sale and consumption of alcoholic beverages, the law also meant, in fact, that the city's most prominent antiprohibitionist, a beer brewer who was currently under federal indictment for violating the Volstead Act, would now determine which applicants were morally qualified to operate a speakeasy. Nevertheless—primarily because none of the other four members of the city commission wanted to assume responsibility for regulating the shops—the ordinance secured passage in early March 1922, thereby significantly enhancing the mayor's influence.[34]

This did not mean that Schwab could always have his way; as one angry city commissioner reminded him, "You're part of the commission, but you're not all of it." Although Schwab's four colleagues on the commission were willing to cede control over soft drink establishments, they jealously defended their authority in other matters, regularly clashing with the mayor and quarreling among themselves. Initially, Commissioner of Public Affairs Frank C. Perkins had hoped to win Schwab over to the idea of municipal ownership of utilities, but when the mayor proved resistant, the commissioner lashed out during a meeting: "I am surprised at you. Good night! I thought you'd stand for something decent." By the summer of 1922, relations between the two men threatened to deteriorate into fisticuffs. On one occasion, after Schwab refused to support a referendum on a municipal electric plant, Perkins charged that instead of representing the "plain people" the mayor was trying to "knock them out." Schwab, visibly outraged, pounded his gavel for silence and shouted, "I won't be insulted by you!" Fortunately, a motion by another commissioner shut off debate on the referendum. The mayor later advised reporters that "If Perkins continues to insult me, I'll eliminate him myself without any motion."[35]

Schwab's relations with Commissioner of Parks and Public Buildings John H. Meahl and Commissioner of Finance and Accounts Ross Graves were also less than cordial. Resentful that the mayor had attempted to influence the awarding of park concessions, Meahl warned Schwab in May 1922 that "I will take orders from no one except the people as to how my department is to be run. If you butt into my department, maybe your department will be butted into." In later months, the pair regularly exchanged insults and sarcastic comments.[36] Ross Graves's difficulties with the mayor stemmed from differences over the city budget, the commissioner accusing Schwab of manipulating public accounts so as to reward his supporters. "Get the idea out of your head that this is Tammany Hall or that Tammany Hall is running Buffalo," he advised the mayor. When Schwab and the three other commissioners united in the spring of 1922 to push through a tax increase, higher salaries for municipal employees, and the creation of a number of new city jobs, Graves was beside himself, denouncing the budget proceedings as "a grand carnival of waste"; at a later meeting concerning city finances, he proclaimed that he was ashamed to be in the company of the other commission members and then stormed out of city hall.[37]

After months of such squabbling, Mayor Schwab had become convinced that he could not effectively work with the existing commission, and he announced his opposition to the reelection bids of Graves and Perkins in the 1923 city elections (Commissioner Meahl's term, like Schwab's, was not due to expire until 1925). "In addition to his hypocrisy as a public official," the mayor said in reference to Graves, "I stand against his reelection because he is rankly inefficient as commissioner of finance and accounts of the city of Buffalo." He also decried Graves's support of prohibition, noting that those "who have the opportunity of seeing him daily know that he not only enjoys a drink, but enjoys a great many of them." The mayor's sarcasm, however, failed to sway the electorate. Both Graves and Perkins had developed strong campaign organizations, and they easily defeated the members of a Citizens' Ticket that had been fielded by local businessmen. To make matters even worse for Schwab, Commissioner of Public Works Arthur W. Kreinheder, the one member of the commission with whom the mayor had managed to forge a relatively amicable relationship, declined to run for reelection and was succeeded by William F. Schwartz, who had already indicated his opposition to Schwab's policies. It seemed very unlikely, therefore, that the open acrimony and petty feuding—what one historian would later refer to as "an hilarious civic circus"—would cease any time in the near future.[38]

Naturally, the unruly behavior on the city commission hardly amused those citizens who desired an efficient and progressive form of government. To one resident who commented on the commission's antics in the spring of 1922, it appeared that "our original generous form of democracy is today plunging us into ruin. That same element which in other days lifted pagan barbarism from the depth, is now dragging our higher civilization into the mud." The editor of the *Buffalo Express* also lamented the apparent lack of idealism and genuine commitment to public service, noting the "enthusiasm with which the mayor and three councilmen . . . voted to increase the salaries of favored ones and otherwise to spend the public money." The blame for such shameless behavior, he argued, ultimately lay with the voters themselves, who had chosen "public servants on the strength of noise and hand-shaking and extravagant promises." The conservative *Buffalo Commercial* likewise felt that democracy had gone astray, with the result that the city had fallen under the control of a "crew of political demagogues and highbinders."[39]

The intense dissatisfaction that many Buffalonians felt over the course of local government in the early 1920s needs to be considered in the context of the broader social concerns of the period. Like most of urban America, Buffalo was caught up in a process of unsettling expansion and change during the years immediately after World War I, producing an impression among some people that—as evangelist Billy Sunday said during a visit to the city— the world was going "crazy, nuts, and bughouse."[40] To many, it seemed that American society had broken loose from traditional moorings and entered a perilous new era in which the basic standards of civilization were under assault. In 1922, a local social observer argued that an unhealthy degree of materialism and a willful abandonment of basic morality had set the nation adrift:

> It needs no argument to prove that a large part of mankind are passing through a crisis. . . . The unreflecting see it. It is upon everyone's lips. Some particulars stand out prominently in American Life. The attendance of multitudes upon the movies, profanity, and multiplied forms of gambling; the addiction of our people to the use of tobacco at a cost of $2,000,000 in 1921; the dance evil with its excesses, the disposition in dress of women to appeal to the baser passions, the relaxed discipline of the public schools, profiteering, demagoguery, or the disposition to play to the crowd in the interest of self or of party; the increase in crime against property and person, notably in the case of highway robbery and killing, once very rare, but now alarmingly frequent.

The major causes of these dangerous trends, he concluded, were "a material development out of proportion to the moral; relaxed home training; . . . the large and irresponsible element in our great cities; [and] lowered standards in the administration of law."[41]

One topic of great interest and extended public discussion at this time was the new behavior of American women. Through newspapers, magazines, and motion pictures, Buffalonians were kept fully informed of the latest provocative trends in female hairstyles and attire, as well as the sexual escapades of film stars and other celebrities; the *Buffalo Courier*, in particular, regularly offered an abundance of titillating stories and photographs featuring attractive, and often scantily clad, young women. Almost inevitably, the new styles of dress and deportment presented by the media influenced local females, promoting fears that traditional values were being undermined. One of the city's Protestant ministers, for example, denounced the modern Buffalo woman's "oddity of dress, her lack of esthetic standards, the hardness and emptiness of face, her uncultured voice, her revolt from customs and conventions which have become almost sacred, her exaggerated sense of freedom and individual expression, and a certain brutal coarseness which shocks lovers of the true, the beautiful, and the good."[42] Another religious spokesman similarly decried the "Buffalo girl of the bobbed hair, rouged cheeks, audacious smile, flippant carriage and daring dialogue." "What moral right have flappers to overstrain manhood?" he asked. "The one who tempts another is as guilty as the one who yields to the temptation."[43]

Alarm over trends in female behavior fueled concerns over the conduct of younger people in general. "The direction in which, for the most part, the young people of America are headed today," the Reverend Robert J. MacAlpine informed his congregation at the Central Presbyterian Church, "spells certain misfortune for the Republic tomorrow. The flagrant personal liberties now conventional between the young men and women of society, the lowered moral ideals of the great mass of our young women, foreshadow the weakening of our nation's future moral integrity."[44] Another Buffalonian felt that the current generation of males, just like their female counterparts, suffered from a lack of positive guiding values: "What [will happen to] the young man of our time, with his easy sense of superiority yet with little sense of the things that make and break, with no real plan of life and no conviction that he needs one, with no breath of purpose in his mentality and no port toward which he definitely moves?"[45]

Such assessments indicated, in many citizens' view, the need for the nation and the community to reinvigorate their sense of social and spiritual purpose. One city resident, in a letter to a local newspaper, argued that "the first thing that ought to be taught [to children] is respect for authority of parents, of preceptors, of the duly constituted civil authorities, and of the laws enacted by the people through their chosen representatives."[46] In a sermon in which he denounced the "excesses and extravagances in the young life of today," the Reverend Dr. Charles H. Stewart asserted that "The real remedy for these great and growing evils of our times is, first, to live right ourselves; next, to enforce, with reasonable firmness, discipline and authority in the home. Last and most important of all, [we must] reinstate the religion which for so long we have treated with such utter indifference and even contempt."[47] The Reverend Leon O. Williams similarly called for a "recovery of spiritual ideas, a deeper sense of spiritual values, a stronger hold on the things of the mind and heart, a new emphasis on culture." "So long as the movie sets manners and morals, so long as education sacrifices culture to utility, so long as material gain counts for more than spirituality," he warned, "[we must reap] the harvest we have so carelessly and thoughtlessly sown."[48]

The resolution of other community problems also seemed to require a renewed commitment to traditional values and standards. Throughout the immediate postwar period, Buffalo and Erie County experienced chronic labor unrest, most notably during the nationwide steel strike of 1919–20; owing to violent clashes between strikebreakers and union members at the Lackawanna Iron and Steel Company (the future Bethlehem Steel Corporation) state troops had to be called in to restore order. This traumatic episode, in association with strikes in other industries across the country, made many people wonder whether the United States might be permanently dividing along class lines; in addition, because most of the striking steelworkers were of "new immigrant" origins, the unrest also seemed to be indicative of serious, and possibly unresolvable, ethnic tensions.[49] As was the case with the various forms of social change that followed the war, the conflict between labor and capital, with its attendant violence, enhanced the impression of a society coming apart at the seams, a society that desperately needed to restore order and recover a united sense of purpose.

Apprehensions over class conflict and labor unrest became especially apparent during the Buffalo streetcar strike of 1922, which began only a few months after Mayor Schwab came into office. Early in July, local members of the Association of Street Railway Employees voted to strike against the International Railway Company (IRC), which refused to negotiate with the union. This brought streetcar traffic inside the city to a virtual halt, greatly inconveniencing and angering residents. Initially, most of the community had considerable sympathy for the strikers, but soon

the protest turned violent, with union members and their supporters hurling stones, bricks, and scrap metal at streetcars manned
by strikebreaking motormen and conductors.[50] The few Buffalonians who dared to ride IRC vehicles ran a considerable physical
risk, and not only from the projectiles. In one episode, a dietician
from a local hospital was attacked by a group of female strike
sympathizers after she stepped down from a streetcar; her attackers grabbed her hair, ripped off her clothes, and viciously kicked
her while a crowd of three hundred union supporters looked on.[51]

By mid-July, the press reported "general rioting" along the car
lines in the heavily Polish east side, where residents greased
streetcar rails and placed boulders, iron girders, and other debris
on the tracks. This violence and destruction of private property
seriously undermined public support for the strikers, Mayor
Schwab—one of the foremost supporters of the union—admitting
that "recent occurrences indicate that there are many people in
the city who do not have the respect for the law and order which
is essential to the very existence of a civilized community."[52] In
short order, mounted and motorized units of the state militia
were moved into Buffalo to put down the rioting, a task they
accomplished with considerable brutality, "hitting children, beat-
ing men with their riot sticks, and using vile language." By this
time, however, many residents agreed with the president of the
Buffalo Chamber of Commerce that "The sole question properly
before the public at this time is whether the law or the mob is to
have its way in Buffalo."[53]

The violence associated with the streetcar strike reenforced the
perception of a general upsurge in lawless behavior. In Buffalo,
as in many other communities throughout the nation, there was
frequent reference to an ongoing "crime wave" during the early
1920s; in January 1922, for example, the editor of the *Express*
observed that a major feature of the previous year had been "the
[large] number and daring character of crimes."[54] Whether, in
fact, there was a significant increase in crime is difficult to ascertain. The arrest records of the Buffalo police department for this
period reveal a pattern that was probably more reflective of political developments than of the amount of criminal activity. During
1921, the last year of the Buck administration, the Buffalo police

made a total of 32,246 arrests, up from 24,436 in 1920. During the Schwab administration the total dipped to 25,524 in 1922, then rose to 29,948 in 1923; in 1924, after local reformers had forced the mayor to appoint a new police chief, the number of arrests increased to 34,563.[55] When one considers that the populations of Buffalo and Erie County were rapidly expanding at this time, and that prohibition had created a large new body of offenders, these figures scarcely seem to indicate a massive breakdown of law and order.

Nevertheless, many citizens remained convinced that their community was under siege by determined criminal elements and that firmer measures were called for. Included in this group was State District Attorney Guy B. Moore, who early in 1922 said that the current "crime wave" could be credited to

> abuse of the probation system, excessive leniency on the part of some courts, undue solicitude for professional criminals in and out of prison, the failure of the public to insist upon a fair, but firm and fearless, prosecution of offenders high and low, and to the lack of support by the public for prosecutors who perform their duties in that manner.[56]

Another local resident agreed that a failure of will lay at the root of the problem: "So the wave of crime goes merrily on, and evidently we like it, or the courts do, because they could stop it in about fifteen minutes if they wanted to, and they don't do it."[57] After sociologist Frank Tannenbaum addressed a local group on the need for prison reform, one Buffalonian suggested that it might be more useful to concentrate on forceful retribution: "With murders daily, holdups hourly, the present need is more for punishment of lawbreakers than of studying how to make life in prison a pleasure."[58] Local resident Ernest L. Green concurred, urging that criminals "be taught that they will be punished and that there is no escape.... As quickly as thunder follows the lightning should punishment follow crime."[59]

In the view of the advocates of strict law enforcement, there was ample evidence of a deteriorating local situation. Buffalo experienced a record forty-three murders in 1921, and a rash of shootings and armed robberies the following spring indicated that such violence was continuing.[60] By October 1922, according to a

city court judge, Buffalo had become "a city of gunmen, a terror-
ized city, where any one of us runs the risk of being killed."[61]
Former Erie County Judge George B. Burd concurred with this
assessment the following year, claiming that the "series of atroci-
ties, crimes committed here—the worst in recent years—has
shown that citizens, however decent and law abiding, are not
immune from attack without provocation."[62] The most fundamental standards of order and decency, therefore, mandated a renewed commitment to the vigorous suppression and punishment
of criminals.

The growing demand for improved law enforcement, quite understandably, intensified doubts about a new city administration
headed by an individual who openly opposed certain state and
federal laws. In the opinion of his most ardent opponents, Mayor
Frank Schwab posed a major threat to the community, being an
unscrupulous demagogue whose lax policies could only result in
further social dissolution. It was imperative, then, that the mayor
be closely watched and forcefully opposed if he attempted to undermine the rule of law. As things turned out, Schwab's enemies
(including those who by now were donning white hoods and
robes) decided to confront the mayor primarily on the issue of
enforcement of the prohibition and vice laws, an issue that was
virtually guaranteed to generate political, cultural, and religious
controversy.

Convinced that his election represented a popular repudiation of
the Eighteenth Amendment, Mayor Schwab took decisive measures to reduce prohibition enforcement as soon as he assumed
office, disbanding the police "dry squad" that had been organized
by the Buck administration and appointing John F. Burfeind, a
fellow antiprohibitionist, as Buffalo's chief of police; the mayor
also tried, unsuccessfully, to have the city commission pass a
resolution calling for the legalization of light wines and beer.[63]
Schwab, it should be stressed, took such actions out of a genuine
belief that prohibition was an illegitimate invasion of personal
liberty, and not because he endorsed the unrestrained use of alco-
hol. As he told a reporter from the *Buffalo Times* in 1922, "I believe
in temperance. I was never intoxicated in my life, and I never

allowed anyone to work for me who was habitually intoxicated. I drink a glass of beer or an occasional highball. That's all." Like many German-Americans, he simply felt that the consumption of alcoholic beverages, provided it was done responsibly, could be a pleasurable and positive part of social life.[64]

The mayor's assessment of the benefits of moderate drinking did not impress prohibition advocates, who were regularly presented with evidence of widespread defiance of the Eighteenth Amendment in Buffalo. By the end of 1921, local, state, and federal officers had made hundreds of arrests and had seized huge quantities of malt syrup and hops, thousands of crocks and barrels, and dozens of stills "ranging in size from the Big Bertha of 100-gallon capacity, down to a tea kettle."[65] Throughout the following year, prohibition agents continued to uncover sophisticated liquor-making operations and large caches of illegal beverages. One facility, located only three hundred feet from the Louisiana Street police station, included two fifty-gallon copper stills and other equipment "as elaborate as that of any Kentucky distillery"; at the site of another large-scale operation, located in the heavily Italian part of the city on the lower west side, authorities confiscated a ton of sugar, seventy barrels of mash, twenty gallons of whiskey, and two huge stills with a total capacity in excess of three hundred gallons.[66] These and other discoveries indicated the presence of a criminal element that not only intended to violate the Constitution but to make extraordinary profits in the process. In the opinion of the dry forces, if the community failed to oppose—or, even worse, if it encouraged—such deviate behavior, then Buffalo would have forfeited all claim to moral and civic integrity.

As they attempted to rally local citizens in defense of prohibition, dry advocates faced a very discouraging situation. Buffalo's many residents of non-Anglo-Saxon origin overwhelmingly opposed the noble experiment, and they had demonstrated their electoral clout during the 1921 city election. The local Democratic party was formally committed to the repeal of New York's strong new prohibition law (the Mullan-Gage Act) and a number of the city's most prominent Republicans—such as United States Representative Clarence MacGregor—were fervent wets.[67] Prohibitionists did, however, have a few influential friends in Buffalo. State

District Attorney Guy B. Moore was fully committed to the cause, warning that "the present decadent public sentiment which openly winks at the violation of one law [will lead to] disrespect for all law"; United States Attorney William J. Donovan also extended his full cooperation to the dry forces.[68] Yet such support could not compensate for the inadequate level of public support, nor for the scant resources allotted to enforcing prohibition. Even during the Republican administration of Governor Nathan Miller, only twenty state prohibition agents were assigned to the Buffalo district, an area that encompassed seventeen counties in western New York; excluding customs officers, the number of federal agents assigned to the local vicinity was even smaller.[69] This meant that it was particularly crucial that Buffalo's city government, with its one-thousand-man police force, be willing to assist in enforcement efforts.

During the spring of 1922, federal officials sent a personal message to Mayor Schwab that they were serious about enforcing the Volstead Act, United States Attorney Donovan announcing that the mayor would soon stand trial on the two-count prohibition charge that had been pending since 1920. This news delighted Schwab's enemies but distressed those who were preoccupied with the community's national image, the *Express* claiming that "It cannot be looked upon otherwise than as a humiliation to Buffalo that the mayor of the city should be placed on trial in a court."[70] Schwab also had no desire for such proceedings, and on May 29 he appeared in court to enter a plea of nolo contendere to one count of possessing a quantity of illegal beer; Federal Judge John R. Hazel fined the mayor five hundred dollars, then dismissed the remaining count. The mayor pulled out a large roll of bills, paid the fine with a flourish, and on the way out of the courthouse informed the press that he had not wanted to waste time "arguing with the government as to my personal liability in the matter"; he also noted that under the provisions of the city charter his misdemeanor conviction did not constitute an impeachable offense. Nevertheless, the mayor decided to tread more lightly from this point on; he became less outspoken in his opposition to prohibition enforcement, and on June 7, 1922, he tendered his resignation as president and general manager of the Mohawk Products Company.[71]

By this time, Protestant reformers in such organizations as the Anti-Saloon League and the evangelical-dominated Buffalo Federation of Churches had launched a major campaign to improve the city's moral conditions, an effort that would continue for more than two years. Convinced that the local vice situation had deteriorated since Mayor Schwab came to power, these activists employed private investigators to gather information and then released detailed reports on the lawlessness and immorality that allegedly prevailed in Buffalo. One report, prepared by an undercover operative working for the Anti-Saloon League, claimed that approximately five hundred young men had entered the city's notorious "tenderloin" district during a one-hour period in early May 1922. Releasing this and other findings to the press, ASL State Superintendent William Anderson observed: "We have a mayor who was elected on a platform of a wide-open town and he is giving the people what they want."[72] In July, a report commissioned by the Buffalo Federation of Churches similarly noted that "vice is carried on undisturbed by police officers on the street and that proprietors of disorderly houses are not afraid of the authorities because they do not disturb the businesses."[73] Four months later, a local Methodist minister announced that another secret investigation had uncovered more than thirty speakeasies operating openly just blocks from city hall, proof, in his opinion, of the "utter indifference, incompetence, and crookedness of certain officials in the city."[74]

By the fall of 1922, many Protestant clergymen had become convinced that the Schwab administration was hopelessly corrupt. "Definite and comprehensive steps must be taken to redeem the moral integrity of the city," warned the Reverend Dr. Robert J. MacAlpine, pastor of the Central Presbyterian Church. "For this state of affairs the chief executive is directly to blame. He has fallen. At the bar of public opinion the Mayor stands convicted." The Reverend Henry S. Palmeter of the Hudson Street Baptist Church argued that local conditions would never improve "with public officials laughing up their sleeves," noting that "If God is to be as hasty in punishing Buffalo as He was in destroying Sodom and Gomorrah, it would be well for us to look for foreign domiciles." "The Mayor and chief of police have clearly [demonstrated] their incompetence," asserted the Reverend Charles C. Penfold of the Sentinel Methodist Church, "and in a thoroughly democratic community it ought to be possible to find a way of relieving them with officials who are both willing and able to act." Others agreed, and during December the Buffalo Methodist Ministers' Association requested Governor Miller to order a formal investigation of Schwab to see if there were grounds for his removal.[75] The governor, who left office less than a month later, declined to act, but it was clear that the mayor's enemies would remain active.

By the close of 1922, the recent course of local affairs gave Buffalonians much to ponder. A controversial new mayor had come to power following a bitter election that had divided the community along religious, ethnic, and class lines; subsequently, many of the city's Protestant leaders had accused this individual's administration of promoting corruption and rampant disregard for the law. At the same time, as throughout much of the nation, there was heightened general concern over the new behavior of women and young people, labor unrest, and a perceived surge in crime—all of which seemed to indicate a marked deterioration in fundamental social values and standards. Increasingly, there was an impulse for citizens to arise and take action against these dangerous trends, to unite the forces of decency and reinvigorate the community with a sense of unified social and spiritual purpose before it was too late. But by what means was this to be accomplished? The most recent city election had demonstrated that "un-American" elements held the upper hand in terms of votes and neither of the major political parties appeared to be a satisfactory reform vehicle. There was, however, a new option—an increasingly popular organization that might, at the least, serve as a striking means of expressing anger, discontent, and defiance. That organization was the Knights of the Ku Klux Klan, a group that hundreds of Buffalonians had been joining since 1921.

Two

The Kluxing of Buffalo

Only very gradually, and in distinct stages, did the Ku Klux Klan establish itself in Buffalo. Throughout 1920 and the early months of 1921, the dramatic expansion of the Invisible Empire remained a remote phenomenon that generated little concern among city residents. The local press featured numerous reports indicating that the Klan's appeal was not confined to the South, but the possibility that the hooded order might develop a significant following in Buffalo or other parts of New York apparently received minimal consideration. Klan organizers recognized, however, that the Empire State might serve as a bountiful source of recruits, and they inaugurated a membership campaign in the spring of 1921, an effort that concentrated on New York City and communities in the lower Hudson River valley. Operating out of a suite in the Hotel Embassy and making use of contacts within fraternal and religious organizations, Grand Goblin Lloyd P. Hooper had by the late summer established klaverns in Manhattan, Brooklyn, and the Bronx. Eventually Gotham's total Klan membership would exceed fifteen thousand, but recruiting proved sluggish and fell far below initial expectations; in addition, Hooper and his associates had to contend with the vehement and active opposition of the administration of New York Mayor John F. Hylan. A number of kleagles therefore began searching for more promising recruiting grounds elsewhere in the state.[1]

Even before the arrival of an official representative, a small group of Buffalonians had developed a strong interest in the Klan. Intrigued by what they had read and heard about the secret order, these residents—who included "at least three prominent Buffalo men," one of whom was a medical doctor—wrote early in 1921 to national KKK headquarters in Atlanta for information and eventually received an ample supply of Klan application forms and pamphlets. The physician later explained that his interest derived from a familiarity "with the work done by the original Klan many years ago in the reconstruction period following the Civil War." His examination of the revived Klan's literature convinced him of the organization's honorable intentions, and he proceeded to distribute KKK booklets and membership questionnaires among his friends and lodge brothers.[2]

In the late summer of 1921, just as the sensational and widely syndicated exposés in the *New York World* and the *New York Journal-American* were directing the nation's attention to the Klan, Buffalonians received the first public notice that KKK recruiting was being carried on within their community. Claiming that it had uncovered certain evidence of a "plan to extend an invisible empire of terrorism" to the city, the *Buffalo Courier* revealed that the secret order had been conducting an "intensive campaign of weeks in Buffalo for members" and that "Ku Klux Klan literature is pouring into Buffalo and is being distributed by Ku Klux Klan sympathizers and advance agents." According to the newspaper, Klan promoters were generally confining their recruiting campaign to members of fraternal organizations, although workers at nearby factories had also been approached. As proof of the Invisible Empire's desire to organize a local klavern, the *Courier* reproduced a letter from Grand Goblin Hooper inviting candidates to a "meeting of qualified citizens now being arranged in Buffalo."[3]

The arrival of the Klan produced a vehemently negative reaction in certain quarters. Convinced that the revived KKK was an "organization of terrorism and hate," a "band of cowardly murderers" that intended to spread Southern-style racism and vigilantism northward, the *Buffalo American* served notice that the community's African-American population would oppose the order with all possible means. Advising the paper's readers to "take time to teach your offspring the manly art of self-defense," one *American* editorialist asserted that

> The Negro has naught to fear of this gang of cowards. Give me the four colored regiments, with full permission to shoot, not in the air, but direct at them, and in thirty days I will sell their long white robes to any junk dealer you designate, make a torch of the castle of the high muck-a-mucks and a jack rabbit of the supreme lizard.[4]

This militant attitude was shared by the *Catholic Union & Times*, which urged Buffalonians to unite in an effort to "Kill the Knavish Klan." "The Ku Klux Klan is a menace to the community and a blight upon civilization," argued the paper's editor. "The sooner the vile thing is suppressed, the better for the world at large." The *Union & Times* later expressed confidence, however, that there would be little local enthusiasm for the "veiled brand of bigotry" espoused by a secret order from the "benighted and bigoted South."[5]

Although they were generally more restrained, the city's major newspapers also made clear that the Klan was not welcome. The *Buffalo Evening Times* and the *Buffalo Enquirer* joined the *Courier* in denouncing the KKK as a money-making scheme that exploited the religious and racial prejudice of gullible citizens, calling for a federal investigation of the organization. The *Buffalo Evening News* presented the *New York World*'s exposé of Klan violence and the *Express* and the *Commercial* offered anti-KKK cartoons, one of which—entitled "The Answer"—showed a Klansman being booted out of Buffalo.[6] The press's stance was almost uniformly characterized by derision and contempt, with the sole exception of the archconservative *Buffalo Truth*, which apparently reserved judgment.[7]

Surprisingly, given the press's overwhelmingly negative depiction of the Klan and the *Courier*'s warning that KKK organizers were "looking toward permanent establishment of a lodge of terror and hatred in this metropolis," the arrival of the Invisible Empire produced little outward sign of alarm among city officials. "If the members of the Ku Klux Klan hold their meetings in an orderly fashion and strive for proper aims in accordance with the law," District Attorney Guy B. Moore announced, "they will no more be in danger of prosecution than any other secret organization." Although he stressed that he was very much opposed to any type of local "vigilance committee," Mayor George Buck also noted that he had no power to "prevent a secret organization from propagating itself." Police Chief James W. Higgins concurred, even acknowledging that there was no municipal ordinance or regulation preventing a police officer from joining the Klan.[8] Nor was there a forceful response forthcoming from civic organizations, fraternal groups, or Protestant religious leaders, with the ironic exception of the Reverend Charles C. Penfold—a future Klansman—who argued that the "Spirit of Christ does not live behind a mask and the sacred name of America does not stand for race hatred or religious prejudice."[9]

The relatively passive stance of city elites at first seemed justified, as the flurry of excitement over KKK activity in Buffalo soon subsided. The press's limited fund of information concerning the order was quickly exhausted and local Klansmen entered an extended period of absolute silence; by late September the *Courier* confessed that "there seems to be increasing proof that a substantial body of citizens looks with no favor on Kluxism."[10] To many residents it no doubt seemed that Buffalo, as a particularly progressive and enlightened community, had proved resistant to the irrational and disruptive intolerance that plagued less fortunate parts of the country.

That Buffalo was not immune from the lure of the Invisible Empire was suddenly made clear late in May 1922. In a statement to local reporters, a visiting Klan official, a district kleagle who would only give his name as "Mitchell," announced that hundreds of city residents—including "some of the finest American citizens, men beyond reproach and of sterling character"—had been inducted into the order and that Klan meetings had been held every two weeks in Buffalo for the past eight months. Mitchell confirmed that a professional Klan organizer had come to the city the previous summer and had given a lecture to several hundred prospective candidates on the fundamentals of the secret order. "Many of these were admitted to membership subsequently and others have since joined," he noted. Although the klavern had not yet received an official charter, it was reportedly well-organized and under the command of thirteen provisional officers. The district kleagle stressed that the group remained in a state of perpetual readiness: "It is just a case of pressing a button and within one hour we can get all the Klansmen in a certain place." Although the Buffalo Klan was currently preoccupied with the teaching of true Americanism, it anticipated "the time when trouble may occur, when [the Klan] will be prepared to throw its strength on the side of the law and government."[11]

This first official announcement concerning the local klavern heralded an intensified recruiting effort that would continue for the next several months. On May 23 the hooded order placed an advertisement in the *Express* featuring a masked Klansman, and a few days later a second Imperial official, New York King Kleagle F. S. Webster, visited Buffalo and held a press conference. Webster informed journalists that the local Klan's membership now stood at nearly eight hundred and that "many persons locally have evinced a desire to become affiliated with the organization since the recruiting began a week ago." He emphasized that, contrary to newspaper accounts, the Klan was not an "anti" organization but merely pro-American:

> Klansmen don't doubt the loyalty, integrity and bravery of Catholics, Jews, negroes [sic] and foreign born persons. We realize that these classes proved themselves good and brave Americans during the recent war and we are not against them. Catholics bar themselves [from the Klan] by their allegiance to the Pope; the Jews because they do not believe in the birth of Christ and negroes [sic] because of their color. We want only Caucasians, who, so far as their allegiance is concerned, have it all confined within the boundaries of the United States. That does not mean that we are opposed to them. We are organized to maintain American principles and are opposed only to lawlessness and lack of Americanism.

The king kleagle further revealed that the Buffalo Klan intended to take an active role in local affairs: "We have elected Mayors in other cities—I don't see why we can't do it here."[12]

The growing and increasingly overt Klan presence in Buffalo naturally unsettled many residents, the *Courier* noting the rise of a "plainly felt agitation for official action to prevent possible racial outbreaks, religious commotions, disorderly assemblages or riots here." Rabbi Louis J. Kopald of Temple Beth Zion denounced the Klan as a "dastardly underhanded group of citizens who are knifing the best interests of every element of our religion, Catholic, Jewish and Protestant, alike," and the *Commercial*—whose staff would eventually include several Klansmen—ran a front-page editorial claiming that the order was composed of "narrow minded bigots and wild-eyed fanatics" who had "no place in the everyday life of the community." This hostile attitude received the full endorsement of the new Schwab administration. Police Chief John F. Burfeind, in contrast to his predecessor, flatly stated his intention to move against the KKK, avowing that he would "leave no stone unturned to call a halt on any organization holding meetings or recruiting members in this city which is of a character calculated to inflame racial or religious hatred. That is my plain duty, and I shall not dodge it." The chief admitted that the police department knew very little about the Klan and urged citizens to relay any information they possessed about the location of the group's meetings.[13]

Although he openly scoffed at the claim that eight hundred Buffalonians had entered the Invisible Empire, Mayor Schwab also informed the press that he did not "see why [the KKK] should be permitted to carry forward its operations here," threatening to break up any type of gathering within the city limits. The mayor challenged Klan leaders to meet with him personally and prove that their group was truly in accord with American principles and ideals. Perhaps to Schwab's surprise, King Kleagle Webster quickly accepted this invitation and spent an entire day at city hall waiting for an audience. The mayor, however, declined to speak with the Klan representative, who soon departed Buffalo because of pressing Imperial business.[14]

Throughout the summer and early fall of 1922, the local Klan generally removed itself from public view and concentrated on quietly expanding its membership. For the most part, this kluxing effort followed a pattern similar to that in other American communities, but the Buffalo klavern appears to have been atypically unconcerned with developing a positive image. Unlike other fledgling chapters that sought to demonstrate their social respectability and civic utility through official proclamations and the ostentatious donation of cash gifts to fund drives and needy citizens, the local Klan apparently preferred to remain a mysterious group outside the scrutiny of mainstream community life. Beyond the announcements of Kleagles Mitchell and Webster, both of whom were outsiders, the Buffalo klavern for months provided no formal acknowledgment of its intentions; indeed, it would not be until 1924 that the chapter made its first official statement (and then only as the result of an ongoing controversy) and disclosed its formal title: Buffalo Klan No. 5. Confronted with unfriendly municipal authorities, a hostile press, and a local population that was largely non-Protestant and non-Anglo-Saxon, Klansmen early recognized and accepted the likelihood that their organization was fated to be primarily a means of defiance, a medium of expressing the intense dissatisfaction and frustration that many white Protestants felt about the conduct of community affairs.

Although acutely aware of their minority status locally, Buffalo Klansmen could take considerable comfort by the fall of 1922 in the remarkable inroads their organization was making elsewhere in the nation. In recent months the KKK had scored impressive electoral victories in Oregon and Texas; the Midwest and western Pennsylvania appeared well on their way to becoming Klan strongholds; and a revived recruiting campaign was meeting with considerable success in New York City.[15] Such gains undoubtedly reassured local knights of the legitimacy of their order and made them feel that they were part of a vast and growing movement that would inevitably transform the fabric of America's social and political life. It was at this time of heady expansion and surging confidence that Buffalo Klan No. 5 decided to hold its first outdoor ceremonial—an event clearly designed to generate interest in the KKK and enhance the group's mysterious image.

At eight o'clock on the evening of October 25, 1922, automobiles arriving from all directions converged upon a stubble-littered field off of Harlem Road, a few miles north of the Buffalo city limits. Here they were met by a "withered old man" who received a secret password and directed drivers up a short winding lane to the top of an adjacent slope. The cars, 297 in all, eventually formed a huge circle that was brilliantly illuminated by the vehicles' headlights. The occupants of the automobiles, forty masked Klansmen in full regalia and approximately eight hundred candidates in civilian attire, stepped out and gathered around a large pulpit in the center of the circle. Suddenly a forty-foot-high cross burst into flame just beyond the ceremonial ring, its light eerily playing off the gaunt trees that surrounded the assemblage. A Klan officer then strode forward and ascended the pulpit. The hooded and masked figure made an impressive sight in his white robes; he wore a band of red silk on one arm, mysterious symbols adorned his sleeves, and a gilded eagle on his breast glistened in the electric light. The Klansman addressed the recruits and explained— primarily for the benefit of visiting reporters—that the Invisible Empire did not intend to promote racial or religious bigotry:

> We are not against the negroes *[sic]*. As a matter of fact, we want to [cooperate with] the colored race, but we do not want them to violate the sanctity of the homes of Americans. As far as Catholics go, we make no discrimination between Catholics and Protestants. The only thing is that Catholics are forced to admit allegiance to a foreign potentate, in other words, the Pope of Rome. That, in our way of thinking, makes them allegiant to a foreign power.

The remainder of the ceremony was dedicated to the initiation of the new class of recruits, who recited the Klan oath and pledged eternal loyalty to the Invisible Empire. Shortly before midnight, the ritual was concluded and the Klansmen drove off into the damp moonless night. Some of the participants returned directly to their homes in Niagara Falls, Batavia, and other communities in western New York, but most of the knights crossed the city line into Buffalo. As the last automobile departed, the giant fiery cross tumbled to the earth. The first open-air ceremonial of the Ku Klux Klan in New York had ended.[16]

News of the Klan initiation on Harlem Road shocked the many Buffalonians who had remained skeptical about the extent of local recruiting. "The majority of the city's residents had no realization that the Klan had been so completely organized," observed the *Courier*. "The secrecy shrouding every movement and meeting of the K.K.K. was complete." The paper's editor seemed bewildered that, despite the numerous denunciations of the Klan by the local press and city leaders, the organization was thriving: "An appeal to the common sense of men ought to be all that is necessary to break up the order, but this appeal has been made time and again, in many parts of the country, . . . and yet this Klan that works at night still grows!"[17] Moreover, as would soon be evident, the KKK now felt confident enough to hold public meetings within the city itself.

During the first week of November 1922, the business secretary of Buffalo Nest No. 1, Fraternal Order of Orioles, was contacted concerning the possibility of renting the Orioles' hall on Genesee Street for a meeting of the National Business Men's Association of America. Buffalo Nest No. 1 gave its consent, and on November 8 a small crowd of 119 men and 17 women attended the meeting, which had actually been arranged by professional organizers for the Knights of the Ku Klux Klan. The gathering featured two speakers, the Reverend Dr. Samuel H. Campbell and the Reverend Basil E. Newton, both of whom hailed from Texas. Dr. Campbell, a tall man with nose glasses and a deep, powerful voice, did most of the talking, focusing on the great peril posed by blacks, Catholics, and Jews. The Negro, according to Campbell, "is a menacing figure, threatening the heart of America today." He produced a purported copy of the oath taken by fourth-degree members of the Knights of Columbus that demonstrated the inherent disloyalty of Roman Catholics, and observed that both President Abraham Lincoln and President William McKinley had been assassinated by "followers of the Pope." Jews were assailed for their plots to "seize Russia and Palestine" and to "destroy the morals of the world" through their domination of the entertainment industry. The speaker also cited an alleged conspiracy between Catholics and Jews to control the United States through manipulation of the press: "[The Catholic], backed by Jewish capital, produces the American newspaper that forces into the mind of the youth in this country what he shall think, how he shall think, and why he should think."[18]

Having delineated the dangers presented by the enemies of white Protestant America, the Reverend Dr. Campbell called on the assembled residents to answer the call to arms and "build up an organization in Buffalo, [so] that you may share in the conquest of all these perils and threatening influences that shadow our national existence." "It's easy to get into this order," he advised his audience. "You rub shoulders with Klansmen every day. Let a whisper go out that you want to join this sacred movement and your worries will cease." Apparently those attending the talk needed no further convincing. Not only did Campbell receive a rousing round of applause at the conclusion of his speech, but every man in the hall rose to pledge his allegiance to the Invisible Empire. No doubt satisfied with the response to their work in Buffalo, the Klan representatives soon departed for Lockport and Niagara Falls, where the same presentation was delivered before a total of six hundred interested citizens.[19]

Throughout the remainder of the year, western New York experienced a furious membership drive by the Klan. By mid-November, kleagles had visited Jamestown, Corning, Bath, Batavia, Salamanca, Elmira, Olean, and Lackawanna, making sales pitches before enthusiastic gatherings of prospective recruits in lodge rooms, lecture halls, and private homes. In the small railroad town of Hornell, less than a week after KKK organizer C. S. Fowler gave a talk at the local Grand Army of the Republic hall, the Klan announced its existence by igniting a huge cross on the side of a mountain, a demonstration evidently intended to intimidate the community's sizable immigrant population. By December, Klan activity had spread throughout the Finger Lakes region and even across the border into Canada, where kleagles reportedly sought recruits by making an anti-Quebec appeal. Continued kluxing was also evident in Erie County, Cheektowaga Chief of Police Emil Capolla reporting that on December 13 "scores" of "mysteriously hooded" men had assembled for some type of induction ceremony at the intersection of Harlem Road and Broadway; although he had kept his distance, the chief strongly suspected that the participants had been members of the Ku Klux Klan.[20]

As a result of the surge in Klan activity in Buffalo and western New York during the second half of 1922, local opposition to the hooded order greatly intensified. In September 1922, a small group of Buffalonians formed the Knights of the Invisible Jungle of the Tiger's Eye, a secret club dedicated exclusively to "destroying the Knights of the Ku Klux Klan, Inc., here." The order set up headquarters on Main Street, near the downtown business district, and pledged to serve as "another link added to the chain that will soon drag the Klan from its hidden realm."[21]

More significant at this time was the increasingly forceful opposition of the African-American community. In a powerful sermon at Shiloh Baptist Church in November, the Reverend E. J. Nichols characterized the KKK as a "cowardly, underhanded organization," warning that "We do not want any Ku Klux Klan in Buffalo, and will resist the invasion of these lawless individuals who preserve a mask of what they term righteousness while committing lawless acts." The editor of the *Buffalo American* similarly noted that the Klan would be well advised to steer clear of local blacks: "Our people are aroused and it is known that we mean business. We feel that we are prepared to check the spread of this infamous organization in our fair city of Buffalo. With the Northern Negro, it will be 'an eye for an eye, and a tooth for a tooth' with this Klan." The Buffalo chapter of the National Association for the Advancement of Colored People also denounced the KKK and called on Governor Miller to take action against the order: "[Thousands] of our people in Buffalo want to see the American Constitution kept inviolate. We will resist with every ounce of our power the invasion of our rights by such a body."[22]

A growing number of other western New Yorkers joined black leaders in taking an open stand against the Klan in the closing months of 1922. Outraged at the KKK's appearance in his community, Rabbi Solomon Fineberg of Temple Beth El, Niagara Falls, denounced the order as the "most insidious menace to American democracy and government ever devised." County Supervisor Frank E. Freedman of Buffalo's Seventh Ward called on Sheriff William F. Waldow to prevent any future Klan gatherings outside the city limits, warning that the "unpopulated fields of Erie County may become the rendezvous of these anti-Americans," and Buffalo Deputy Police Chief John S. Marnon announced that "We cannot tolerate any of this kind of business in our city and I intend to put a stop to it [the Klan] immediately." In a speech before the Zonta Club at the Statler Hotel, District Attorney Guy B. Moore likewise (if somewhat belatedly) acknowledged that "The time has come to crush the Ku Klux Klan," pledging "to do all in my power to punish and to prosecute it swiftly and surely."[23]

For the first time, Protestant religious leaders also began to speak out against the hooded order. Although he was careful to note that "our judgment on the Ku Klux Klan must be hypothetical until we have [more] knowledge," Dr. William L. Sullivan of Buffalo's First Unitarian Church argued in November 1922 that if the KKK "excites bigotry of race or bigotry of sect, it is wrong." In a sermon before his congregation at Tonawanda First Presbyterian Church a few days later, the Reverend Earl L. Douglas stressed his aversion to the secret methods of the Invisible Empire: "I want to see crime reduced. I want to see the illicit selling of liquor broken up, but I'll say so without a mask on my face, and I am perfectly sure that to put a mask on my face would be to cultivate cowardice in my own heart." At the same time, Bishop Charles H. Brent, head of the Episcopal Diocese of Western New York, called on authorities to "uproot" the Klan and early the next year the Reverend Dr. Robert E. Brown, pastor of Richmond Avenue Methodist Church, opined that the KKK was potentially dangerous and "based upon distrust and denial of democracy."[24]

The tension and uncertainty resulting from the local kluxing campaign contributed to a pair of unpleasant episodes at the close of 1922. On December 20, Edward Wild, a motorman for the International Railway Company, received a note—via a brick hurled through the window of his home—warning him to "Look out. More on the way. Stay home. This is our last warning." The ominous missive bore the initials "K.K.K."[25] That same month, seven prominent Polish-American businessmen also received letters signed "K.K.K." that denounced three Polish Roman Catholic pastors on Buffalo's east side. Although the letters were not on official Klan stationery, they seemed to confirm suspicions that the Reverend Walter Chrzanowski, pastor of the First Polish Baptist Church, had affiliated with the secret order. The situation became even more serious when rumors began to spread that the Klan intended to hold a meeting in the Polish Union Hall, a local paper citing the "scare among the people of the east side recently [owing to] the circulation of letters and pamphlets signed by the

Klan." It was soon learned, however, that not a Klan meeting but rather a theatrical production—entitled "Ku Klux Klan" and sponsored by Polish Protestants—would be held at the east-side site. Local authorities nonetheless remained on guard, posting seventy-five police with riot guns outside the hall on the evening of the play and insisting that the presentation's title be changed to "Ku Klux Klub." On the orders of the mayor, a police captain attended the event to make sure that there were "no speeches or words referring to the Ku Klux Klan."[26]

The Klan's increasingly disruptive impact on community affairs placed pressure on the Schwab administration to take some form of forceful action. "The very minute that the Klan question is brought to a definite issue in Buffalo, then I will take steps," avowed the mayor late in November. "We all know that the Klan is unconstitutional, un-American and against the better interests of all good citizens." Soon, two police detectives were assigned to full-time duty "investigating the affairs of the Ku Klux Klan," and on December 11 Schwab—despite the lack of any legal authority—promised to discharge any municipal worker who joined the hooded order: "We don't want the Klan in Buffalo. . . . I will dismiss any city employee or official who becomes a member. I don't think any will be foolish enough to join."[27]

Beyond such actions, however, the mayor found his options severely limited. Other than the meetings on Harlem Road and at the Orioles' hall, the Buffalo Klan's activities had taken place under a shroud of absolute secrecy. No local knight had been positively identified, the regular meeting place of the order remained unknown to the authorities, and the group had severed all contact with the press; the klavern truly appeared to be part of an invisible empire. Moreover, despite the newspapers' and local leaders' consistent depiction of Klansmen as irrational bigots and hooded terrorists, the chapter had thus far acted in a manifestly law-abiding manner, violating no state or municipal ordinance and avoiding any type of confrontation with opponents. "Until some unlawful action is committed [by the KKK]," admitted Deputy Chief John Marnon, "it would seem that the hands of the police are tied so far as arrests are concerned." Sheriff William

Waldow concurred, promising action only in the case of a specific violation.[28] Thus, for the time being, the Buffalo Klan could proceed without fear of legal harassment.

During the winter months of early 1923, as would regularly be the case during extended periods of cold weather, Buffalo Klan No. 5 entered a period of relative quiescence and the organization temporarily ceased to be a matter of pressing concern. The precise nature of the klavern's activities at this time must remain largely a matter of speculation, but the chapter was evidently nurturing friendly contacts with select Protestant clergymen, an effort that seemed particularly promising because of mounting frustration over inadequate enforcement of the vice and prohibition laws. Confronted with a former beer brewer as mayor and the antiprohibitionist Al Smith returning to the governor's office, moral reformers found themselves in a deteriorating situation and in dire need of effective allies. Despite their initial aversion to the Klan's practice of masked secrecy, Buffalo's evangelical activists had begun to assure themselves of the group's honorable intentions; no doubt a number of them had learned or suspected that certain respected friends and colleagues had entered the fold. Indeed, some reformers had almost certainly begun to wonder whether the Klan, which had taken admirable stands on key issues and conducted itself in a restrained and disciplined fashion, might not be effectively utilized in the ongoing campaign to improve community conditions.

With the spring thaw came clear evidence of the KKK's growing association with Protestant churchmen. On Sunday morning, March 25, during the course of his sermon before the congregation of Kenmore Presbyterian Church, the Reverend Frank H. Smith suddenly fell silent and directed his attention toward the last row of pews. There, to the astonishment of most of those in attendance, stood three masked Klansmen in full uniform. As women in the audience gasped and a few nervous members edged toward the exit, the trio of knights marched side by side up the church's center aisle, the Klansman in the middle bearing a small red cross. After reaching the altar and turning to face the congregation, one of the hooded figures, speaking in a "slow, monotonous voice," read a short message expressing the KKK's devotion to the Christian faith and the order's goals as a patriotic organization. The speaker then placed a letter and a small purse on the altar, whereupon the Klansmen, holding hands, briskly walked out of the building, entered a closed automobile, and sped away in the direction of Buffalo.[29]

The Kenmore church visitation, which had taken place on the verge of the city line, reactivated the controversy surrounding the Klan. Despite the Reverend Smith's protestation that the visit was "totally unexpected," the minister remained strangely evasive about the precise contents of the letter and purse left by the Klan; that Smith had immediately resumed his sermon after the Klansmen's departure—making no comment or observation concerning the bizarre intrusion—also seemed manifestly curious. The clergyman's behavior displeased many church members, one of whom warned that Klansmen would "leave minus their hoods and white bed sheets" if a return visit was attempted. Soon the congregation of Kenmore Presbyterian was engaged in a bitter internal debate over what type of action to take in regard to the episode. At a meeting of the Young People's Society of Christian Endeavor (the church's youth auxiliary), an anti-Klan proponent presented a resolution accusing the KKK of fomenting the "bitter passions of bigotry and intolerance"; the society, however, refused to take an official stand against the secret order. A diversity of opinion likewise characterized the church's ten-member board of trustees, which engaged in a rancorous discussion before instructing the Reverend Smith to read a formal statement expressing disapproval of the Klan visit. Although the minister complied, emphasizing that this was the "final word" on the matter, considerable tension evidently persisted: early in June, reportedly owing to pressure exerted by the trustees, Smith announced his resignation from the pastorate at Kenmore Presbyterian.[30]

Additional efforts to place the Klan on a stronger footing in western New York accompanied the organization's growing involvement with the Protestant clergy in 1923. On March 31, three hundred Buffalonians attended a spirited pro-Klan lecture at Mizpah Hall, a Masonic auditorium located at the intersection of Ferry and Herkin streets on the west side. The Reverend John

H. Moore, a professional speaker dispatched from Atlanta, addressed the gathering on the topic of "Ideals of the Ku Klux Klan" and urged nonmembers to enlist in the Klan's noble cause. The meeting was punctuated by frequent applause and laughter, and at its conclusion approximately two hundred of those in attendance signified their desire to enter the Invisible Empire.[31] At this same time, the *Express* relayed word that the Buffalo Klan would soon formally institute a new klavern in the suburban community of Tonawanda. Although for the past several months they had been meeting in private homes, Tonawanda Klansmen had recently relocated to more spacious facilities and anticipated a sizable growth in membership in the near future.[32] Niagara Falls was also the site of renewed kluxing, as the Reverend Dr. Oscar Haywood—whose pro-Klan activities had recently led to his removal as associate evangelist of the Calvary Baptist Church in New York City—explained the order's goals to an enthusiastic crowd at the Church of Christ in early April.[33]

One month later, a particularly elaborate and awe-inspiring Klan ceremonial took place on Grand Island, in the middle of the Niagara River. On the evening of May 23, hundreds of knights from Erie and Niagara counties ferried across to the island and assembled at a remote southern location on the edge of Tonawanda Bay. Dressed in their white-hooded regalia, members ignited a "flaming cross of huge proportions" on top of a hill and set off a series of giant bonfires along the beach. A large number of motorists traveling along the River Road on the opposite shore witnessed the eerie spectacle, and word was soon relayed to the Tonawanda police, who claimed they could not take action because of a lack of jurisdiction. Spared any intrusion by the authorities, the Klansmen conducted an hour-long induction ritual and then dispersed into the night, thus ending "one of the most picturesque illuminations on [the] Niagara River that has ever been seen." A short while later, a man identifying himself as the "Kleagle of Niagara Falls" called the *Express* and announced: "We have just put through a class of 148 on Grand Island and they will now receive their charter."[34]

Although the Klan could certainly take comfort and pride in its growing strength in western New York, recent developments elsewhere in the state presented a serious challenge to the secret society's very existence. Throughout late 1922 and early 1923, as KKK recruiting surged in major communities such as Buffalo, Rochester, Troy, Schenectady, Albany, and Syracuse, many state and local officials became convinced that the time had come for drastic action. In New York City, where local klaverns had taken on new life and wildly exaggerated rumors placed the total Klan membership at nearly fifty thousand, Mayor John Hylan launched an all-out war on the organization, ordering police to break up chapter meetings and secure a list of members.[35] At the same time, state lawmakers began to agitate for anti-KKK legislation, Senator John H. Hastings of Kings suggesting that steps be taken to "destroy the vicious secrecy of the outfit." Late in February 1923, Senator James J. (Jimmy) Walker of New York City, the Democratic majority leader in the upper house, introduced such a measure, a bill that would require oath-bound associations to file their membership lists with state officials. Walker's proposal experienced clear sailing in the senate, survived a surprisingly close vote in the assembly, and was signed by Governor Smith on May 22.[36]

Though it does not mention the Ku Klux Klan by name, New York's Walker Law—which still remains on the books—suggests which aspects of the Invisible Empire legislators found most threatening and objectionable. The law's most significant feature is that it restricts the freedom of association, targeting the practice of organizational secrecy. With the express exceptions of labor unions and officially chartered benevolent orders, the statute requires that

> Every existing membership corporation, and every existing unincorporated association having a membership of twenty or more persons, which corporation or association requires an oath as a prerequisite or condition of membership . . . file with the secretary of state a sworn copy of its constitution, by-laws, rules, regulations, and oath of membership, together with a roster of its membership and a list of its officers for the current year.

Such associations are also required to submit biannual statements "showing the names and addresses of such additional members as have been received."[37]

Klan opponents touted the Walker Law as a great victory for civil rights, and to a certain extent they were correct; despite the restrictions the measure places on the freedom of association, it is manifestly necessary and proper that state governments be involved in the monitoring and regulation of sizable organizations that may infringe upon the rights of others. This should not, however, obscure the political motivations that contributed to the law's passage. By 1923, the Invisible Empire's electoral clout had been well-demonstrated across the nation and New York klaverns appeared poised for political action. The incumbents in Albany recognized the uncertainty and instability that the Klan might bring to Empire State politics and hoped through the Walker Law to reduce the KKK's influence. This is clearly indicated by the statute's requirement that oath-bound societies "file in the office of the secretary of state every resolution or the minutes of any action of such corporation or association, providing for concerted action of its members or a part thereof to promote or defeat legislation, federal, state, or municipal, or to support or to defeat any candidate for political office." It would be fair to say, therefore, that a desire to maintain the political status quo contributed in no small measure to the legislature's taking action against the Klan.[38]

The enactment of the Walker Law constituted a major turning point in the development of the Klan in New York. Although the measure proved to be an awkward and largely ineffective means of attacking the KKK, its passage meant that the Klan, which steadfastly refused to divulge its membership, was now an illegal organization. Having consistently presented themselves as the true champions of law and government (in contrast, for example, to officials who openly winked at violations of the prohibition and vice statutes), Klansmen confronted an uncomfortable new role as lawbreakers. For many in the order, the dubious benefits of continued affiliation did not compensate for such status, and thousands drifted away. In the case of others, however, the appearance of the Walker Law crystallized commitment and engendered a desire to strike back at opponents. "Governor Al Smith, by signing that bill, barred himself from the Presidency of the United States," New York King Kleagle Emmitt D. (E. D.) Smith avowed before a crowd of eight thousand knights on Long Island. "The Klan pledges itself never to reveal the names of its members. We will fight to the last breastwork to prevent public disclosure of our identities."[39]

This belligerent attitude also characterized the Buffalo Klan, which signified its defiance by an unprecedented open-air meeting in the heart of the city three days after the Walker Law went into effect. Gathering on a large vacant lot near the intersection of Jefferson and Main streets, several hundred non-costumed kluxers conducted a Klan ritual on the evening of May 25, 1923, burning a twelve-foot-high cross constructed of wood wrapped with kerosene-soaked burlap. The fiery spectacle soon attracted a large crowd that spilled out into Main Street, and police rushed to the scene, only to discover that all members of the hooded order had departed; left behind were the fiery cross (which was extinguished by the fire department), an American flag, a few KKK pamphlets, and a canvas streamer emblazoned with "Ku Klux Klan." Subsequent questioning of onlookers and nearby residents by the police produced little useful information; no Klansman had been positively identified, and witnesses could not recall the automobile license numbers of departing knights.[40]

That same evening, the Invisible Empire was on the move in other communities. At midnight, three carloads of Klansmen entered the small village of Lancaster, where they proceeded to distribute Klan literature under the doors of homes and businesses. A village constable in a patrol car detected the "silent, hooded figures" and set off his siren; suddenly, "from all directions there scrambled hooded [Klansmen] stumbling over themselves in their frantic effort to pile into the waiting motors." The kluxers made their escape and the next morning Lancaster residents awoke to find copies of *Ideals of the Ku Klux Klan* on their doorsteps. The secret order also paid a nocturnal visit to Batavia, where members "canvassed the city, throwing their pamphlets on front porches." The knights worked until long after midnight, scaring a number of Batavians in the process.[41]

Two days later, a reporter for the *Express* received a telephone call from an unidentified Klan officer, inviting him to a gathering of the local Klan; the newspaperman was instructed to be at the corner of High and Washington streets at 8:30 p.m. and to carry his hat in his hand. At the designated time, a closed vehicle carrying two masked Klansmen and an unmasked driver picked up the reporter, who was immediately blindfolded. In route to the meeting, the Klansmen kept their identities secret, referring to each other by number ("Next left turn, No. 23."), and attempted to obscure the direction they were traveling by making numerous detours. The *Express* man, however, managed covertly to peer beneath his blindfold and discovered that the automobile had entered the village of Williamsville, then turned south on Transit Road. Here it had joined a large cavalcade of vehicles, each bearing a "white streamer or flag, presumably to mark them as Ku Klux conveyance," which rolled through the small communities of Depew and Lancaster with a noisy tooting of horns. Eventually the procession reached the site of the Klan affair, an open field near the corner of Transit Road and William Street, and the reporter was permitted to view the subsequent proceedings.[42]

By midnight, approximately thirty-five hundred knights representing "lodges from all parts of the western end of the state" had assembled, some of them carrying red flares. After an opening prayer "such as might have been delivered in almost any church," the Grand Kleagle of Western New York inducted a large class of recruits, asking them the questions required by the Kloran (Klan constitution): "Are you a native-born, white, Gentile American citizen? Do you believe in the tenets of the Christian religion? Do you believe in clannishness and will you faithfully practice same toward Klansmen? Do you believe in and will you faithfully strive for the eternal maintenance of white supremacy?" After receiving the appropriate response, the Klan officer sprinkled the heads of the candidates with water from a goblet and proclaimed them knights of the Invisible Empire, at which time a gigantic cross burst into flame. The ceremony was concluded with the singing of "America." Many Klansmen soon departed, but others remained at the site, fraternizing until the break of dawn.[43]

During the early morning hours, the *Express* man—his sight unencumbered—was conducted back to the city and permitted an interview with the grand kleagle. The KKK official stressed the pervasive influence of the hooded order in Buffalo: "Our organization is far reaching. We have members in every section of the city. At a meeting [yesterday] morning there were five members of the Buffalo police force and they have been Klansmen for a long time. The Klan has more than five offices in Buffalo and about the same number of meeting places." He pledged to resist the Walker Law and asked the reporter to notify the public of the local klavern's absolute support of prohibition: "You can say through your paper that the Governor had better not sign the repeal of the Mullan-Gage [state prohibition] act. We stand for law enforcement and enforcing the Constitution. Regardless of our feelings on the eighteenth amendment, we will see it enforced while it is in the Constitution." The grand kleagle and his companions then released their newspaper contact and drove away.[44]

Not surprisingly, the Klan's open defiance of the Walker Law and its claims of influence on the police force angered local authorities. "The Ku Klux Klan is not wanted in Buffalo and will not be tolerated," proclaimed Chief Burfeind. "I will send out the entire police department, if necessary, to put a stop to any meeting or ceremonial conducted by the Ku Klux Klan if they appear in disguise or robes"; the chief additionally promised to dismiss summarily any officer who joined the order. Deputy Chief Marnon likewise indicated that the organization would have a "merry time in Buffalo": "This department will not tolerate any Klan activities here and the first hooded man we find will be locked up, no matter who he is." Evidently convinced that the police needed additional incentive, Mayor Schwab posted a fifty-dollar bounty for "the first arrest and conviction of a member of the Klan."[45]

The overt hostility of local authorities enhanced the Buffalo klavern's appreciation of the serious problems posed by the Walker Law. Although the precise fashion in which the statute might be applied remained unclear, it appeared that the Schwab administration might use the law as the basis for a raid on the Klan. The arrest of even one Klansman could conceivably lead to the exposure of the chapter's entire membership and other untold damage. Even in the absence of some sudden move by the authorities, recruiting (and thus revenue) would surely slump as long as the organization was forced to exist beyond the pale of the law. It therefore became a matter of pressing urgency that Klansmen discover some manner of neutralizing the legal threat to their order.

A plan was soon devised. On May 31, 1923, four "representatives for the Ku Klux Klan for the Buffalo district," accompanied by their lawyer, appeared before New York Supreme Court Justice George E. Pierce and filed for state incorporation of the Knights of the Ku Klux Klan. Justice Pierce signed the provisional charter and the Klansmen carried the document to the county clerk's office, which would send it to Albany for final approval. Before delivering the charter to the county clerk, however, the KKK representatives erased the name "Knights of the Ku Klux Klan" and inserted the name "men's fraternal organization." If undetected, this illegal maneuver would have enabled the Invisible Empire to claim status as a "benevolent order," one of the two groups exempted from the membership-disclosure requirements of the Walker Law.[46]

Unfortunately for the Klan, the alteration was almost immediately discovered and the group found itself embroiled in a major scandal. District Attorney Moore indicated that the hooded order might be charged with falsification of official records, and New York Attorney General Carl Sherman secured an injunction preventing the KKK from making any future attempts to incorporate as a fraternal organization. Perhaps most crucially, the incident undermined the absolute secrecy that had earlier surrounded the Buffalo Klan, the press revealing the names of the chief culprits involved in the scandal: New York King Kleagle E. D. Smith (a resident of Binghamton) and Buffalo Klansmen Kenneth G. Scott (the Grand Kleagle of Western New York), George C. Bryant, and James B. Mincher.[47]

As might have been anticipated, Klansmen did not passively deliver themselves up to their enemies. E. D. Smith admitted that changes had been made in the charter, but dismissed them as "unimportant," and Kenneth Scott emphasized the necessity of such tactics given the patent unconstitutionality of the Walker Law and the Klan's pressing mission: "We cannot be compelled lawfully to reveal the lists of those affiliated with the [KKK]. The very fact that the advent of this organization has aroused to protest all the un-American forces in this nation is proof positive of its absolute necessity at this time."[48] Yet there can be little doubt that the altered-charter affair—the fallout of which, although it never resulted in formal indictments, persisted throughout the summer—hurt the Klan, solidifying the group's widespread image as a rogue organization given to deviousness and deceit. Even Imperial officials in Atlanta felt moved to distance themselves from the scandal, the *Imperial Night-Hawk* stressing that "the national organization has nothing to do with the New York Klan's attempt to incorporate to evade the Walker Law."[49] By mid-1923, the Empire State KKK, and the Buffalo klavern in particular, appeared to have forfeited all claims to public respectability and acceptance.

Three

Fraternity, Moral Reform, and Hate

Despite their failure to circumvent the provisions of the Walker Law, the Klansmen of western New York continued to hold large gatherings over the next several months. On July 4, 1923, Niagara Falls hosted the first annual convention (Klorero) of the New York Klan, an event that attracted thousands of participants, including a large delegation from Buffalo. After a day spent relaxing with family and friends, a company of three hundred knights assembled on Riverway Drive at 6:00 p.m. and paraded some four miles through the city to a large tract of land just beyond Porter Road and Gill Creek. The "klavalcade" was a colorful affair, featuring six robed riders astride "fiery piebalds," a five-Klansman fife and drum corps, and scores of uniformed (but unmasked) knights marching in military formation. The procession attracted thousands of onlookers who lined the parade's route "four or five deep," often jeering—but occasionally cheering—the hooded kluxers.[1]

Once they had arrived at the Porter Road site, the Klansmen donned their masks and mingled with nearly fifteen thousand fellow Klan members and invited guests. At ten o'clock the knights joined hands and formed a huge circle around a grassy knoll surmounted by a flag-draped altar and three giant crosses; surrounding the scene were ceremonial urns that glowed with a mysterious red fire. Klan officials set the large crosses ablaze and King Kleagle E. D. Smith proceeded to induct a new class of five hundred recruits. Upon the completion of the ritual, the night sky exploded with a fireworks display and Smith asked the assemblage, "What is the penalty for revealing the secrets of the Klan?" "Death!" roared those in attendance. A visiting reporter later acknowledged the powerful impact of the convention's concluding ceremony: "The psychology of the Klan's existence in this state became apparent at once. There was something romantic, almost savage, in this sort of a gathering, out in the open, the emotion stimulated by the mysterious garb, pyrotechnics, and blazing crosses."[2]

The success of the Klorero contributed to a new surge in Klan activity. On the evening of July 25, the Buffalo klavern conducted yet another "spectacular ceremonial" outside the eastern city limits, at the intersection of Transit Road and Main Street. The headlights of hundreds of automobiles illuminated the scene as approximately three thousand knights and "neophytes" witnessed the official chartering of the "Williamsville unit of the hooded order." Two evenings later, five hundred carloads of Klansmen assembled on the outskirts of the village of Hamburg, arranging their vehicles in a large semicircle around a flaming cross. The kluxers took care that the subsequent initiation ritual remained undisturbed, sentries turning away a number of unwanted onlookers. Late in August, "about 2,000 Klansmen from Buffalo and 800 from Erie, Pa., all in white robes and hoods," traveled to the Chautauqua County community of Sherman "for the purpose of establishing a local body"; the visitors ignited crosses and inducted the klavern's fifty charter members.[3]

Given the frequency and size of the Invisible Empire's open-air meetings in the summer and fall of 1923, a clash with the order's enemies was perhaps inevitable. On October 18, one thousand knights from Niagara County assembled at the farm of Henry H. Pletcher, a few miles east of Niagara Falls, to perform a nighttime initiation of six hundred recruits from Lockport, North Tonawanda, Pekin, Ransomville, Youngstown, Wilson, Newfane, Olcott, and La Salle. The hooded affair soon attracted the attention of passing motorists, who were kept from the scene by armed guards. One of the sentries, Klansman Roy Cramer, pointed a gun at several parties of onlookers and then discharged the weapon beneath the car of Edward P. Clifford, a resident of Lockport, who immediately departed to notify Niagara County Sheriff Benjamin F. Gould.[4]

Before the sheriff could arrive, approximately 150 Klan opponents from Lockport, some armed with revolvers and sawed-off shotguns, attempted to disrupt the initiation. According to a *Courier* reporter who witnessed the encounter, the attackers quickly overpowered the KKK's outer guards, but the sentries succeeded in crying out for help. Their hooded brethren immediately launched a wild counterattack, discharging "automatic double-barreled weapons and Texas Steer variety revolvers" in the air as the intruders fled before the "wave of white-robed figures sweeping down on them." The anti-KKK forces rapidly departed by automobile, and the kluxers, flushed with victory, completed their initiation. At the ceremony's conclusion, however, Sheriff Gould arrived and arrested two Klansmen for wearing masks in public. Although it took nearly three weeks, county authorities later charged Roy Cramer with first degree assault.[5] Kluxing, it increasingly appeared, was not without its perils.

As the numerous ceremonials and outdoor meetings in western New York demonstrated, the bonds of mystic fraternalism constituted a major part of the Klan's appeal; in this respect, the organization fulfilled many of the same social and emotional needs catered to by other ritualistic societies such as the Odd Fellows and the various branches of Masonry. The Invisible Empire's lack of social acceptance and its outlaw status, however, mandated particularly stringent standards of solidarity, discipline, and dedication that enhanced a sense of mission missing in mainstream fraternal groups. Although outsiders ridiculed almost every aspect of the hooded order, Klansmen remained confident that they were pursuing noble ends, that each knight represented another soldier in a crucial struggle to reorder and revitalize the community and nation.

By the latter half of 1923, the mysterious lure of the Klan had enabled the order to achieve an impressive foothold along the

Niagara frontier, with a total of approximately two thousand knights in Buffalo and roughly the same number in outlying communities in Erie and neighboring counties. Yet if the KKK intended to retain and expand upon this membership, the organization would need to develop a course of action that would address the specific concerns of the rank and file. As was the case with most chapters across the nation, the Buffalo klavern had early considered an involvement in politics, and rumors occasionally circulated of Klannish influence in electoral matters. Although the order had apparently lacked sufficient strength to play a significant role in the 1922 general elections, it seemed that the races for three seats on the city commission in 1923 proffered a promising opportunity; indeed, in June a former Klan officer informed a local reporter that the klavern had decided to field a three-man ticket in the fall contest. But the chapter soon abandoned these plans.[6]

The hooded order's reluctance to mount a formal political effort in 1923 can be readily appreciated. The most obvious problem was that a large percentage of voters were Roman Catholic or of new ethnic stock and thus hardly likely to support the apostles of Protestant nativism. Moreover, issues with which the Klan might have rallied the white Protestant vote had been largely co-opted. Commissioner Frank C. Perkins had a firm hold on labor's support (stressing his opposition to the International Railway Company), and incumbent Ross Graves, despite a personal taste for liquor, emphasized his endorsement of strict prohibition enforcement. Both men, as well as the other eventual victor, William F. Schwartz, had established themselves as political enemies of Mayor Schwab, occupied populist ground in opposition to the Citizens' Ticket backed by elements of Buffalo's commercial-civic elite, and commanded efficient campaign organizations; their candidacies simply did not present the Invisible Empire with an effective entering wedge into municipal politics. Nor were opportunities available in state and county races, where the great majority of incumbents—only one of whom was KKK-affiliated—scored easy victories.[7] Relatively small in numbers, confronted with a predominantly hostile ethnocultural environment, and unable to lay exclusive claim to a major issue, Buffalo Klansmen possessed little hope of assuming a dominant role in politics.

This did not mean, however, that the Invisible Empire was consigned to total political impotence. If the order did not possess the ability to displace its enemies at the polls, it still might take steps to force officials to modify their policies. Indeed, the Klan would soon assume a major role in the ongoing campaign to improve enforcement of the vice and prohibition laws in Buffalo and Erie County, an effort that had taken on increasing urgency during the first two years of the Schwab administration. It bears emphasizing that prior to this time the Klan had not openly involved itself in advancing the cause of moral reform, beyond general statements in support of better law enforcement. The preponderance of open Klan activity—the nighttime ceremonials and cross-burnings—had constituted a form of overt defiance and civil disobedience, but the klavern, as a group, had not undertaken a specific course of civic action. Thus only gradually did the Buffalo Klan embrace the cause of moral reform.

By the spring of 1923, the local crusade on behalf of improved moral conditions and better law enforcement had become exceedingly intense and bitter. Late in May, the Buffalo branch of the Anti-Saloon League released a new report on the collapse of prohibition enforcement, complaining that "We should not have to wait until a mayor commits a felony or his four-year term expires before we can put in a man who will do his duty."[8] Other evangelical groups also kept up the pressure, eventually persuading city authorities to hold special hearings in July and August on vice and alleged corruption in the police department. Although Mayor Schwab dismissed most of the reformers' claims, the hearings produced more than twenty-five hundred pages of testimony detailing prostitution, drug trafficking, gambling, and bootlegging in Buffalo, resulting in a widespread demand for a major reorganization of the police department.[9] Eventually succumbing to public pressure, Schwab in November ordered Chief of Police John Burfeind to step down and replaced him with Charles F. Zimmerman, a highly respected officer acceptable to reformers.[10]

This victory for Protestant activists was offset by two other

developments in 1923. One was Al Smith's return to the governor's office at the beginning of the year. Smith's most recent
campaign had largely focused on his opposition to prohibition,
and in June 1923 he secured repeal of the Mullan-Gage Act,
thereby greatly undermining prohibition enforcement in the Empire State.[11] A serious scandal in the New York Anti-Saloon
League constituted another major setback. In July, a New York
grand jury indicted State Superintendent William Anderson on
several counts of larceny, forgery, and extortion, charges related
to his fund-raising activities for the league. Although Anderson
consistently denied any wrongdoing, the indictment left his organization in disarray and significantly reduced the ASL's credibility in the struggle for better law enforcement. The situation would
become even worse early in 1924, when Anderson was convicted
of forgery and sentenced to two years in the state penitentiary.[12]

Confronted with a deteriorating situation and in dire need of
effective allies, eleven local Protestant ministers had entered the
ranks of the Invisible Empire by this time. Included among these
were three of the city administration's most vocal and prominent
critics: George A. Fowler, district supervisor of the New York Anti-
Saloon League and a prominent member of the Buffalo Methodist
Ministers' Association; Charles C. Penfold, pastor of Sentinel
Methodist Church and chairman of the Social Committee of the
Buffalo Council of Churches (formerly the Buffalo Federation of
Churches); and Littleton E. H. (L. E. H.) Smith, pastor of Ontario
United Presbyterian Church and also an active member of the
Buffalo Council of Churches.[13] Ambitious, energetic men in their
mid-thirties, Fowler, Penfold, and Smith shared an ardent, and
apparently sincere, interest in promoting a more moral and law-
abiding community in accordance with the standards of evangelical Protestantism; they had, however, become increasingly frustrated by a perceived worsening in local conditions and by what
they viewed as the uncooperative attitude of Buffalo authorities.

Since the advent of the Schwab administration, George Fowler
had attempted to rally the Protestant community against city
hall, releasing detailed reports that showed rampant disregard for
the law. These revelations, however, did little to change the local

situation, convincing Fowler in the summer of 1923 to explore other modes of civic activism. As he later explained,

> When the [Klan] started I was interested in an organization of citizens because municipal control of vice in the city was at low ebb. At the same time I heard that [the Reverend Oscar] Haywood was in the city and that he was a member of the Ku Klux Klan. A friend of mine, interested in the order, invited me to meet and hear Haywood. We met at the Ford hotel and talked for about an hour and a half. These gentlemen indicated to me that the Klan was a patriotic organization. No hint of bigotry which has been attached to the Klan was stressed by them and I assumed that it was not the case. They told me the Ku Klux Klan had been misrepresented by the press and that the organization stood for the maintenance of law and order and that it was not opposed to Jews, Catholics, negroes *[sic]*, and so on. . . . We went to an office on the east side of the city. I don't know whether I signed a card or whether somebody else did. But it was done with my consent.[14]

Yet membership in the Invisible Empire could not compensate for the scandal that soon overwhelmed the Anti-Saloon League. Although Fowler remained active in local affairs, his influence and credibility were severely diminished by the league's difficulties; thus other Klansmen assumed a more prominent role in advancing the cause of moral reform.

Throughout 1923, the Reverend Charles C. Penfold established himself as one of Buffalo's leading Protestant activists. Calling for a renewed campaign to address the community's "deplorable conditions," Penfold focused on the alleged breakdown of vice and prohibition enforcement in the downtown area, particularly the lower west side and the "tenderloin" district in the vicinity of Eagle Street. Skeptical about whether a police crackdown during July had improved the vice situation, the minister organized a team of undercover operatives (including two federal agents) who roamed the city at night gathering information. Penfold, designating himself Investigator No. 1, contributed to the effort by spending several evenings strolling past suspect cigar stores, soft drink shops, and residences. After being brazenly solicited by a number of prostitutes, he concluded that wide-open conditions generally prevailed in the heart of Buffalo. Testifying at the special city hearings on the vice situation in August, the pastor and his associates painted a graphic picture of a community wallowing in corruption and sliding toward absolute moral ruin.[15]

Penfold's spirited activism helped keep evangelicals convinced of the need for a major cleanup of city government, particularly the police department. The Buffalo Council of Churches endorsed his efforts and formally called on Mayor Schwab to improve law enforcement. Several weeks later, the Buffalo Baptist Union, representing twenty-eight local churches, similarly proclaimed its revulsion "at conditions which have existed, apparently with the consent of the police authorities," and demanded that the mayor "call to account those who are chiefly responsible for the shameful conditions revealed."[16] When mounting pressure resulted in the resignation of Chief Burfeind early in November, Penfold and his associates continued to attack city hall, claiming that the mayor's attitude toward prohibition had produced a general disrespect for the law. "Our whole trouble grows out of the fact that the whole Schwab administration seems to have decided to enforce only such laws as they personally believe in," argued Penfold. "In the matter of prohibition, they substitute their own views for the law and the result is bound to be anarchy." Non-Klansmen such as the Reverend Leon O. Williams agreed, warning that "What we as a people are facing is not merely a breakdown of the means of law enforcement, but it is a breakdown of our sense of the imperativeness of the need to maintain all the laws or to sink into the mire of social and political chaos."[17]

By the close of 1923, Protestant reformers had abandoned what little hope they may have possessed of changing the attitudes and policies of the Schwab administration. Accordingly, throughout the following year, they began to argue that the mayor's removal was an essential prerequisite for any improvement of local conditions, thereby elevating the animosity between city hall and its critics to an unprecedented level. It was in this atmosphere of increasing bitterness that the Klan began to appear as the best means of achieving results to certain Protestant activists, most notably the Reverend L. E. H. Smith. A resident of the Twenty-First Ward in northwest Buffalo, a married man with three small children, and a leading figure within the Buffalo Council of

Churches, the Reverend Smith had three years previously arrived from a pastorate in Philadelphia, where he had earned a reputation as a strong advocate of prohibition and the banning of Sunday sports. Smith enjoyed posing as a fearless man of action at war with the forces of evil and corruption, and it was he, more than any other Klansman, who spurred the Buffalo klavern into action.[18]

In the early morning hours of March 12, 1924, hooded and robed (but unmasked) members of Buffalo Klan No. 5 visited a number of roadhouses, saloons, and hotels located just outside the city line. The Klansmen notified the startled patrons and owners of these establishments that they were in violation of the law and that the klavern found this to be an intolerable situation; at one location the knights warned that "sales of liquor to young girls must cease." Four days later, another intrusion took place at the Auto Rest Inn, near the intersection of Main Street and Transit Road. Shortly after midnight, fifty costumed Klansmen suddenly entered the inn, sending several female customers into hysterics. A Klan spokesman ordered some 150 patrons to calm down and keep their seats; he then accused the Auto Rest Inn of breaking the law "every day and night" and of receiving special protection from the authorities. If the establishment did not change its ways, he admonished, the Klan would close it down. Having delivered their message, the white-robed vigilantes departed. In a subsequent interview, the proprietor of the inn, Mrs. Minnie "Jew Minnie" Clark DiCarlo, observed that the knights had "acted like gentlemen and molested no patron in the place."[19]

The Invisible Empire's open involvement in prohibition enforcement naturally angered local authorities. Erie County Sheriff Frank Tyler announced that "[If] the Ku Klux Klan attempts to take the law into its own hands, or resorts to any lynching methods, there will be trouble." The sheriff subsequently conferred with Mayor Schwab and Police Chief Charles F. Zimmerman about taking action against the hooded order, Schwab noting that the Klan visitations might easily "lead to bloodshed." "Someone is going to get excited about this nonsense and take a shot at these fellows," he explained. "Then it's going to be serious."[20] The klavern remained defiant, however. In a letter sent to the mayor on

March 17 (apparently the group's first official message in nearly two years), the Klan protested that "Klansmen have conducted themselves like gentlemen and have done no more than law abiding citizens would want to do to secure justice in the rottenness of your regime." "Make no mistake about our power," the missive warned: "There might have been a time when you could have done things with impunity, but not now." After the klavern sent copies of the letter to local newspapers, Schwab openly scoffed at the KKK's assertions: "I am not going to get into any controversy with any damn fools who call themselves Klansmen and are looking for notoriety. That's all they are looking for—notoriety." Nonetheless, he repeated his longstanding offer to meet personally with local knights.[21]

Buffalo Klan No. 5 felt that the time had indeed come for a personal meeting, albeit on the Klan's terms. On the evening of March 22, Mayor Schwab was an invited speaker before a gathering of five hundred west-side residents at the Unity Masonic Temple, in the Black Rock section of Buffalo. The unsuspecting mayor had just begun a talk on road construction when nine masked Klansmen in full regalia (some of them reportedly carrying spears) marched into the hall. Their unidentified leader stood before the mayor and reminded him that he had asked to meet with Klansmen: "That's what we are doing now. We're calling your bluff." Schwab, caught off guard, attempted to defend his administration's law enforcement efforts, but the Klansmen remained unconvinced. "The Knights of the Ku Klux Klan of this city do not think you are doing as much as you could," challenged the KKK spokesman. "We have already sent in complaints and named places where the law is being broken. No action has followed. What we want is to see the notorious dens of vice in and around Buffalo closed." After a few more inconclusive verbal exchanges, the knights departed, leaving behind a visibly shaken mayor.[22]

The encounter in Black Rock outraged Schwab and more than any other incident convinced him that the Buffalo klavern had to be crushed. The following day he called for a formal grand jury inquiry into the episode, pledging that "I am going through with the investigation if I have to go down with colors flying. The

Klansmen acted in a cowardly way. A cur would give an enemy more of a chance than they did." Police detectives were ordered to discover the identities of the Klansmen who had interrupted the talk, and District Attorney Moore vowed to prosecute the knights on a charge of unlawful intrusion, which carried a maximum penalty of one year in prison.[23] Perhaps alarmed by the possibility of legal action, the klavern on March 25 informed the press by letter that the west-side gathering had been a regular meeting of the local KKK chapter, that the three hundred men and two hundred women who had been in the audience were all Klan-affiliated; Klansmen therefore were not liable to prosecution because they could not possibly have "intruded" on their own meeting. The letter additionally stressed that Mayor Schwab was overreacting to an innocent prank: "The Mayor was done no harm. . . . In future years he may be able to appreciate the whole affair as a joke."[24]

The Klan's explanations only hardened Schwab's resolve to rid Buffalo of the hooded order. Less than two weeks later, he succeeded in securing the services of an informant within the klavern who began producing highly detailed reports of KKK activities; the spy also revealed the identities of a number of previously unidentified Klansmen, thereby adding to a list of 126 known or suspected knights that the Buffalo police had compiled the previous year. This agent, however, was unable to obtain the klavern's closely guarded membership files—the key to shattering the Invisible Empire's secrecy. Thus, for the time being, the mayor had to bide his time.[25]

Unaware of the threat to their order, Buffalo Klansmen for the next several weeks pushed ahead with their moral reform program. Letters affixed with the official Klan seal were mailed to city officials and to Frank Perry, manager of the Gaiety Theater, complaining about illegal Sunday theatrical performances, and the Reverends Penfold and Smith directed yet another major undercover investigation of vice and liquor violations.[26] Once sufficient information had been amassed, Klansman Smith secured warrants from the office of District Attorney William Donovan and personally accompanied officers on a series of highly publicized raids. On March 29, the crusading pastor and prohibition agents descended on a "soft drink" shop at 145 High Street and uncovered a cache of more than ten thousand dollars worth of liquor; the following evening, raids on a variety of other establishments resulted in the seizure of an even larger amount of illicit booze. Similarly successful raids—prompted by official complaints filed by Smith and his close associate and fellow Klansman David D. Mayne, a former Erie County sheriff's deputy and railroad detective—continued through the spring and well into the early summer, enhancing the impression that the local authorities had been shamelessly remiss in enforcing prohibition. One particularly revealing episode took place in early April, when four government agents accompanied by David Mayne raided a bowling alley and discovered a group of sheriff's deputies and city hall employees consuming alcoholic beverages; also present was a sheepish Sheriff Tyler, who held an open bottle of beer in his hand.[27]

Klansmen cited the results of the raids as clear evidence that conditions in Buffalo would never improve as long as Mayor Schwab remained in office. "I publicly charge the Mayor with having winked at lawlessness," announced L. E. H. Smith. "Second, I charge that he has broken the law himself, and, third, I charge that he advised others to become lawless." When a new report of the Buffalo Council of Churches claimed that "conditions of vice and lawlessness in Buffalo are worse than they have been in many years," Klan member Charles Penfold asserted that the document confirmed that Mayor Schwab "alone is to blame for the present deplorable state of affairs in Buffalo."[28]

Such sentiments were not confined to the Invisible Empire. The Reverend Robert J. MacAlpine of the Central Presbyterian Church avowed that "the disgusting moral situation in Buffalo is due to the impeachable infidelity of the Mayor to the duties for which he was elected," and the Reverend John D. Campbell, pastor of the Covenant Presbyterian Church, said that because of the Schwab administration "Buffalo has become a stench in the nostrils of other cities. Her fair name is besmirched." The minister of the Glenwood Avenue Baptist Church, the Reverend Alva W. Bourne, similarly wanted the mayor to know that "the cultured, law-abiding, country loving, child loving and God loving people of Buffalo will no longer wade through the vomit of the underworld." By early April, it was the opinion of the *Courier* that evangelical leaders had launched a "concerted campaign" against Schwab and his administration.[29]

By this time, the embattled mayor had abandoned any desire to placate moral reformers. "I am convinced," he announced, "that the ministers of Buffalo are not trying to make any constructive campaign of what they call improvement of conditions of the city. [Their campaign] is based on a bitterness and hatred that ill becomes those who profess to be ministers of God."[30] Owing to the secret reports that he had just begun receiving, Schwab was also well aware that the Ku Klux Klan was intimately involved in the current surge of moral reform activity. On April 12, he openly accused the Reverend Smith of having headed the delegation of Klansmen who interrupted his talk at Unity Masonic Temple: "Smith was the man who spoke to me behind the Ku Klux Klan mask. I have certain knowledge to that effect, and I challenge him to deny it." The mayor went on to argue that "any group of ministers which endorses the activities of a recognized Klansman, who is admittedly a member of an intolerant organization, is not deserving of consideration."[31]

Schwab's accusations made little impression on his critics. "God bless the K. of C. or the K.K.K. or any other organization that will cooperate to give us a cleaner city," commented one non-Klan pastor. Indeed, there were signs that the Klan might at last be achieving a degree of open acceptance among local Protestants. On April 13, Woodside Methodist Church invited Klan organizer Oscar Haywood to give a talk on his order's aims; Haywood promised that "If you will turn this church over to the Ku Klux Klan, we will make it the biggest church in Buffalo within six months, and the biggest in the state within a year."[32] That same month, Mrs. Alma Smith (no relation to the Reverend Smith), a teacher at School No. 16, told her eighth-grade class that "Our mayor ought to be the next one tarred and feathered and it would be a good thing for Buffalo if the K.K.K. did something."[33] The Buffalo Council of Churches continued to extend full support to the Reverend Smith (who consistently, if unconvincingly, denied Klan affiliation), and even District Attorney Moore, who despised the KKK,

felt obligated to cooperate with Smith and his undercover operatives.[34] Thus, by the early summer of 1924, largely as a result of
its success in focusing the Protestant community's attention on
the shortcomings of Mayor Frank Schwab, the Klan appeared to
be easing itself into a role as a legitimate force in local affairs.

Although the Buffalo Klan's increasing involvement in moral reform provides some indication of the goals, values, and motivations that guided at least part of the klavern's membership, many
basic questions about the hooded order obviously remain: What
did Buffalo knights say and do at their secret meetings? Where
did the Klan meet? Who were the leaders of the Klan? In sum,
how did the Klan function as an organization? In the case of the
Buffalo klavern, a remarkable collection of documents—detailed
reports of Klan activities produced by two informants operating
from April to August 1924—permits such queries to be answered
with unusual specificity. The bulk of these reports were prepared
by an unidentified individual who had joined the hooded order
sometime during the first half of 1923; the reasons for his becoming an informer for Mayor Schwab are unclear, although he seems
to have been very displeased with the quality of the Klan's local
leadership.[35] The other source was Edward C. Obertean, who was
appointed as a "special patrolman" by the mayor and assigned the
task of infiltrating the klavern; he entered the Invisible Empire on
June 16, 1924.[36] The reports of both men appear to be straightforward and balanced, although it is evident that their primary task
was to relay information that could be used to discredit the KKK.

Despite the Buffalo Klan's claims that it was not a racist or
religiously intolerant organization, the informers' reports reveal
that bigotry pervaded the klavern. Meetings of the hooded order
often featured speakers who employed crude negative stereotypes
of Jews, African Americans, and Catholics. At one meeting late in
June 1924, a visiting lecturer avowed that "The Jew's God is the
almighty dollar and his creed is commercialism and greed"; he
also noted that Klansmen "wanted nothing to do" with blacks and
hoped to introduce a bill in the state legislature "prohibiting the
marriage of a Negro and a white person."[37] The great bulk of the
KKK's spite, however, was reserved for Roman Catholics, who

were routinely referred to as "fish," "crossbacks," and, whether
they were Irish or not, "micks," "harps," and "flannel mouths."[38]
The pope was described at one meeting as a "big bellied, poisoned
toad," and stories circulated that the Catholics controlled the
press, had poisoned President Warren G. Harding, and were plotting, in association with the Jews, to install Governor Alfred E.
Smith in the White House. Some Klansmen believed that Catholic
agents in the United States Treasury Department had succeeded
in putting hidden religious symbols on a certain type of one dollar
bill in preparation for the arrival of the pope in America. One
informant observed Klansmen Raymond Goss and Harry A. Kiefer
tearing bills in half and asked what they were doing:

> Kiefer said that particular series of one dollar bills have the Pope's
> picture, a cross, the word "Leo" and a rosary. He showed me what
> was supposed to represent each of these. He said however it was
> only necessary to tear off the corner of the bill which contained the
> Pope's picture. . . . Goss informed me he had torn up about 100 of
> these bills in the last two weeks. Kiefer and Goss . . . seemed of
> the opinion that clansmen *[sic]* can finally eliminate the bill from
> circulation by tearing every one [they] get hold of and thus making
> it necessary to replace them by some other issue. Kiefer said, "The
> bunch that designed the bill are the ones Harding canned. That's
> the reason the Catholics poisoned him."[39]

Many knights viewed themselves as participants in a life-or-
death struggle to keep the forces of Roman Catholicism at bay.
Klansman Louis H. Conshafter said that "someone in the organization [KKK] should bomb the next president of the U.S. if he
appointed any Catholics to office," and another member, Albert C.
Acker, expressed a desire to "shoot some of these d——m K. of C."
At a meeting in May, members were formally advised that the
Klan had decreed that "no son of Rome would ever sit in the
president's chair."[40] Yet the klavern was not totally inflexible in
regard to religion. The knights regularly praised District Attorney
William J. Donovan, who, despite his Catholicism, was "the only
official in the County who will give us a square deal."[41] There is
also no evidence that the Klan concerned itself in a specific way
with Buffalo's large populations of Italian and Polish Catholics;
the KKK's sectarian animosity focused upon the predominantly

Irish Knights of Columbus and Mayor Schwab, who were political, as well as religious, enemies.

The klavern spent more time discussing politics than religion, although the two topics were often intertwined. According to the mayor's informants, most members belonged to the Republican party but felt that local party leaders were hopelessly corrupt. "Before we can clean up the Republican party in Erie County," the Reverend L. E. H. Smith explained at one Klan meeting, "we must clean up the Republican organization." One prominent county official the Klan particularly disliked was Sheriff Frank Tyler, who had done little to strengthen prohibition enforcement. The news that federal officers had caught Tyler drinking beer (during the Klan-sponsored raid in April 1924) produced jubilation in KKK headquarters. "That's great," exulted Grand Kleagle George C. Bryant. "This will make great reading in the newspapers." Another Klan officer observed, "We have been laying for the Sheriff for some time."[42]

Not surprisingly, the Klan also spent considerable time plotting against Mayor Schwab (dubbed "Frank Xzema Slob" by one klavern wit). Throughout early 1924, the KKK sought concrete evidence linking the mayor with illegal liquor interests and hoped in the near future to file charges. At a general meeting of the secret order, the Reverend Smith, the group's chief investigator, claimed to be on the verge of success:

> Mr. Chairman and Brothers: You have been calling for action and we have decided to give you action. We have discovered a large bootlegging ring in Buffalo which seems to be guided by some master mind. We have reason to believe that party is the Honorable Mayor. We have the assurance from the District Attorney [William Donovan] that if we can connect him [Schwab] up with it [then he will be] brought up on a federal charge. We also happen to know the Mayor and other city officials frequent places where booze is sold and we are going to make an effort to raid one of these while he is paying a visit.[43]

The mayor, however, perhaps because he was well aware of the Klan's intentions, avoided being caught in a compromising situation, prompting one Klansman to comment, "Boys, the only way for us to get Schwab out of there is for about five men to go out and get him and take him out and never bring him back." Other knights nevertheless felt that the secret order had succeeded in permanently crippling the mayor's political career. One member believed that Schwab would certainly go down to defeat at the next election, even if "we are not able to get him out of there before then." "No, no, he won't ever run again," opined another. "He knows he hasn't a chance."[44]

Their confidence about the eventual removal of the mayor notwithstanding, Buffalo Klansmen possessed few illusions about their political strength. In contrast to many Klan chapters elsewhere, the klavern consistently declined to field a slate of municipal candidates, opting instead to determine which non-Klan candidates were "right," then casting the Klan's votes as a bloc. Prior to the city elections in the fall of 1923, a committee headed by Klansman William J. Casper (a clerk at the National Aniline Company) selected the three "best qualified" candidates for the city commission; one of their choices was the eventual winner William F. Schwartz, whom the klavern, ironically, later denounced as one of the "biggest bootleggers in Buffalo." With a mayoral election scheduled for 1925, the Klan hoped that a satisfactory reform candidate would emerge, but recognized, as one knight noted, that "it will take more than the Clan [sic] vote to elect him."[45] For the present, and probably for the future, the KKK had little choice other than to accept a role as a minority interest group with limited access to governmental power.

Despite its lack of electoral prospects, the Klan aspired to be a significant factor in community affairs. One informant observed that the secret order's leaders carefully scrutinized press reports of Klan activities, studying "the newspapers hungrily to see if anything is published that will react to their advantage—at the same time telling their followers the newspapers are Catholic controlled and fighting the clan [sic]." The Klan distrusted most of the local press but felt that the *Commercial* and the *News* were relatively balanced in their reporting; on one occasion George Bryant angrily denounced the *Express* because "every time anyone burns a cross around here [that paper] always says, 'Boys did it.' "

The KKK was delighted that the undercover investigations of the Reverend Smith and David Mayne had garnered so much favorable publicity, and hoped that this would improve the group's poor public image. In order that Buffalonians might more readily associate the Invisible Empire with the purity crusade, the klavern issued an official statement praising Smith and Mayne, offering "to assist them financially and to give them all the information in our possession relative to the rotten conditions in the city and county."[46]

During the spring and summer of 1924, KKK headquarters were regularly abuzz with excitement over the Klan-sponsored raids of bootlegging establishments. Smith and Mayne frequently rushed into the klavern offices for important conferences with Klan officers, then dashed away on urgent business. One knight admiringly noted that Mayne was a "fighter." "He sure is," agreed another Klansman, "and he will keep on until he gets that man Tyler out of office." Mayne and Smith personally conducted most of the Klan's undercover work, obtaining samples of illegal alcoholic beverages with a small rubber syringe in order to secure federal warrants. Such work was perhaps not totally unpleasant: late in June an informer spotted the minister and his assistant sitting with two attractive young women in the back of a tenderloin district cafe, evidently in preparation for having the place "pinched." The two investigators updated fellow Klansmen on their activities at general meetings of the order, Smith at one point emphasizing "the great personal sacrifice he was making to carry on this work."[47]

In addition to a sense of participation in the campaign to improve law enforcement, the klavern offered its members the standard features of fraternal life. General meetings took place approximately every two weeks, usually at Mizpah Hall on Buffalo's west side. Klan rituals, the induction of recruits, and speeches by visiting lecturers and klavern officials dominated these gatherings; occasionally an outdoor ceremonial would be held. "Nothing of importance is discussed [at these meetings]," noted an informant, "on account of it being considered too open." Indeed, secrecy so permeated the Buffalo Klan that most rank-and-file knights knew the identities of only a small percentage of the membership, a situation that enhanced security and diminished the possibility of an internal challenge to the klavern's leadership. Klan headquarters notified knights of forthcoming functions by mail, but there was growing fear that the group's mailing list might fall into the wrong hands. In order to prevent this, the Klan devised a "block system," the "idea being to have each man on record at the office by a number, so it would not be necessary to carry their names on the record cards at the office. Then when a meeting is called one man in each ward would be notified and he would notify a man in each district and so on down to each individual." The klavern planned to have this new mode of mobilization in place by November 1924, in time for the general elections.[48]

Klan headquarters were located in a suite of offices at the Calumet Building in downtown Buffalo; the site had been rented by the Kay-Bee Adsign Company, which served as a KKK front. Numerous Klansmen passed in and out of headquarters, exchanging news, gossiping, and making sales contacts, but the organization's serious business was conducted by a handful of klavern officers in closed session. During the period 1921–1924, four men had headed the secret order as Grand Kleagle: a man identified only as Batty; Kenneth Scott, a professional Klan organizer; Stewart Queer, a former minister who was employed at different times by the Westinghouse Electric and American Brass companies; and George C. Bryant, a former manager of the Pentix Petroleum Corporation who also held the position of Grand Titan of the Province of Western New York. None of these individuals had proven to be a particularly talented or inspirational leader; in fact, two of them had nearly wrecked the Klan. Batty, who probably had been an outside organizer dispatched by Atlanta, embezzled the klavern's entire treasury and had departed by 1922. His successor, Kenneth Scott, possessed "a good personality and [was] well liked by the men for awhile," but he was removed from office after becoming too familiar with married members of the Klan's women's auxiliary. Stewart Queer had probably been the Klan's best leader, yet he resigned when the klavern declined to pay him a salary of fifty dollars per week; he later commented that the Klan "had not given him the right deal and he was sick of it."[49]

By early 1924, George Bryant, under orders from the KKK hierarchy to straighten out the situation in Buffalo, had assumed control of the klavern. Bryant infused the group with a new enthusiasm, but there was growing dissatisfaction with his leadership. The failure of Klan officers to render a full accounting of the organization's finances angered many members. At a meeting in February, Klansman and State Assemblyman Henry W. Hutt requested that Bryant prepare monthly reports of klavern expenditures, and many knights subsequently refused to pay dues until they learned where their money was going. Bryant's appointment of his father-in-law, William B. Royal, and brother-in-law, Walter B. Hawke, as financial secretaries helped fuel suspicions. One dissident Klansman, Milo F. Jarden, declared his intention to "find out whether this is a family affair, a money-making scheme or what"; another unhappy member speculated that there were "a couple of 'black legs'" at the head of the local Klan.[50] By the summer of 1924, it did not appear that Bryant would prove any more successful than his predecessors.

The reports prepared by Mayor Schwab's informants depict an organization that possessed few redeeming features. On the other hand, they do not reveal a warped collection of antisocial fanatics and terrorists. The KKK's scheming against the mayor and other officials had its repugnant aspects but probably was quite similar to the plans that were being formulated in the anti-Klan camp. The religious and racial bigotry embraced by the Invisible Empire, while repellent by today's standards, hardly distinguished the Klan in the 1920s; similar sentiments, almost surely, were at that time routinely expressed in lodge halls, private clubs, executive board rooms, and around Protestant family dinner tables. Also, despite its anger at local officials, the Klan never seemed to consider any type of drastic extralegal action (beyond refusing to comply with the provisions of the Walker Law). The hooded order followed standard legal procedure in securing warrants against illegal establishments, never engaged in violence against local African Americans and immigrants, and hoped to establish itself as a legitimate force within the existing power structure. To characterize the KKK, therefore, as a hopelessly aberrant and lawless fringe group would be manifestly inaccurate. Indeed, the most frightening aspect of the Invisible Empire was its ability to attract ordinary, law-abiding citizens.

Four

The Knights of the Queen City

While the reports of undercover investigators enhance our understanding of the Buffalo Klan, these sources focus on the activities of klavern officials and only vaguely describe the chapter's rank and file. Exactly who composed the main body of the Klan, these masked men who gathered around fiery crosses at night? Often Klan studies are hampered by a dearth of reliable membership data, but a detailed evaluation of the Buffalo klavern is made possible by the existence of a rare document: a list, culled from the Klan's official files, of the chapter's active membership as of early July 1924. With the exception of minor clerical errors and misspellings, the roster appears to be both accurate and comprehensive, providing the names of 1,910 individuals. Of these 1,747 resided within the city limits, thirty-three lived in the neighboring village of Kenmore (which never had a klavern of its own), and ninety-nine came from a variety of other communities; the addresses of thirty-one Klansmen remain unknown. In addition to names and addresses, the document provides the ages of 93.8 percent of the membership, the occupations of 96.4 percent, and the employers of 94.1 percent. In sum, the roster and its associated data constitute one of the most comprehensive and detailed sources of information concerning the Invisible Empire in a large urban area yet discovered.[1]

When considering the major themes that have been addressed in Klan historiography, the most important information in the membership list is probably that concerning occupation. Contemporary opponents of the hooded order routinely argued that the KKK could hold little appeal for intelligent, rational, and respectable citizens; a Buffalo newspaper editor, for example, asserted in 1923 that the Klan attracted "the chinless and those of the slanting brow" and consisted of "morons attired in sheet and pillow case."[2] Although most scholarly evaluations have not been this extreme in their depiction, many have emphasized the alleged ignorance, unsophistication, and socioeconomic marginality of Klansmen—even in the absence of supporting data. Because occupation often serves as the nexus of important social and psychological variables—intelligence, family life, education, ethnicity, class standing, and personality—it provides a valuable means of assessing the general types of men recruited by the KKK in Buffalo.

Individuals from a wide variety of occupations joined the local klavern: doctors, lawyers, engineers, accountants, bank tellers, mail carriers, jewelers, machinists, janitors, and common laborers. Klansmen included blue-collar workers who earned their livelihood by making steel, operating cranes, navigating tugboats, and repairing railroad cars, and men who pursued gentler trades: photographers, florists, interior decorators, commercial artists, secretaries, and a nurse. Beneath the white robes and hoods could also be found firemen and policemen, architects and surveyors, clergymen and clerks, butchers, bakers, and, at the American Brass Company, candlestick makers. Altogether, the Klan was drawn from 129 major types of occupations.

In order to determine the occupational distribution of the local klavern, the 1,707 knights residing in Buffalo for whom occupation is known (89.3 percent of the entire chapter, 97.7 of those living inside the city) have been organized into the six occupational status categories utilized by Robert A. Goldberg in his study of the KKK in Colorado.[3] Table 1 presents the percentage of klavern members in each category, along with percentages for Buf-

Table 1

Occupational Distribution (by Percent) of Buffalo Klansmen,
1921–1924, Compared with the Occupational Distribution
of Buffalo' s Male and Native-White Male Working
Populations in 1920

Occupational Status Group	KKK Residing in Buffalo	Male Working Population	Native-White Male Working Population
High nonmanual	6.1	3.6	4.7
Middle nonmanual	18.5	10.3	10.4
Low nonmanual	27.7	17.6	22.6
Skilled	30.6	24.9	25.3
Semiskilled and service	16.4	28.9	30.2
Unskilled	.5	14.5	6.5

Sources: Buffalo Klan Membership List; U.S. Bureau of the Census, *Fourteenth Census of the United States, 1920: Population* 4: 1068–70.

falo's 1920 male and native-white male working populations. As
can be seen, judged by their occupations the city's knights were a
remarkably high-status group, with significantly higher percentages of members in the high and middle nonmanual categories,
and lower percentages in the semiskilled/service and unskilled
classifications, than the other two groups of working males. To a
certain extent, this contrast could have been anticipated: the KKK
confined its membership to native-born white Protestants—a distinctly advantaged group socioeconomically—and the working
populations with which Klansmen are compared included large
numbers of first- and second-generation ethnics. Nonetheless, the
Klan's overall occupational prestigiousness remains impressive,
particularly when one considers that these were the occupations
listed on application forms from the period 1921–1924; it may
well be that some Klansmen on the list rose in occupational status
during this period. In addition, the list presents information only
on members who had not ceased affiliation by mid-1924. It is
likely that prior to the implementation of the Walker Law in 1923
and the intensified activism of local Klan opponents, the klavern
had contained an even higher percentage of high-status members,
who resigned because of increased legal liability.

It might be argued that to compare the Klan's occupational distribution with that of working populations containing a large percentage of members of recent immigrant stock produces an exaggerated sense of the Klan's occupational prestigiousness. Prestige and status, after all, are largely relative. Perhaps a better group with which to compare Klansmen would be native-white male workers of native parentage, a group that enjoyed generally higher occupational status than the native-white male working population at large. Not only does the native-white-of-native-parentage category exclude many native-white Catholic workers of Polish, Italian, Irish, and German origin, but it was also the group from which a majority of Klansmen were probably drawn. In other words, the native-white-of-native-parentage male working population is probably as close to a socioeconomic (and to a limited extent, ethnic and religious) peer group as federal census data enable us to construct for the Buffalo Klan. It should be recognized, however, that the native-white-of-native-parentage population included many non-Protestants—most of Irish and German ancestry—who were not eligible for Klan membership. In addition, as will be discussed later, a large contingent of the klavern was composed of Protestants of German ancestry, who may well have had at least one foreign-born parent, particularly in such a city as Buffalo, which had a sizable German foreign-born population; moreover, a significant percentage of non-German Klansmen may have had at least one foreign-born parent (those of English and Canadian descent, for example). Thus the Klan's membership and the native-white-of-native-parentage male working population may have been mutually exclusive to a significant degree.

A comparison of the two groups nevertheless gives a clearer sense of the Invisible Empire's occupational status locally. As is indicated in table 2, even compared with Buffalo's native-white males of native parentage—the most occupationally prestigious group detected in the 1920 federal census—Klansmen as a group clearly enjoyed higher occupational status. The distinctly privileged position occupied by both of these groups is, in turn, demonstrated by comparison with the occupational distribution of Buffalo's foreign-born white male workers, who constituted nearly 35 percent of the total male work force. In terms of occupation,

Table 2
Occupational Distribution (by Percent) of Buffalo Klansmen,
1921–1924, Compared with the Occupational Distribution of
Buffalo' s Native-White-of-Native-Parentage Male and Foreign-
Born Male Working Populations in 1920

Occupational Status Group	KKK Residing in Buffalo	Native-White-of-Native-Parentage Male Workers	Foreign-Born White Male Workers
High nonmanual	6.1	5.9	1.9
Middle nonmanual	18.5	11.5	9.9
Low nonmanual	27.7	25.4	8.9
Skilled	30.6	24.0	24.1
Semiskilled and service	16.4	28.4	26.3
Unskilled	.5	4.5	28.6

Sources: Buffalo Klan Membership List; U.S. Bureau of the Census, *Fourteenth Census of the United States, 1920: Population* 4: 1068–70.

therefore, the Buffalo Klan can best be viewed as a generally prestigious group within a native-white male population that it-self enjoyed relative prestige and advantages.

In addition to indicating the general economic and social status of Buffalo Klansmen, occupational data reveal the types of employment in which knights were either over- or underrepresented compared with the native-white male working population at large. Perhaps occupation, which both profoundly influences and reflects social and personal behavior, can provide clues as to why certain Buffalonians did or did not join the Invisible Empire. A convenient way to begin such analysis is by looking at Klan employment patterns within each of the occupational status categories utilized above.

High Nonmanual

If the Buffalo klavern members residing inside the city had consti-tuted a perfect cross section of the 1920 native-white male work-ing population, then 1.61 percent of the native-white men in each occupation would have belonged to the KKK. Some obvious problems with this calculation, of course, are that Klan occupational data come from a later period (1921–24), some Klansmen may not even have lived in Buffalo in 1920 or been employed at that time, and the occupational profile of the city may have been altered between 1920 and 1924 by certain forms of economic growth and/ or decline (the expansion of the local automobile and chemical industries, for example). Nonetheless, the 1.61 percent benchmark is probably a fairly reliable, if inexact, means of evaluating patterns of Klan employment—at least for the purpose of determining the occupations in which Klansmen were over- or underrepresented.

In table 3, the percentage of Klansmen (among the city's native-white males) in eight of the sixteen high nonmanual occupations held by KKK members has been calculated. Two professions, cler-

Table 3
Representation of Buffalo Klansmen in High Nonmanual
Occupations, 1921–1924

Occupation	Number of Klansmen	Number of Native-White Males, 1920	Percent Klansmen
Architect	1	149	.67
Chemist	3	392	.76
Chiropractor	4	NA	NA
Clergyman	11	283	3.88
Dentist	4	287	1.39
Editor	1	NA	NA
Engineer	41	926	4.42
Lawyer	5	689	.72
Optometrist	5	NA	NA
Pharmacist	13	NA	NA
Physician	9	622	1.44
Publisher	1	NA	NA
School Principal	2	NA	NA
Teacher	3	622	.48
Veterinarian	2	NA	NA

Sources: Buffalo Klan Membership List; U.S. Bureau of the Census, *Fourteenth Census of the United States, 1920: Population* 4: 1068–70.

gyman and engineer, were significantly overrepresented in the klavern. The special appeal the KKK held for certain men of the cloth—its advocacy of moral reform, strict prohibition enforcement, and militant Protestantism—can be easily understood. Indeed, it should be recognized that many of the native-white clergymen tabulated by the 1920 census were non-Protestant, thus making the KKK's recruiting among clergymen eligible for membership all the more impressive.

The possible explanation for the overrepresentation of engineers is not as readily apparent. Four types of engineering professionals could be found in the local Klan: thirteen chemical engineers, seventeen mechanical engineers, seven electrical engineers, and four civil engineers. These men were generally older than their fellow knights, with an average age of a little more than thirty-seven years; most of them worked for large industrial and manufacturing concerns, more than a fourth for the National Aniline and Chemical Company. Of those listed in the 1924 city directory, 86.6 percent headed households; a majority resided in middle-class neighborhoods in Buffalo's northern wards. Although these men's specific occupational activities remain unknown, it can be reasonably surmised that they spent much of their work day calculating, measuring, planning, and testing, as well as supervising and coordinating the activities of others. No doubt they had acquired habits based upon a sense of orderliness and precision. Perhaps a desire for a better ordered, formally bound community—a desire sustained both by their occupational experiences and the cultural values of native-white Protestantism—had led them into the Invisible Empire, an organization committed to the reordering of society in accordance with traditional Protestant standards.

Three high nonmanual professions were notably underrepresented in the Klan: chemists, lawyers, and teachers, all occupations in which native-whites predominated. The explanation for the small number of chemists is not known, but surely lawyers and teachers had steered clear of the Klan for legal and job-security reasons. Klan-affiliated attorneys risked disbarment after the enactment of the Walker Law, and many teachers, especially those in the public schools, were vulnerable to removal by anti-Klan elements. Legal vulnerability could likewise explain the dearth of high government officials in the order.

Middle Nonmanual

The manner in which the 1920 federal census grouped occupations hinders an evaluation of this status category, but two occupations —accountant/auditor and manager/superintendent—showed notable overrepresentation (see table 4). As was the case with engineers, these men earned their living by measuring, calculating, coordinating, and supervising, but they were somewhat younger (an average age of 29.3 years for the accountant/auditor group, 36.1 for the manager/superintendents) and less concentrated in Buffalo's north-side wards. A wide variety of business concerns employed Klan-affiliated manager/superintendents, ranging from large industrial concerns to small retail establishments.

Table 4
Representation of Buffalo Klansmen in Middle Nonmanual
Occupations, 1921–1924

Occupation	Number of Klansmen	Number of Native-White Males, 1920	Percent Klansmen
Accountant/Auditor	19	757	2.50
Businessman, small	163	NA	NA
Buyer/Department Head	16	NA	NA
Draftsman	7	516	1.35
Farmer	1	NA	NA
Government Official, middle	2	NA	NA
Inspector	22	NA	NA
Manager/Superintendent	82	2,118	3.87
Nurse	1	NA	NA
Student	2	NA	NA
Surveyor	1	NA	NA

Sources: Buffalo Klan Membership List; U.S. Bureau of the Census, *Fourteenth Census of the United States, 1920: Population* 4: 1068–70.

Small businessmen, for whom census data are unavailable, composed the largest single group of middle nonmanual Klansmen. One of the KKK's strongest selling points was its practice of "klannishness," which obligated Klansmen to direct as much of their trade as possible toward fellow knights. For the small white Protestant entrepreneur, often beset by economic uncertainty and perhaps envious of the perceived ethnic solidarity that assisted "un-American" businesses, such an appeal could prove enticing. Census data shed little light on what type of small businessmen were most receptive to the Klan, but it appears that in at least one occupation—restaurant owner—the Klan was overrepresented (3.17 percent) among the native-white male work force. Nearly half (48.5 percent) of the restaurants, cafes, and lunch rooms in Buffalo in 1920 were owned by foreign-born residents, and perhaps this had enhanced the Invisible Empire's appeal among restaurant owners; the intertwining of nativistic and economic concerns may have also influenced the Klan's sizable contingent of independent grocers.

One means of ascertaining which types of small businessmen may have been particularly attracted to the Klan is to examine listings in the Buffalo klavern's business directory, the chief device by which klannishness was to be implemented. As is revealed by undercover reports, the directory was regularly used, and no doubt a small businessman who had joined the Klan primarily for economic reasons would insist on having a listing.[4] Excluding those types of businesses with less than three klavern members, the directory most comprehensively lists Klan-affiliated barbers, building contractors, painters, photographers, plumbers, and realtors. With the exception of barbers and building contractors, these were professions in which the foreign born were markedly underrepresented; thus it can be reasonably doubted that "un-American" economic competition led the bulk of these small businessmen into the Klan. A more probable explanation is simply that these were very competitive fields (particularly real estate marketing, building contracting, and painting), where businessmen were especially willing to use novel means of making sales contacts.

Low Nonmanual

As is shown in table 5, salesmen, foremen, and private detectives were overrepresented among Buffalo Klansmen. Klan-affiliated salesmen worked for a wide variety of business concerns. Of those who identified their employers, 36 percent were employed by manufacturing and wholesale enterprises, and 34 percent were engaged in retail trade. The remainder sold real estate, insurance, advertising, and securities. Owing to the vagaries of census data, it is difficult to ascertain in which specific sales fields Klansmen

Table 5
Representation of Buffalo Klansmen in Low Nonmanual
Occupations, 1921–1924

Occupation	Number of Klansmen	Number of Native-White Males, 1920	Percent Klansmen
Agent	8	859	.93
Bank Teller	7	NA	NA
Bookkeeper/Cashier	18	1,300	1.38
Clerk	121	8,278	1.46
Decorator	5	NA	NA
Detective, Private	6	220	2.72
Dispatcher	7	NA	NA
Foreman	99	2,783	3.55
Government Official, low	1	NA	NA
Mail Carrier	4	NA	NA
Mortician	2	NA	NA
Newspaper Reporter	2	NA	NA
Salesman	171	5,309	3.22
Stenographer/Secretary	3	358	.83
Tax and Title Searcher	2	NA	NA
Telephone Operator	2	NA	NA
Timekeeper	4	NA	NA
Trainmaster	8	NA	NA
Truant Officer	1	NA	NA
Weighmaster	2	NA	NA

Sources: Buffalo Klan Membership List; U.S. Bureau of the Census, *Fourteenth Census of the United States, 1920: Population* 4: 1068–70.

were either over- or underrepresented, but a sizable KKK presence among automobile salesmen and securities brokers appears
particularly notable. These were highly competitive occupations
in which salesmen typically worked on commission; this was also
true of the insurance field, in which Klansmen constituted an
impressive 3.79 percent of Buffalo's native-white sales force. Thus,
almost surely, the lure of business contacts drew numerous sales
representatives into the fold.

More than fifty businesses in Buffalo had at least one foreman
who was a Klansman. Two-thirds of KKK-affiliated foremen
worked for manufacturing concerns, most for large industrial concerns such as National Aniline (thirteen Klan foremen), Donner
Steel (nine), and American Brass (nine); the remainder were engaged in transportation and service. The foremen's median age at
the time of entering the Invisible Empire was 37.6 years, almost
exactly the same as that of Klan engineers and only a little older
than the average age of the klavern's manager/superintendents.
Out of those listed in the 1924 Buffalo city directory, just under 89
percent were classified as heads of household. Mature and successful members of the working class, these Klansmen were accustomed to supervising, coordinating, and regularly making important decisions. Far from being the hapless victims of industrial
growth, they were the skilled overseers of such expansion.

Six private detectives joined the Buffalo Klan; three worked for
detective agencies, two for railroads, and one for the Manufactur-
ers & Traders Trust Bank. An affinity for undercover activity apparently helped bring at least one of these men into the Invisible
Empire: David D. Mayne, a railroad detective at the time he
joined the KKK, later became one of the klavern's most zealous
investigators.

Although agents, bookkeeper/cashiers, clerks, and stenographer/
secretaries composed nearly 9 percent of the chapter's membership, the Klan appears to have been generally underrepresented
in these occupations. Economic factors may have contributed to
this underrepresentation; these workers were often poorly paid,
and Klan fees and dues were steep for the 1920s. Another factor
may have been that these occupations attracted a larger percentage of non-Protestant native whites than more prestigious types of

nonmanual work, thus reducing the pool of potential Klan recruits. In addition, those holding such positions may have shied away from the hooded order because they were more vulnerable to losing their jobs than were supervisory personnel such as foremen, managers, and engineers.

Skilled

Just over 30 percent of Buffalo Klansmen followed skilled manual trades. As is shown in table 6, the KKK was most strongly represented among patternmakers, mechanics, electricians, carpenter/woodworkers, boilermakers, locomotive firemen, and compositor/printers. Klan machinists composed the largest group within this status category (22.1 percent). These were among the most prestigious blue-collar occupations, requiring a considerable amount of intelligence, training, and aptitude; they were also among the most thoroughly organized by craft unions. On average, these Klansmen were in their late twenties to early thirties; of those listed in the 1924 city directory, a solid majority were reported as heading a household.

It might be speculated that the Buffalo Klan's large percentage of skilled workers resulted from economic and/or social competition between rival ethnic groups. Perhaps, as has been posited by Klan scholar Kenneth T. Jackson, the rise of the Invisible Empire represented a defensive reaction to the growing aspirations of

Table 6
Representation of Buffalo Klansmen in Skilled Occupations,
1921–1924

Occupation	Number of Klansmen	Number of Native-White Males, 1920	Percent Klansmen
Artist	5	NA	NA
Baker	4	357	1.12
Barber, nonproprietor	2	433	.46
Blacksmith	3	347	.86

Occupation	Number of Klansmen	Number of Native-White Males, 1920	Percent Klansmen
Boilermaker	9	426	2.11
Bookbinder	3	NA	NA
Brickmason	5	484	1.03
Butcher	10	NA	NA
Cabinetmaker	2	283	.70
Carpenter/Woodworker	72	3,111	2.31
Carpet, Floor, and Tile Layer	5	NA	NA
Chef	1	NA	NA
Compositor/Printer	17	841	2.02
Dairyman	3	NA	NA
Electrician	56	1,899	2.94
Engineer, locomotive	22	1,116	1.97
Engineer, marine	3	NA	NA
Engineer, stationary	5	1,431	.34
Engraver	1	NA	NA
Ferry Boat Captain	1	160	.62
Fireman, locomotive	20	860	2.32
Furrier	1	NA	NA
Jeweler	3	186	1.61
Leatherworker	2	NA	NA
Machinist	116	6,824	1.69
Mechanic	39	1,230	3.17
Miller	3	NA	NA
Millwright	8	398	2.01
Moulder	4	NA	NA
Musician	3	357	.84
Painter	24	1,949	1.23
Patternmaker	13	314	4.14
Pipefitter	19	NA	NA
Plasterer	1	114	.87
Plumber, nonproprietor	4	1,578	.25
Roofer	3	NA	NA
Shipbuilder	1	NA	NA
Steamfitter	11	NA	NA
Steamforger	1	NA	NA
Toolmaker	9	510	1.76
Upholsterer	7	363	1.92
Weaver	1	NA	NA

Sources: Buffalo Klan Membership List; U.S. Bureau of the Census, *Fourteenth Census of the United States, 1920: Population* 4: 1068–70.

non-native-white workers. In order to test this hypothesis, the change in the percentage of foreign-born and African-American workers during the period 1910–1920 has been calculated for five skilled occupations—patternmaker, carpenter/woodworker, boilermaker, compositor/printer, and locomotive engineer—in which the KKK was overrepresented; calculations have also been made for machinists (owing to their large contingent within the klavern) and for cabinetmakers, stationary engineers, and plumbers, groups with among the lowest percentages of Klansmen.[5] In seven out of nine occupations, the percentage of foreign-born workers declined during the decade prior to 1920, and for all of them the increase or decrease of the percentage of black workers was negligible. There is also little evidence that a large percentage of foreign-born workers within an occupation promoted Klan membership. Cabinetmakers—in whose occupation the foreign born composed a decided majority—displayed a relative dearth of enthusiasm for the hooded order; locomotive firemen and compositor/printers, who had relatively low and declining percentages of foreign born, were more likely to have joined. This does not mean, however, that ethnic conflict in the work place had no impact on Klan recruiting. The precise dynamics of inter-ethnic relations surely varied from company to company, and skilled workers may have entered the KKK in response to perceived threats from second-generation ethnics (fellow native whites), particularly those who were non-Protestant.

Another possible factor in the entry of skilled workers into the Klan was membership in a craft union. Labor organizations often pursued racist policies and stood in opposition to foreign immigration, and thus union membership might have primed certain individuals for Klan membership and/or reinforced attitudes that assisted Klan recruiting. Unfortunately, craft union membership records for such key groups as electricians and machinists are largely missing for Buffalo in the 1920s and no adequate comparison with the list of klavern members is possible.[6] One can reasonably suspect, nevertheless, given the particular skilled trades in which the Klan was concentrated, that at least some union members proved susceptible to KKK overtures.

Semiskilled and Service

Other than railroad and streetcar conductors and private police-men, the Klan was underrepresented within all the occupations in this status category for which information is available (see table 7). The underrepresentation among factory workers is particularly notable because native-white Protestants in this group were almost certainly experiencing potentially stressful economic and social interaction with non-Protestants, the foreign born, and African Americans; they were also among the most likely to suffer

Table 7

Representation of Buffalo Klansmen in Semiskilled and Service Occupations, 1921–1924

Occupation	Number of Klansmen	Number of Native-White Males, 1920	Percent Klansmen
Attendant	4	NA	NA
Brakeman	11	717	1.53
Conductor, Railroad	16	736	2.17
Conductor, Streetcar	9	482	1.86
Deliveryman	4	701	.57
Driver (car, truck, streetcar)	33	NA	NA
Factory Operative	130	10,756	1.20
Fireman	8	740	1.08
Heavy Machinery Operative	7	NA	NA
Janitor	3	385	1.03
Meterman	2	NA	NA
Oiler	3	225	1.33
Policeman, City	10	1,063	.94
Policeman, Private	8	453	1.76
Repairman	19	NA	NA
Sailor	1	233	.49
Soldier	1	304	.32
Switchman	5	1,472	.33
Trainman	5	NA	NA
Waiter	1	264	.37

Sources: Buffalo Klan Membership List; U.S. Bureau of the Census, Fourteenth Census of the United States, 1920: Population 4: 1068–70.

during periods of labor unrest. Economic vulnerability, the considerable expense of Klan fees and dues, and a general lack of interest in middle-class fraternalism and political activism may have hindered recruiting. Whatever the primary cause, it is clear that the Klan did not thrive in the lower reaches of the proletariat.

Considering the patterns of Klan recruiting in other status categories, the order's overrepresentation among conductors and private policemen might have been anticipated. Conductors served essentially as the foremen of mass transportation, spending much of their workday ordering, coordinating, and calculating; they were also accustomed to serving as authority figures and resolving disputes. The private policemen in the Klan likewise occupied positions of authority. Six worked for major railroads, one for National Aniline, and one (Chief of Police Herbert N. Davis) for the Bethlehem Steel Corporation. They had an average age of forty-three, and according to the city directory most headed households; they appear to have been well-established residents.

Unskilled

Out of the approximately seven thousand native-white unskilled workers in Buffalo in the early 1920s, the Klan roster lists only nine: three baggagemen, one gardener, and five laborers. Whatever the Ku Klux Klan may have been elsewhere, in Buffalo it absolutely did not represent a mass movement of the socioeconomically marginal.

Judged by the occupations of its membership, the Buffalo klavern was drawn from a broad cross section of the native-white community, but one in which nonmanual and skilled workers were overrepresented and semiskilled, service, and unskilled laborers were underrepresented. The Klan proved particularly attractive to white- and blue-collar employees whose work involved managing and supervising, small businessmen and salesmen in highly competitive fields, and workers in the more prestigious blue-collar trades. This recruitment pattern no doubt resulted, at least in part, from the Klan's membership requirements (native-born white Protestants probably were concentrated in certain forms of employment, thus contributing to Klan overrepresentation), but available data do not permit a closer evaluation of this influence. Some Buffalonians may have joined the Klan because of ethnic conflict in their workplace or business field, yet evidence of such conflict is sketchy at best. In fact, local Klansmen appear for the most part to have been remarkably secure, established, and accustomed to leadership roles relative to the male working population at large.

Additional occupational information supports the conclusion that the klavern was drawn from a broad economic cross section of local native-white society. The Buffalo Klan roster lists 670 individuals and businesses that employed Klansmen; 1,573 knights worked for these employers (the remainder of the membership was either self-employed or listed no employer). Nearly 75 percent of the employers (502) had only one Klan employee, and 91 percent had three or less; Klansmen working for such employers constituted 38.7 percent of the members who listed employers on application forms. On the other hand, nearly 33 percent of klavern members listing employers worked for enterprises that employed twenty or more knights. Without knowing the percentage of native-born white males in individual businesses (let alone the percentage of employees who were native-white male Protestants residing inside the city limits), it is difficult to evaluate Klan representation within specific firms. But it is evident that the hooded order attracted members from a large number and variety of enterprises, ranging from the smallest retail establishments to the largest industrial corporations. Indeed, the occupational profile of the Buffalo Klan was so diverse and wide-ranging, both in terms of type of occupation and type of employer, that perhaps it would be advisable to explore factors other than occupation in an effort to determine why certain individuals entered the Invisible Empire.

One possible factor differentiating Klansmen from most other native-white Protestants was the part of the city in which they resided. Klavern members might have been fairly typical citizens who faced particularly stressful or unusual circumstances in their immediate neighborhoods—an acute crime problem or a growing number of foreign-born residents, for example—and thus were primed for recruitment. At the least, residential information should provide a better understanding of the general environment in which Klansmen developed at least part of their social and political outlook.

Figure 4 shows the residential distribution of Buffalo Klansmen based on information on application forms for the period 1921–1924. The hooded order attracted members from all parts of the community, but knights clearly tended to concentrate in the outlying districts. Nearly 40 percent of klavern members lived in just four wards: the Twentieth, Twenty-First, Fourth, and Fifth, all located far from the heart of the city and near the municipal boundary. Another 40 percent lived in nine other wards that ringed the older districts. Only 59 percent of Buffalo's total population lived in these thirteen wards. Thus, compared with their fellow city residents as a whole, Klansmen were significantly more likely to reside in the newer, more middle-class parts of the city.

Calculations for Klansmen as a percentage of ward populations of adult (twenty-one and older) native-white males are presented in figure 5. These percentages confirm that the Invisible Empire most successfully recruited among those residing in outlying areas, particularly in the extreme northern and southern wards. In the inner-city districts, where one might reasonably have expected to find the most anxious native-white Protestants, the Klan experienced little recruiting success. A major factor limiting Klan recruiting in these wards was, of course, that most native-white males were non-Protestant, and thus unqualified for KKK membership. Yet, this being the case, one might have anticipated that such native-white Protestants as there were would have been all the more eager to join the Klan—if in fact the order appeared to be a promising agency of ethnoreligious solidarity and self-defense. Possibly, precisely because they lived in close proximity to large populations that could be expected to be intensely anti-Klan, the KKK seemed to be a particularly unpromising organization to these residents, or maybe economic and class factors hindered recruiting. Whatever the reason, the Invisible Empire did not prosper in the heart of Buffalo.

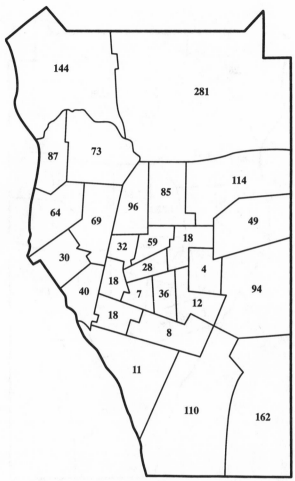

Figure 4
Number of Klansmen in Buffalo Wards,
1921–1924

This is not to say that ethnic conflict played an insignificant role in the development of the Buffalo klavern. Although the outlying wards where most Klansmen lived generally contained lower percentages of foreign-born residents than the inner city, they were far from homogeneously native-white. For example, Ward

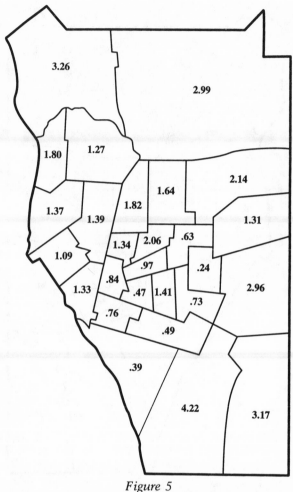

Figure 5
Percentage of Klansmen in Native-White Male
Population, Age 21 and Older, by Ward

Twenty-One, which had the second highest percentage of Klansmen among native whites, encompassed large enclaves of Poles
and Hungarians, and more than a fourth of the residents in heavily kluxed Ward Eleven had been born outside the United States;
by 1925, a majority of the Klansmen listed as residing in these

two wards by the state census had at least one foreign-born neighbor or their former residence was occupied by non-natives. Even in Ward Twenty, which had the lowest percentage of non-natives in the city, more than 15 percent of the population was of foreign birth.[7] Thus assessing the relationship between the ethnic composition of wards and Klan residential patterns presents a considerable challenge.

In an attempt to detect whether Klan recruiting might have been influenced by certain ethnosocial and/or economic factors, scatterplots and Pearson correlation coefficients have been produced for ward-level percentages of Klansmen (among the male adult native-white population) with population percentages of foreign-born whites, foreign-born Poles, foreign-born Germans, foreign-born Irish, foreign-born Italians, native-born African Americans, and native whites of native parentage; the percentage of Klansmen has also been compared with the ratio of homeowners to renters and the ratio of dwellings to families for each ward. The percentage of Klan members demonstrated practically no linear association with the percent of foreign-born Irish ($-.027$), Germans ($.064$), and Italians ($-.165$), and only a slight one with Poles ($-.240$) and African Americans ($-.268$). The correlation with the percentage of foreign-born whites ($-.431$) and native whites of native parentage ($.452$) was significantly stronger, but still quite nonlinear. Variables related to economic circumstances demonstrated the most linear relationship, $.597$ for homeowner-to-renter ratio and $.640$ for dwelling-to-family ratio, with both being statistically significant at $.001$ (one-tailed test). These calculations reflect what was already known: the bulk of Klansmen lived in relatively prosperous outlying wards characterized by large populations of native whites of native parentage, yet such wards also contained numerically significant foreign-born populations. The proximity of foreign-born residents surely influenced Klan recruiting, but the precise dynamics of such influence remain unknown. Moreover, other factors—most notably religion and the ethnic composition of the native-white population of foreign and mixed parentage—may have played important roles in shaping Klan recruitment patterns.[8] Until a closer analysis can be made, all that can be concluded is that Buffalo Klansmen, considering their race, nativity, and general socioeconomic status, mostly lived where expected—assuming that the Invisible Empire exercised a broad cross-sectional appeal within the local native-white Protestant community.

The breadth, if not depth, of successful Klan recruiting is further indicated by data concerning the ethnicity of Buffalo knights. Although KKK rhetoric and literature regularly extolled the distinctive accomplishments of Anglo-Saxon institutions and culture, in practice the order eagerly accepted applications from almost all native-born white Protestants, whatever their ancestry. The thousands of German-American Protestants in Buffalo constituted a particularly rich source of potential recruits, and evidently the kleagles made considerable headway: by 1924, more than 34 percent of the klavern members residing inside the city had distinctively German surnames.[9] When one considers that many Germans Anglicized their names after arriving in the United States and also that some Klansmen with non-German surnames probably had German or German-American mothers, then it becomes clear that a very large percentage of the klavern—maybe 40 percent or more—was of German ancestry.

Upon first reflection it may seem strange that German-Americans would join a superpatriotic, nativist society, particularly given the recent anti-German excesses of the war era. Perhaps the Klan provided a means of certifying a commitment to nation and community (at least the white Protestant community); it also proffered an opportunity to turn the tables and denounce certain antagonistic groups as un-American. Even more importantly, by the early 1920s the bulk of young German-Americans had been thoroughly assimilated into U.S. society and thus shared many of the beliefs, values, problems, and concerns that helped lead other white native-born Protestants into the KKK. A comparison of the occupational status of German-surnamed Klan members with that of non-German-surnamed knights reveals remarkable similarity between the two groups, although the occupations of German-American Klansmen seem to have been slightly less prestigious overall—as might have been anticipated of a group derived from non-English-speaking origins.[10]

The residential patterns of German-surnamed members also

indicate considerable assimilation. More than 61 percent lived in outlying wards adjacent to the city line, with the remainder being generally scattered across the community; in Ward Twenty, a district with one of the highest percentages of native whites of native parentage, 32.3 percent of Klan members were German-surnamed, almost the same percentage as the total representation of the German-surnamed within the klavern. Klan recruiting among German-Americans appears to have been particularly successful in the east-side wards (where the growing Polish population may have enhanced the order's appeal), but it is still clear that German-surnamed Klansmen came in significant numbers from all parts of the city. Just as it did among Buffalo's native-white Protestants as a whole, the Klan attracted a broad, albeit occupationally prestigious, cross section of the qualified German-American population.

The surnames of the Klan's non-Germanic majority also suggests the order's wide-ranging appeal. The bulk of the Klansmen in this group could probably trace their ancestry to the British Isles, but sixty-eight had the Scandinavian "son" at the end of their name (although a number of these may have been British), fifteen names were clearly Dutch, eight French, five Polish, and two each Spanish and Italian. Without reliable figures for the ethnic origins of Buffalo's native-white population, it is difficult to assess which groups may have been over- or underrepresented within the Invisible Empire, but it seems likely that the KKK developed at least a token following among most major local populations of Protestant European stock.

Klan recruiting apparently traversed ethnic divisions among Protestants with greater ease than it did age groups. Knights residing in the city had an average age of 32.7 years at the time of entering the hooded order, with nearly 77 percent being below the age of 40. As is indicated in table 8, Klansmen as a group were significantly younger than the adult male and native-white male populations from which they were drawn. A number of factors might have contributed to the order's relative youthfulness. As we have seen, the Buffalo klavern attempted to serve as a medium— albeit an unusual one—of civic action, and younger men might have been more willing to give their time, energy, and money to

Table 8

Age Distribution (by Percent) of Buffalo Klansmen at the Time
of Joining the Klan, 1921–1924, Compared with the Age
Distribution of Buffalo's Male and Native-White Male
Populations, Age 18 and over, in 1920

Age	Klansmen	Males	Native-White Males
18–19	2.3	4.7	6.3
20–29	43.1	28.5	33.6
30–39	31.5	25.3	25.2
40–49	14.9	18.0	16.7
50–59	5.7	12.8	10.9
60–69	2.1	6.7	5.3
70 and over	0	3.3	1.4

Sources: Buffalo Klan Membership List; U.S. Bureau of the Census, *Fourteenth Census of the United States, 1920: Population* 2: 290.

such an organization. Nearly two-thirds of the Klansmen listed in the 1924 city directory headed households (of whom 30.7 percent were in their twenties, 36.3 percent in their thirties, and 21.5 percent in their forties), and state census data from 1925 indicate that many of them had started families.[11] Considering the serious social problems faced by Buffalo in the early 1920s, young family men, beset by the pressures and obligations of caring for the welfare of others, may well have been particularly drawn to the KKK as a means of improving local conditions; they may also have seen the group as a means of establishing business and social contacts that could advance their careers.

When considering other generational experiences that may have made the Klan particularly attractive to younger men, the recent world war comes readily to mind. The first scholars who evaluated the KKK attributed much of the order's success to the intolerance, passion, violence, and general irrationality that the war experience had generated; one sociologist even suggested that the Invisible Empire was composed largely of angry, restless war veterans, hard-minded militants who threatened to turn the Klan into a form of homegrown fascism. In order to examine this assessment, the Buffalo Klan roster has been compared with a list of

17,797 World War I veterans who resided inside the city at the time they entered the military. One obvious, and major, limitation of these sources is that they do not indicate the number of Klan-affiliated veterans who moved to Buffalo after the war; nevertheless, a comparison of the two lists yields much valuable information. According to these sources, 118 Buffalo Klansmen (6.75 percent of the klavern members residing inside the city) served in the Great War. Of these, seventy-five were in the Army, thirty-six in the Navy, six in the Marine Corps, and one in the Coast Guard; by the end of the war, thirteen had been commissioned as officers, thirty-five were noncommissioned officers, and seventy held lower enlisted ranks. A number of Klansmen had experienced combat duty, at least four being wounded in action; one future knight, Erwin C. McIndoo, received a citation for valor. The klavern also included one of the community's best-known war heroes, Major Edwin G. Ziegler, who had been officially praised for his "exceptionally meritorious service characterized by untiring zeal and intelligent grasp of his duties in the battle of the Hindenburg Line."[12]

Did the KKK attract a disproportionate share of the city's war veterans? In Buffalo, in 1920, there were 143,709 males between the ages of twenty and thirty-four. If one assumes, theoretically, that all 17,797 Buffalo war veterans were members of this group, then 12.3 percent of this generational cohort would have seen wartime military service. By 1923, the year during which most of the men on the Klan roster probably filled out their application cards, the members of this cohort would have been between the ages of twenty-three and thirty-seven, including all 118 of the Klan-affiliated veterans who had resided in Buffalo during the war. Since there was a total of 983 Klansmen in this age range, a simple calculation reveals that the KKK members for whom veteran status is known constituted 12 percent of this cohort within the klavern, a figure comparable to the percentage for the city as a whole. However, there may have been—and probably were—a number of veterans in the Klan who had not resided in the city at the time of the war, in which case the percentage would have been higher; unfortunately, available data do not permit an estimation of the size of this group. It nonetheless seems virtually certain that World War I veterans composed only a small minority of the Buffalo Klan.[13]

Probably more than war-veteran status, membership in other men's fraternal societies helped bring Buffalonians into the Invisible Empire. From the time of the KKK's arrival in the late summer of 1921, rumors persisted of Klan recruiting in such organizations, particularly the various branches of Masonry.[14] Not only were these societies largely composed of native-born white Protestants, but their common practice of secrecy afforded Klan recruiters a degree of security. Moreover, because these groups often employed bizarre rituals and unusual costumes, their members were generally more likely than nonfraternalists to be amenable to the strange practices of the Klan.

Buffalo in the early 1920s offered kleagles an abundance of men's societies in which to solicit recruits: twenty-four lodges of the Free and Accepted Masons, seven chapters of the Royal Arch Masons, four lodges of the Ancient Accepted Scottish Rite Masons, two commanderies of the Knights Templar, a temple of the Mystic Shrine, thirty-seven chapters of the Odd Fellows, eight lodges of the Knights of Pythias, five courts of the Foresters of America, eleven tribes of the Improved Order of Red Men, eight camps of the Woodmen of the World, and various units of the Maccabees, Elks, Moose, Orioles, and Eagles. Most of the official records for these groups are not available for examination, but one important document, a directory listing all of Buffalo's Masonic lodge officers in 1922, sheds light on the local Klan's connection with leading Masons. Of the 642 officers listed in the directory, forty (5.9 percent) were members of the Klan by 1924. The Invisible Empire was particularly well represented in the leadership of two Masonic bodies: Zuleika Grotto No. 10, Mystic Order of Veiled Prophets of the Enchanted Realm, and Northeast Lodge, Free and Accepted Masons.[15]

By 1923, the future Grand Kleagle of Western New York, George C. Bryant, had become "monarch" (chapter president) of Zuleika Grotto No. 10, a sixteen-hundred-member social organization associated with the Blue Lodge Masons. A colorful group that wore fezzes and green and blue uniforms, the "veiled prophets" participated in a large marching band, drum corps, and military drill team that performed on special occasions. Throughout 1923 and 1924, Bryant used his position as leader of the grotto to solicit members for the Klan, at one point allowing a KKK lecturer to address a regular meeting of the chapter. These efforts evidently produced a mixed reaction, a Klansman later noting that Bryant had "nearly wrecked the Erie County Masons." Nevertheless, Bryant retained his Masonic office and continued his recruiting among lodge brothers.[16]

The Northeast Lodge, a relatively small group of Masons located in Ward Twenty, had been established in 1921 and was still engaged in developing a substantial membership at the time of the KKK's arrival. Perhaps because they felt less constrained by the official anti-Klan stance of Masonry than did the leadership of older, better-established Buffalo lodges, at least five of the group's fourteen officers had joined the Klan by 1924.[17]

In Buffalo, there clearly was a significant link between the Masons and the Klan; this was shown by the KKK's regular use of Masonic facilities such as Mizpah Hall and the Unity Masonic Temple. But this connection should not be overemphasized. The great majority of Masons steered clear of the Invisible Empire, and the KKK only significantly infiltrated the leadership of the two lodges mentioned above. The Klan did, however, have at least one member serving as an officer in twenty-five of the forty-two Masonic bodies listed in the 1922 directory. Whether all of these men solicited recruits for the hooded order is unknown, but it does seem that the KKK was very well situated to develop a healthy following among Masons. In addition, at least one knight headed a major civic organization that also may have contributed members to the klavern. Besides holding the rank of Chief Rabban in the Masonically affiliated Ismalia Temple, Klansman Albert H. Zink was president of the Kiwanis Club in 1924.[18] Thus the Buffalo klavern certainly possessed influential contacts within some of the groups that dominated the city's mainstream organizational life.

One final factor that may have influenced Klan membership remains to be discussed: religious affiliation. Did the KKK attract a balanced cross section of the local Protestant community, or was its membership concentrated in certain denominations?[19] Adequately addressing this question requires, at the least, a determination of the religious affiliation of a sizable random sample of the Buffalo Klan. Unfortunately, such a sample cannot be derived from local records, primarily because the membership lists of many Buffalo churches from the 1920s are missing or otherwise unavailable.[20] Confronted with this difficulty, this study has attempted to construct a sample of Klansmen's religious affiliations through a telephone survey of 5,400 Buffalonians who share the same last names as the men on the klavern roster. The survey succeeded in locating 206 descendants and other relatives of local KKK members who were willing to provide information about the denominational affiliation of 219 local knights (12.5 percent of the Klansmen residing inside the city). It should be stressed that the results of the survey do not constitute a statistically reliable random sample and are therefore only suggestive; nevertheless, this is the best that could be done under the circumstances.[21]

One hundred and seventy-eight of the Klansmen in the sample produced by the telephone survey were identified as church members; fifty-six were described as being "just Protestant" or as being unaffiliated with a particular denomination. Table 9 presents the results of the survey compared with the denominational profile of Buffalo's white Protestant church members in 1926. As can be seen, the Klan apparently attracted members from a number of major churches across the Protestant religious spectrum. Perhaps the most intriguing finding is the high percentage of Lutherans, but this may be the result of the survey's methodology: relatives of Klansmen with German surnames were generally easier to locate in telephone directories than relatives with more common English surnames. Another problem hindering the survey was that very few of the relatives of Lutheran Klansmen could recall whether their kinsmen had belonged to evangelical or nonevangelical denominations.[22] Nevertheless, the survey information does suggest that the Invisible Empire enjoyed wide-ranging and relatively balanced support among residents who belonged to the major Protestant denominations.

The Buffalo Klan's overall religious orientation is also suggested by the group's activities. Meetings of the hooded order featured prayers and speeches by evangelical ministers, and, as

Table 9

Survey Results Concerning the Denominational Affiliation of
Buffalo Klansmen Compared with the Denominational
Distribution of Buffalo's White Protestant Church Members,
Ages 13 and over, in 1926

Denomination	Number in Sample of Church Members	Percent of Sample	Percent Among White Protestant Church Members in 1926
Baptist	13	7.3	7.4
Congregational	3	1.6	1.5
Evangelical	22	12.3	14.7
Episcopalian	23	12.9	14.3
Lutheran	65	36.5	20.4
Methodist	28	15.7	11.9
Presbyterian	23	12.9	13.9
Quaker	1	.5	.1
Other	0	0	15.8*

* Reformed Church and numerous smaller denominations.
Sources: Telephone survey of Buffalo residents conducted February–May 1992; U.S. Bureau of the Census, *Census of Religious Bodies, 1926* 1: 381–82.

has been related, by 1924 the Klan had assumed a prominent role in the evangelical crusade to improve enforcement of the liquor and vice laws. In addition, ten of the eleven clergymen who affiliated with the Invisible Empire were evangelicals. It would be a mistake, however, to view the local KKK as an organization that was uniformly infused with evangelical zeal; undercover reports depict a group that was more preoccupied with secular political maneuvering than with advancing the cause of moral reform—although these concerns often overlapped.[23]

One religious matter that the Klan, as an organization, apparently ignored was the doctrinal dispute that raged between Protestant modernists and fundamentalists during the 1920s. In no source—newspaper articles, the sermons of Klan-affiliated pastors, the secret reports prepared by Mayor Schwab's spies, or oral interviews—is there any evidence that the klavern ever took a stand on Protestant doctrinal issues. There may well have been numerous representatives from the fundamentalist and/or modernist camps within the klavern; if so, they never let their convictions undermine the group's commitment to Protestant solidarity. Indeed, many knights probably agreed with Klansman Mark H. Hubbell, editor of the *Buffalo Truth*, who warned that the "unseemly squabbling between opposing theorists within the [Protestant] church means a loss in religious values that cannot be compensated for by anything that either side has to offer."[24]

The foregoing examination of Klansmen's place of residence, ethnicity, age distribution, veteran status, fraternal connections, and religious affiliation—although far from exhaustive—significantly advances our understanding of the Buffalo klavern. Compared with fellow native-born white adult males, local knights were relatively young and more likely to reside in outlying wards. The hooded order attracted citizens of both British and non-Anglo-Saxon ancestry and appears to have developed a balanced following among the city's Protestant church members; war veterans and fraternalists may have been particularly drawn to the Invisible Empire, but available data do not indicate the extent of their presence within the klavern. Overall, considered in association with what is known about Klansmen's socioeconomic status, this additional information lends strength to the conclusion that the KKK exerted a broad appeal among Buffalo's white middle-class Protestants and attracted hundreds of otherwise ordinary and respectable citizens from the social mainstream. But this was not recognized at the time, particularly by the Invisible Empire's enemies; they remained convinced that the Ku Klux Klan was a fanatical and violent organization that needed to be crushed by any means necessary. Eventually these enemies would strike at the Klan, and they would do so mercilessly.

Five

The Destruction of the Buffalo Klan

In the summer of 1924, the enemies of the Invisible Empire launched an all-out war on the Ku Klux Klan in Buffalo, an assault from which the secret order never recovered. Although to many residents this appeared to be a rather sudden development, the anti-Klan campaign is best seen as the culmination of a gradually intensifying effort that had originated months earlier, during the previous summer. In June 1923, as the Klan conducted numerous ceremonials throughout western New York in defiance of the Walker Law, anti-KKK elements began to organize in earnest. Meeting in the office of a "prominent business man" in Ellicott Square, a group of professional and business people laid the groundwork for the formal incorporation of the United Sons of America. Pledging to combat any "group of individuals who have plans for the breaking down of this government, or the destruction of law and order," the organization served notice that influential citizens believed that the time had come to deal with the Klan.[1] Other residents, including Mayor Schwab, endorsed the efforts of the regionally based Liberty League, which sponsored a series of lectures dedicated to exposing the Klan as a money-making scheme. A third organized group, based in the Crosby Building, gathered information from a former Klansman from New York

City. Although little is known about the specific activities of these organizations, it can be assumed that like similar groups elsewhere (such as the American Unity League in Chicago) they hoped to undermine the Klan by exposing its membership. Given subsequent events, it appears quite likely that these groups took an active, albeit covert, role in the assault on the local Klan.[2]

The situation remained relatively quiescent until the spring of 1924, when the Buffalo klavern inaugurated its moral reform campaign and confronted Schwab at the meeting in Black Rock. From then on, tensions steadily increased, as it became evident that Klansmen intended openly to exert their influence in community affairs. Much of the animosity of the anti-Klan forces focused on L. E. H. Smith, who had emerged as the chapter's most visible and outspoken activist. After spending three weeks visiting local roadhouses, hotels, restaurants, and soft drink places, the crusading pastor informed a gathering of reformers at the Ontario Street Presbyterian Church late in March that he was convinced that "there is not another place in the country as corrupt as Buffalo," going so far as to allege that the mayor "is crooked and the sooner the people of the city realize it the better." He also praised the numerous unidentified Klansmen he said were attending the meeting: "I believe that you have done more to crystallize public opinion than any force in a generation. I hope that you will keep on in your attempt to bring about a universal demand for different civic conditions."[3]

Smith's provocative assertions and his increasingly open relationship with the Ku Klux Klan produced a vehemently negative response in certain quarters. Mayor Schwab threatened to sue him for slander, and soon the controversial minister began receiving threatening notes. "Count your days until the 13th," warned one missive. "Beware!" "A bullet is too good for you," another stated. "Your legs ought to be tied behind a young colt and dragged through the streets of Buffalo. You are an undesirable citizen and not worthy to live here." The Reverend Charles Penfold also received threats, one particularly vicious letter saying, "Stop your attacks on our mayor or you are going to get it. . . . I will blind your child on his way home from school, and will attack when you least expect it. I know that we can get your wife."[4]

Apparently the opponents of moral reform decided to deliver a more forceful message. Shortly after midnight on the morning of April 18, a large fused bomb exploded on the porch of the Reverend Smith's residence at 34 Gallatin Street. The force of the explosion ripped through the house, the front of the residence being "crushed in like an eggshell." Although the pastor and his family were away visiting friends for the evening, the bomb had probably not been intended as a warning: the Smiths had left their house lights on, and the size of the device suggested a murderous intent. The police never discovered who bore responsibility for the attack, but it was evident that the controversy surrounding the Klan had escalated to a dangerous new level.[5]

Continued activity by Klansmen kept tensions high for the next several weeks. The KKK released a letter promising to "use every means at our command to apprehend the ones responsible for the recent outrage [bombing]," and early in May a group of knights ignited a large cross at the foot of Ashton Place, in the heavily Irish part of South Buffalo.[6] The Klan-sponsored raids on suspect establishments continued unabated, and L. E. H. Smith wrote to Governor Smith asking if he would remove the mayor from office if "we introduce into your office definite proof that Frank X. Schwab has committed misdemeanors while in public office." Late in May, the increasing boldness of the Invisible Empire was well demonstrated when scores of members in civilian attire drove through Hamburg, Lackawanna, and "nearly the entire section of South Buffalo" late at night and put up pro-Klan posters reading "God Give Us Men, Knights of the Invisible Empire." Thousands of placards were placed on telephone and telegraph poles before the police succeeded in arresting twelve Klansmen for illegally posting bills.[7]

The increasingly militant attitude of the city administration also promoted tension. Following his humiliating encounter with the Klan at the Unity Masonic Temple late in March, Mayor Schwab refused to countenance any sort of open support for the secret order. After schoolteacher Alma Smith commented before her eighth-grade class that the KKK should tar and feather the mayor, Schwab immediately launched a personal investigation, taking statements from more than a dozen students; on April 10, without citing a specific regulation, he removed Smith from her position. The dismissed teacher denied having "ever uttered one word that might be construed as Ku Klux Klan propaganda," but she did admit that "if everyone were moved by Klan principles, affairs of the public weal would be better off."[8] A few days later, on the evening of April 14, the police department went on full alert upon receiving word that white-robed Klansmen were parading near the vicinity of Main and Chippewa streets, in downtown Buffalo. Officers immediately notified the mayor and rushed to the scene, but they soon learned that the procession was composed of two hundred University of Buffalo students conducting a fraternity initiation. Although the youths had previously secured a parade permit, seven of them were taken into custody for questioning. One participant clad in a cheese-cloth gown adorned with black felt KKK's was forced by the police to remove his offending costume.[9]

Although the skirmishing between the pro- and anti-Klan forces had its near-farcical aspects, most thinking Buffalonians realized the considerable potential for major trouble. One particularly disturbing trend was the discernible hardening of religious divisions. The local Klan episode had always been characterized by strong undertones of Protestant-Catholic hostility, but both camps had taken care to avoid open warfare. By 1924, however, certain developments had increased the likelihood of unrestrained conflict. Governor Al Smith's strong bid for the Democratic presidential nomination imparted new saliency to the concerns of many Protestants, while the growing opposition to his candidacy fueled Roman Catholic resentment. Locally, the sense of a final reckoning on religious issues was enhanced by the spectacle of a Roman Catholic mayor, the newly reelected Supreme Commander of the Knights of St. John, openly feuding with Protestant activists, the Buffalo Council of Churches, and a secret society dedicated to Protestant solidarity—a quarrel that had already resulted in the bombing of a man's home. Nineteen twenty-four seemed to be a year when important decisions would have to be made, when judgments would be rendered, when old scores and grievances would be settled.

For more than two years Mayor Schwab had tried to avoid

turning the moral reform and Klan issues into a religious fight, but he became much less restrained after the confrontation in Black Rock. In April 1924 he dismissed the leadership of the Buffalo Council of Churches as "wholesale scandal-mongers," and a few weeks later he ordered police to investigate the council's chairman, the Reverend Don B. Tullis, whom he suspected, incorrectly, of being a Klansman. "Mr. Schwab seems to be insistent upon stirring up some religious prejudice in this vice campaign," Klansman L. E. H. Smith observed. "We have tried to keep that out." [10] As the situation worsened, the mayor openly exploited his religious ties. Late in May, at the annual convention of the Catholic Press Association, Schwab accused the Invisible Empire of "conducting guerrilla warfare against the Catholic church" and urged the journalists in attendance to "fight this battle for the church. Don't pass it up." Also present was the Bishop of Buffalo, the Right Reverend William Turner, who argued that Catholics must "shoulder the burden" of opposing "undesirable Protestant citizens," an assessment that the mayor publicly endorsed. A few weeks later, in a speech before the national convention of the Knights of St. John, Schwab again called on Catholics to "battle against all bigotry and lies that are welling up in the country through such agencies as the Ku Klux Klan." [11]

Ignoring the gathering storm clouds, the Buffalo Klan pressed ahead with its activities. On May 30, the klavern conducted a large outdoor ceremony on private land near Clarence Center, an event attended by hundreds of knights; when a state trooper in pursuit of a traffic violator arrived on the scene, KKK pickets turned him away. [12] Much of the following month was spent preparing for the New York Klan's second annual Klorero, which was to be held in Binghamton. In early July, several hundred knights from Buffalo and surrounding communities traveled by train and automobile to the four-day gathering. Despite a couple of unpleasant incidents—a Klan sentry was pelted with bricks and a load of buckshot was fired into the KKK encampment—the approximately four thousand knights in attendance appeared to have had a good time. The most notable event was a parade of two thousand robed and hooded kluxers through the heart of Binghamton on the Fourth of July. King Kleagle E. D. Smith headed the klavalcade astride a white horse, followed by floats, a band, and marchers from both the Klan and the Kamelia (the order's female auxiliary). One of the more boisterous contingents in the procession represented Buffalo Klan No. 5. Led by a costumed individual masquerading as Frank Schwab, the two-hundred-man unit carried signs identifying themselves as "Mayor Schwab's Pets." When told about the klavern's demonstration, Mayor Schwab commented, "God forgive them; they don't know what they are doing."[13]

The mayor's desire for forgiveness did not extend to himself. For months he had been planning to take decisive action against the hooded order, and the Binghamton Klorero presented an ideal opportunity to strike. His spies had informed him of the location of the Klan's membership files and mailing lists, and he knew that most of the chapter's officers would be out of town for at least a couple of days. Who served as his agent or agents remains unknown; possibly it was the police, his operatives within the Klan, or members of one of Buffalo's anti-Klan organizations. It is certain, however, that late on the evening of July 3 a burglar or burglars broke into Klan headquarters (ostensibly the offices of the Kay-Bee Adsign Company) on the third floor of the Calumet Building. Early the next morning, a janitor discovered that the suite had been completely ransacked, papers scattered about, equipment smashed, and all the office's file cabinets jimmied open; a subsequent investigation revealed that a number of important documents were missing. Denying that they had previously known the location of KKK headquarters, the Buffalo police speculated that the burglary was the work of a dissident faction within the Klan.[14]

Quite naturally, the break-in greatly distressed Buffalo Klan No. 5. Klavern leaders had promised to take all necessary steps to prevent exposure of the rank and file, and now unknown parties had gained access to the chapter's most sensitive records. In order both to squelch panic among Klansmen and to plant doubt in the minds of their enemies, klavern officers issued a press release playing down the importance of the illegal intrusion, claiming that only two Bibles, an American flag, $250 in cash, and "a mailing list of eligible prospects and a few enquiries from those desir-

ing information" had been taken. "The files of the actual membership of approximately 18,500 names together with financial
records," the letter bluffed, "are not kept at the office."[15]

The Klan also tried to keep up members' spirits by continuing
to hold large initiation ceremonies. Only three days after the burglary, the hooded order conducted its first outdoor meeting in
Tonawanda, burning a large cross erected on a canal barge; attending Klansmen informed the newspapers that they planned a
public parade in the near future. On the evening of July 15, more
than four hundred knights in full regalia gathered on private land
near Swormsville and initiated a new class of recruits, a ritual
that lasted until well after midnight. The state Klan publication
Vigilance said that the gathering was "the answer of the Klan to
the enemies of the order in Buffalo that attempted to secure the
membership list by robbing the Buffalo headquarters recently."[16]

As it became evident that the theft of klavern records had not
dissuaded Klansmen from further activity, Mayor Schwab decided to apply additional pressure. On July 25, he informed local
reporters that he had received a letter from an anonymous Klansman offering to sell the Buffalo Klan membership list for two
hundred dollars. The letter claimed that "there are many good
citizens in this organization," but vehemently denounced the "un-
American, unprincipled, law-defying, money-grabbing, face-cov-
ered ministers who call themselves the inner circle of the Ku Klux
Klan of Buffalo." In both tone and structure, the message revealed
a strong similarity to the secret reports that Schwab had been
receiving from one of his informants since April—which suggests
that the writer and the mayor were far from unacquainted. Indeed, Schwab almost surely was trying to use this "anonymous"
offer as a means of orchestrating the appearance of the KKK
roster while disassociating himself from the break-in at Klan
headquarters. This approach, however, presented a serious legal
obstacle, the mayor being liable to charges of receiving stolen
property if he bought the list.[17]

Schwab quickly resolved this difficulty. On August 1, the mayor
announced that he had received another "anonymous tip" that
important materials concerning the Klan could be found in the
basement of the Calumet Building. Police officers dispatched to

the scene soon located a large sugar bag that contained KKK literature, uniforms, and nearly two thousand index cards bearing the names of city residents; they then took the items to downtown headquarters to be "counted and checked." When pressed to elaborate on this sensational discovery, the mayor remained evasive: "I will not talk about it because I do not wish to give anyone the opportunity to say that I am prejudiced."[18]

The Buffalo klavern wasted little time in responding to the mysterious reappearance of the stolen items. Attorney Julius Grass, acting as legal representative for the chapter (of which he was an active member), demanded the immediate return of everything that had been taken from the basement and threatened to sue for libel if the newspapers published the alleged membership list. When officers returned the materials on August 3, Grass protested that they had retained transcripts of all the information on the index cards. Admitting that this was true, the police argued that it was standard procedure to have an "itemized and descriptive record" of stolen property on file.[19]

Exposing the klavern's membership still posed problems. Although the authorities had no doubt that they possessed an accurate list of Klansmen, they had no way of proving this if it came to a legal showdown; the roster had been inscribed on plain index cards (not official membership application forms) and carried no signatures. The local newspapers would not publish the roster without more substantial verification, and the city risked legal action for libel if it openly claimed that the citizens named on the list belonged to the Invisible Empire. Thus a degree of official disingenuousness was required when the police department, on the orders of Mayor Schwab, placed a copy of the roster on public display the afternoon of August 4. "We do not know," explained Assistant Corporation Counsel Andrew P. Ronan, "whether the list is a list of Klansmen or not. We are taking no chances in making the list public." He argued that the names simply constituted part of an official record of stolen property that was available to all concerned residents, adding that "Anybody may copy the list if he desires."[20]

Public interest in the "record of stolen property" steadily grew over the following days. On August 6, seventy-five residents came to police headquarters to view the document, taking turns carefully reading through the names as armed guards stood nearby. "I always suspected that bird," commented one visitor. "See that fellow there—well he lives next door to me, can you beat it," another exclaimed. Two days later, the number of visitors had increased to three hundred; viewing was now done by groups, and an additional copy of the list was put on display. Police soon had to extend visiting hours and make a third copy available, a spokesman acknowledging that the department was not prepared for such an influx. On August 13, when the ranks of the curious swelled to more than three thousand, officers transferred the copies of the roster to a more spacious location in the Franklin Street station. As those in the crowd read through the lists, there were numerous "outbursts of anger, displays of bitterness and exclamations of astonishment"; many residents jotted down names from the document, particularly those of tradespeople and neighbors.[21]

Most Klansmen responded to their exposure with silence. The *Courier* contacted a number of the men listed on the roster, all of whom either denied affiliation or refused to comment. When asked if he was a member, State Assemblyman Henry Hutt replied, "Absolutely not. I never was connected with the organization, nor am I now." After being informed that the authorities possessed evidence that he had attended a Klan meeting in January, however, he admitted that "I may have, but I don't think so." Although he initially denied any connection with the KKK, the Reverend Charles Penfold also eventually indicated his involvement: "I believe I have addressed some Klan meetings—but so has Mayor Schwab; so that does not mean anything. I have addressed meetings that looked very much like Klan meetings to me—maybe that is the reason for my name appearing among a number of prospects."[22]

The loss of its secrecy threw the klavern into disarray and fueled discontent among the rank and file. One angry Klansman argued that the chapter's officers should be formally censured, claiming that the theft of the membership files represented "a pure case of neglect." The exact degree of anxiety, embarrassment, and anger that exposure produced can only be speculated on, but in at least one instance it resulted in a tragic incident. For several months prior to the break-in at Klan headquarters, Henry H. Lyon had been one of the klavern's most active members. A highly respected electrical engineer and a longtime employee of the Buffalo General Electric Company, Lyon suffered from a progressive neurotic condition and found public humiliation to be more than he could endure. Shortly after midnight on August 7, 1924, less than three days after the KKK roster went on display, he took a revolver and fatally shot his wife and two young sons, ages eight and ten, while they slept. Lyon then fired the weapon into his own right cheek; he died a few hours later. A newspaper report of his death provided a description of his work habits that is particularly intriguing in light of what we know about the Klan's concentration in certain occupations:

> It was said that Lyon was a conscientious, painstaking man in his work and all employees under him respected him. Lyon was chief engineer of the drafting department of the [Buffalo] General Electric Co., which position involved a vast amount of mathematical work. The men under Lyon were required to figure everything strictly according to scale, a fact which reveals the exactness Lyon desired and demanded.

Perhaps an obsession with order, regularity, and precision had helped lead Lyon into the Invisible Empire; perhaps, as well, it ultimately led him into madness.[23]

The enemies of the Klan did not let the Lyon tragedy deter them from their assault on the Invisible Empire. "The murderer and the suicide joined an organization whose sole reason for existence is to persecute the Catholic Church, to revile her priesthood and sisterhood," argued the *Catholic Union & Times*. "Conscience makes cowards of us all." Soon others felt the wrath of the community, Police Lieutenant Austin J. Roche observing on August 11 that "business men whose names were found on the list have been boycotted by many of their customers since the list at police headquarters was thrown open to the public. One west-side milk dealer said he lost 106 customers the first day the list was made public." Rumors also circulated that insurance salesmen and stockbrokers had "lost considerable business" and that a number of Klansmen had been dismissed from their jobs. Shortly after the list was put on display, the Seneca Flower Shop, owned by klavern member Anson C. Beeman, was painted with yellow KKK's, and a downtown shoe store was covered with strips of wallpaper advising "Catholics, Jews, and Negroes" to take their business elsewhere. On the evening of August 13, seven south-side homes and businesses, all belonging to Klansmen, were marked with large KKK's painted in white lead paint; Klan opponents also posted a sign with the names of south Buffalo knights at the intersection of Seneca Street and Norman Place, a display that attracted hundreds of curious Fifth Ward residents. The following night, vandals covered at least half a dozen residences just across the city line in Cheektowaga with black and white KKK's of various sizes.[24]

The surge of anti-Klan activity worried local authorities. "If these demonstrations continue," warned Police Chief Charles Zimmerman, "we will be forced to withhold the list from further exhibitions. Displaying of the lists is not intended to incite any such activities." Even Mayor Schwab, whose actions had encouraged such demonstrations in the first place, voiced strong reservations: "While some may think that retaliation is justified, I appeal to them as civic-spirited citizens and as true Christians not to despoil the fair name of the city of Buffalo by any such occurrences which would resemble in any way the tactics of the organization at which they are aimed."[25]

This did not mean that the mayor had finished with Klansmen. Correctly anticipating that most knights would deny membership, Schwab had held additional records in reserve. On August 19, he announced that a disgruntled Klan officer had mailed him a new membership list, one that included not only the names of nearly two thousand Buffalo Klansmen but also those of a like number residing in over seventy towns, villages, and hamlets in western New York. Schwab indicated that, unlike the earlier list, this roster consisted of a comprehensive set of official application cards bearing the signatures of members; the forms additionally provided detailed information concerning place of residence, occupation, age, religious belief, and rank within the Klan. In order to convince others that he had fairly and legally acquired the KKK records, the mayor released a copy of a letter that had accompanied the roster:

Frank X. Schwab
Mayor of the City of Buffalo

Because you have proven to be such a good sport and because these confirmed liars of the Klan have repeatedly denied their membership and defied you to prove their identity with the hooded anti-Americans and are now crying for help and putting the responsibility upon the shoulders of others, I am sending you by express the remainder of the property taken but not stolen from the Ku Klux Klan headquarters July 3, 1924, by those who had a right to enter for their own protection and whose cards have been removed from this file but who will be ready to reveal the rottenness of the Buffalo Klan when the proper time comes.

Remember, Klansmen are sworn to lie when asked if they belong to the Ku Klux Klan.

A Klansman Was I

One of Mayor Schwab's spies within the klavern had at times signed his reports "A Klansman I Am" and "A Klansman I Was," and he had regularly criticized the corruption that he believed pervaded the chapter's leadership. His reports had also stressed the unfair way in which the Klan had treated the mayor, as was likewise indicated in the letter. Although there is no absolute proof, one can strongly suspect that the membership files had been acquired by this operative, a person with whom the mayor had been in close contact for months.[26]

Almost immediately, a "corps of stenographers" went to work copying the Klan records, and Mayor Schwab gave every indication that he planned to put the new list on public display. He also hoped to use the membership cards to confront and humiliate those Buffalonians who had dared to join the Invisible Empire, announcing that instead of returning the materials in bulk to a Klan representative, "I am going to insist on the [men] whose names and signatures are in the new list personally coming to police headquarters if they wish to recover their membership cards." The mayor added a religious twist to this approach by writing an open letter to the city's Protestant clergymen, asking them to "inform the public from their pulpits next Sunday that we will insist upon the Klansmen retrieving their cards." One week later, the police began sending out postcard notices to all the residents on the list, requesting them to pick up their property.[27]

Some city officials felt that the mayor was being excessively vindictive in dealing with Klansmen and that his actions would only breed trouble. The most vocal among these was Police Chief Zimmerman, who had been very disturbed by the recent outbreak of anti-Klan activity. A Protestant, an admired figure among local reformers, and the uncle of Klansman Andrew Zimmerman, the chief possessed a considerable degree of understanding as to how otherwise respectable citizens might have been led into the Invisible Empire. "If it is up to me," he informed the press on August 21, "I will under no circumstances allow anybody to see the Klan list. The open inspection of the [first list] led to many disorders and unnecessary strife." Zimmerman warned that "People are ready to commit murder over the accusations made that they are members of the Klan. A man called up only yesterday and said he would kill anyone who chalked the letters K.K.K. on his home as someone attempted to do." Only if he were presented with an order from the state supreme court, advised the chief, would he open the records to public scrutiny. Police Lieutenant Austin Roche also voiced reservations about revealing the roster, commenting that "I believe that it is unfair to allow persons indiscriminately to view the lists, especially when their reason for wanting to see the list is a malicious one."[28]

Desiring to avoid a controversy within his administration, Mayor Schwab tried to compromise. Rather than giving the public free access to the Klan materials, he suggested that only the newspapers be allowed to examine the records; then, "They [the newspapers] can take it or leave it. I am not giving out the list and neither is the chief. If the newspapers wish to make public a public record, it is up to them." In order to avoid further delay, Schwab on August 25 issued a direct order to Zimmerman: "You will immediately permit members of the press to view the said list in the hands of the property clerk." Having no choice, the chief allowed reporters to look at the roster—angrily avowing that he had "washed his hands of everything"—but he refused to allow the journalists to copy down any information from the documents. "I have received several requests from officials of industrial plants and other organizations to do all in my power to keep the list a secret," he explained. "They informed me that several of their employees have caused disturbances in the stores and plants and they fear further disorders if the new list is made public."[29]

The chief's arguments against full and open disclosure did not convince the Klan's most zealous opponents. On August 28, Charles S. Desmond, an ambitious young Catholic attorney and Democratic candidate for the state assembly seat held by Klansman Henry Hutt, indicated that he would take legal action against Zimmerman. "As a public official in charge of public records," argued Desmond, "[Zimmerman] must show any document in his possession vital to the public interest in reasonable time when asked to do so by a citizen." The anti-Klan attorney pursued this legal effort and secured a special hearing before New York Supreme Court Justice Charles A. Pooley early in September 1924. Desmond's main line of argument was that the Buffalo city charter guaranteed residents access to public records. In an opposing affidavit, Chief Zimmerman asserted that the Klan documents were not public records and that unrestricted access to them might lead to civil disorder. On September 15, Judge Pooley rejected Zimmerman's argument and ruled that the Klan list and associated materials fell within the charter provision allowing citizens access to public records; he declared that not only could the documents be put on display but that they could be copied by anyone who desired to do so.[30]

By the time it was delivered, Pooley's ruling had become largely moot. Early in September, rumors surfaced that copies of the new Klan membership list were secretly circulating throughout the city. This received confirmation on September 10, when a number of vendors began openly selling a published version of the roster in downtown Buffalo; soon more than five thousand copies of the pamphlet, which listed klavern members by trade and profession, were available in local newsstands. Entitled *Exposé of Traitors in the Interests of Jews, Catholics, Negroes and All Respecters of the American Principle of Civil and Religious Freedom* and selling for fifty cents, the pamphlet became an instant bestseller. This unauthorized appearance of information culled from records in police custody did not please Chief Zimmerman, who ordered the arrest of Gabriel J. Vestola, one of those vending the publication. It was soon learned, however, that Vestola possessed a valid peddler's license and that there were no legal grounds for holding him. When asked what further action the city was contemplating, Mayor Schwab disavowed any personal interest in learning how the list had fallen into unauthorized hands: "If Chief Zimmerman wishes to arrest any persons for the publication of the list, that's his affair, not mine." The Klan's attorney, Julius Grass, tried to take the publication of the list in stride, commenting: "Now I know where to buy my butter, eggs and milk. [The list is] a good business directory for the Klan."[31]

It remains uncertain which person or persons acquired the list and published it. Given the tone of some of the writing in the pamphlet, one suspects that one or more of the city's predominantly Catholic anti-Klan organizations bore major responsibility.[32] Yet, this was at least to some extent an ecumenical effort: the unnamed publishers were represented by Jewish attorney Samuel M. Fleischman, who provided the press with an illuminating assessment of the sense of personal outrage that had convinced him to participate in the assault on the Klan:

> I have no malice against any person named in the pamphlet. I am, of course, opposed strenuously to the organization [KKK] for this reason. When it attempts to say that my boy, dearer to me many times than my own life, because he was born unto me a Jew is to be barred from holding public office in this country, and should be voted against in the event he did run for office, by the members of any association, purely because he is a Jew, [then it] is vicious and un-American, and every bit of energy that I possess will be used in wiping out such an organization.[33]

The appearance and distribution of the published Klan list coincided with a new spate of anti-Klan activity. At least four additional business establishments were adorned with KKK's, including the automobile service station of Edgar H. Herning. "I believe in what the Klan stands for," a defiant Herning stated following the incident. "I was brought up Protestant and I have a right to believe in the principles of religion which were taught me. I don't see why anyone should object to that as long as I don't harm anyone." He promised that the letters painted on the window of his service station would remain there until the responsible parties removed them. Fenton H. Dimmick, the principal of

Buffalo Public School No. 1, exhibited considerably less resolve after anti-Klan students sent him a note saying "Old Man Dimmick, If you don't get out, we will get you." Dimmick immediately requested police protection, protesting that he had attended only one klavern meeting and did not consider himself to be currently affiliated with the secret order.[34]

By this time, one of the most unfortunate and violent episodes associated with the exposure of the Klan had kept the community on edge for more than a week. Immediately following the theft of its records on July 3, Buffalo Klan No. 5 notified Imperial headquarters in Atlanta and requested assistance. Shortly afterward, an official Klan investigator, Thomas H. Austin, received instructions to travel to Buffalo; perhaps anticipating trouble, he stopped off in Binghamton on July 7 and acquired a license to carry a revolver. Once in Buffalo, Austin checked into the Graystone Hotel under an assumed name and in association with local klavern officers tried to determine who had been involved in the break-in.[35]

Gradually suspicions focused upon Edward C. Obertean, a former policeman who had joined the Klan in June. A member of the vice squad from 1919 to 1920, Obertean had been dismissed in a well-publicized episode that many believed was politically motivated. Most Klansmen probably assumed that he harbored resentment against the police department and other city officials; they also assumed that he was Protestant because he had designated his religious affiliation as Baptist on his membership application. In actuality, Obertean was a Roman Catholic operating as a special officer under the direction of Police Lieutenant Roche and Mayor Schwab.[36]

By late August 1924, Klansmen had begun to piece together the truth and confronted Obertean at a meeting of the order. A number of outraged knights brandished weapons at him, claimed he was a traitor, and made a variety of dire threats. Although released, the special officer still feared for his life, confiding to a friend, "If they try to get me, you can bet your life that I will mark a couple of them."[37]

This was the tense situation on the evening of August 31, when a car bearing Klan investigator Thomas Austin, Kleagle George C.

Bryant, and Klansman Carl W. Sturm arrived at Obertean's home at 159 Kensington Avenue in north Buffalo. The three men soon saw Obertean pass by in an automobile driven by Floyd A. Victor, a non-Klansman, and they gave chase. Eventually, Victor pulled over in front of a residence at 128 Durham Street, and George Bryant, the driver of the pursuing vehicle, stepped out and said to Obertean, "Just a minute, Ed, I want to talk with you." Obertean simultaneously alighted, declaring, "We might as well settle this right here and now." Suddenly, according to witnesses, two flashes of light flared from Obertean's coat pocket, where he had concealed a revolver. A bullet struck the unarmed Bryant in the groin and he collapsed in the street; the other slug grazed the leg of Carl Sturm, who had exited the car and now ran away, wounded, into the night. Thomas Austin then stepped out and, standing only five feet away from Obertean, shot the special officer once in the chest; as Obertean spun around, the Klan investigator shot him three more times in the back. Obertean fell to the ground, managed to lift his weapon a final time, and fired two steel-jacketed bullets directly into Austin's heart, killing him instantly. Less than an hour later, Obertean died in a local hospital, never managing to make a final statement.[38]

In the wake of the north-side shoot-out, religious tensions in Buffalo soared. "My brother Edward," announced the slain officer's sister, "was a martyr to his religion and church." The subsequent distribution of the *Exposé of Traitors* and Charles Desmond's successful legal action against Chief Zimmerman soon added fuel to the fire, producing a very unpleasant state of affairs that persisted for several months. Early in September, Mayor Schwab, observing that "Buffalo has changed from a city noted for its religious tolerance to a city in which bigotry and race distinction [have] been forced to the attention of the great mass of citizens," called on the leaders of the community's major churches to form a tolerance committee around the theme of "One God and One Country." In the following days, however, he was decisively rebuffed by prominent Protestant clergymen. The Roman Catholic Bishop of Buffalo, William Turner, also refused to cooperate, despite his personal friendship with the mayor. "Catholics of Buffalo have been the chief sufferers from religious intolerance," he explained in an open letter. "We did not start the conflagration and it is not up to us to get scorched and smudged in the attempt to put out the flames." The bishop went on to assert that "The blame and the shame are to be placed elsewhere. The churches that have contributed to the membership of the Klan, the churches that have harbored and encouraged the hooded knights can, if they have the inclination and the authority to do so, bring the matter to a speedy head."[39]

In this atmosphere of growing hatred and distrust, many Catholics desired nothing less than the total destruction and humiliation of the Klan. Accordingly, on September 4, Henry W. Killeen, an attorney and close associate of Charles Desmond, initiated proceedings in city court to determine whether there were grounds for prosecuting local Klansmen under the provisions of the Walker Law. Over the course of the next several weeks, Killeen subpoenaed forty-one Buffalonians whose names appeared on the KKK roster, pressing them in court to reveal how and why they had joined the Invisible Empire. Most Klansmen continued, even under oath, to deny affiliation; others testified that they had filled out application forms and attended "patriotic" meetings, but insisted that they did not consider themselves to be members of the hooded order. A few individuals—most notably the Reverend George A. Fowler, the Reverend L. E. H. Smith, and Klan attorney Julius Grass—readily admitted that they had joined. State Assemblyman Henry Hutt also decided that it was time to come clean: "I am a member of the Klan and I am proud of it. I hope the day is near when the state of New York shall receive a charter from national headquarters for a regular Klan."[40]

Such comments notwithstanding, the Killeen investigation seriously damaged Buffalo Klan No. 5. Members now realized that at any moment they might be hauled into court and subjected to further public humiliation; they also clearly risked prosecution under the Walker Law. A powerful message had been delivered: Abandon any type of disruptive activity or suffer serious consequences. Ultimately, most knights decided to accept the inevitable. From September 1924 on, the order greatly reduced its activities within the city limits; there were no more cross-burnings, anonymous messages were no longer promulgated, and the campaign for improved moral conditions gradually faded away. The klavern continued to hold secret lodge meetings, but increasingly these were exclusively social occasions. By late 1924, the Buffalo Klan had been largely neutralized, permanently removed as a serious factor in the community's political life.

Had the Klan's opponents desired to do so, they could have pressed ahead with the prosecution of every local knight under the Walker Law. After Judge Pooley ruled that the documents taken from Klan headquarters were public records, the anti-Klan forces had ample evidence to use against their enemies, particularly the signed membership cards. Such an effort, however, promised to be complicated, time-consuming, and expensive. Strangely enough, it was Klansman Julius Grass who suggested an alternative approach during the Killeen inquiry:

> I admit that the Ku Klux Klan did not comply with the Walker act in not having filed a list of members and officers. I admit that George C. Bryant [who was recovering from his gunshot wound] is the kleagle of the Klan in Buffalo. Now that is all that my friend Killeen is after in this proceeding. Let him issue a warrant for Bryant's arrest and bring him into court. We—when I say, we, I mean that I represent the Invisible Empire of the Ku Klux Klan— are ready to test the constitutionality of the Walker act.[41]

As Grass and other Klan leaders were no doubt aware, such a course would not only simplify matters, but, by focusing the attention of the authorities exclusively on Bryant, would ease pressure on the KKK's rank and file, increasing the likelihood that they would continue affiliation.

The hooded order's opponents agreed that a test case would be the best way to proceed. Late in September, District Attorney Guy Moore issued a warrant for Bryant's arrest, charging him with violating the Walker Law. On October 1, Bryant surrendered to authorities, but his legal counsel secured the kleagle's release pending a ruling by Supreme Court Justice Pooley on the constitutionality of the anti-Klan measure. Five days later, Pooley heard arguments for and against the Walker Law. Bryant's chief attorney, Louis C. Fuller, a prominent criminal lawyer from Rochester, argued that the act constituted a "vicious, pernicious form of class legislation" because it exclusively targeted the Invisible Empire:

> Everybody knows that the Walker act was aimed solely at the Ku Klux Klan. This statute is a dishonor to the state of New York. I am frank to state that the law is anarchistic in spirit and far worse than anything ever suspected of the Klan. Evidently it was enacted because a few politicians, members of the Republican and Democratic parties, by concerted action thought the Klan could disturb the balance of power now controlled by the two major parties in the state legislature.

In rebuttal, District Attorney Moore and Henry Killeen presented a bitter and emotional denunciation of the KKK, stressing that the state clearly had the right to regulate organizations that posed a threat to the public good.[42]

One month later, Judge Pooley delivered yet another blow to Buffalo Klan No. 5 by upholding the constitutionality of the Walker Law. "It is a matter of common knowledge that this organization functions largely at night, its members disguised by hoods and gowns and doing things calculated to strike terror into the minds of the people," he observed. "It is claimed that they are organized against certain of the citizens by reason of race and religion." Therefore, because the Invisible Empire clearly struck at "fundamental principles of our government," the state should have the power "to eradicate it and . . . is not required to await violations before enacting legislation." The decision angered the Klan's legal representatives, who continued to claim that the Walker Law was "unreasonable, arbitrary, and discriminatory." On November 10, just as George Bryant was preparing to be arraigned in city court, they appealed Pooley's ruling to the New York appellate division. Bryant then posted bail pending the decision of the five-justice tribunal, which would not hear the case for several months. Meanwhile city officials indicated that they would not use the act against other knights until the appeal had been settled.[43]

This did not mean that Klansmen would be able to evade the enforcement of other laws. Already legal action had been taken against Albert C. Acker, sales representative for the National Life Insurance Company and active klavern member; he was also, as Mayor Schwab had learned from his undercover sources, a part-time dealer in rubber condoms, which could be distributed legally only by physicians. On August 9, the police arrested Acker on a charge of possessing and selling "illegal merchandise." Unable to make bail, the Klansman was taken to county jail; one month later he pled guilty in city court and received a fifty-dollar fine.[44] At the same time, city authorities charged Stewart Queer, former kleagle of Buffalo Klan No. 5 and one of the chief organizers of the encounter with Mayor Schwab at Black Rock, with failing to provide adequate financial support to his estranged wife and three children. On September 17, a city court judge ordered him to pay an increased amount of support.[45] A few weeks later, Klansman E. Laverne Buell, the display manager at the Walter E. Bedell Company, was convicted of assaulting a seventeen-year-old girl; the young woman had willingly spent the night with him in a local hotel, but her age had left Buell legally liable.[46]

Easily the most sensational charges directed at a Klansman at this time were those leveled against the Reverend Charles C. Penfold. On the evening of September 19, 1924, three constables in the town of Cheektowaga discovered the pastor's car parked in an unlighted area at the side of East Delevan Avenue, just across the Buffalo city line. Inside the vehicle were Penfold and a woman, who had jointly assumed an "improper position." Once aware of the officers' presence, the clergyman quickly exited the car and began explaining that the woman was his wife and that she was merely adjusting her clothes after being stuck with a pin. This explanation did not convince the constables, who immediately brought Penfold and his partner before Justice of the Peace Jerome F. Rozan on charges of "outraging public decency." The justice questioned both of the defendants and became suspicious when "Mrs. Penfold" had difficulty remembering her full name and the age of her only son. "You're both lying to me," he stated, rendering a verdict of guilty; Rozan then ordered the pair to return for sentencing the following week.[47]

News of Penfold's nocturnal activities created a great stir in Buffalo, the press promptly dubbing him the "parking parson." The Klansman insisted that he had been set up, that the whole episode was "a preposterous lie framed by my enemies who have long threatened to rid the city of me." Protestant leaders promptly leapt to his defense. The Reverend Robert E. Brown of the Richmond Avenue Methodist Church, a non-Klansman, said that the incident constituted "a cowardly and dastardly attempt to intimidate those who are fighting for law and decency in Buffalo," and the Buffalo Council of Churches extended an unqualified vote of confidence. The pastor's congregation at the Sentinel Methodist Church remained particularly loyal, one member asserting that their leader was "a martyr to the cause of righteousness. We will back him to the last man and the last dollar until complete vindication has been secured." When Penfold conducted Sunday services on September 21, those attending greeted him with "many warm handclasps and heartening words of welcome."[48]

The minister's defenders soon learned that their support was undeserved. For two days, Cheektowaga detectives had followed the alleged Mrs. Penfold, discovering that she actually was Mrs. Freda Lohr, a member of the Sentinel Methodist choir. They confronted her, and she subsequently visited Judge Rozan and admitted having lied in court; as Mrs. Lohr signed an official statement retracting her earlier testimony, her husband stood nearby softly saying, "Tell the truth, dear. That is the only thing to do." In short order, Edward P. Volz, the deputy chief of the Erie County probation department, interrogated Charles Penfold, who confessed that he had also made false statements under oath. On September 26, the minister presented himself at the Cheektowaga fire department for sentencing on his earlier conviction. As an unruly crowd of anti-Klan partisans, unable to gain admittance, jeered and hooted outside the building, Judge Rozan sentenced Penfold to thirty days in the Alden penitentiary, to begin immediately. The pastor was taken to the facility, but just as guards were preparing to shave his head, he secured release on bond pending appeal. Waiting to take him home was a small group of friends, including fellow Klansman and moral crusader L. E. H. Smith.[49]

Penfold's hooded brethren did what they could to show displeasure with his sentence. On the evening of September 27, roving bands of knights ignited crosses in various parts of Cheektowaga, hoping to intimidate the authorities. Unfortunately for the Klan, however, town constables succeeded in arresting six of those responsible for the fiery displays. Cheektowaga Chief of Police Emil Cappola, who had previously seemed reluctant to take decisive action against the KKK, now left no doubt about his intentions: "There will be no more burning of crosses in this village. I have given my men orders to shoot to kill if the hooded order shows its head here again." Klansmen wisely took the chief at his word and refrained from further demonstrations.[50]

The Reverend Penfold's problems were far from over. District Attorney Moore indicated that he would file perjury charges against the clergyman, and Methodist Bishop Adna W. Leonard, putting integrity before sectarian solidarity, removed Penfold from his pastorate. By mid-October, according to a local reporter, the "parking parson" seemed to be a broken man. As he faced his interviewer, he appeared "unstrung. . . . The bolt of scandal that has singed him seemed to have left him dazed, helpless." On November 28, Penfold received more unwelcome news when the Erie County grand jury indicted him for perjury. He entered 1925 completely discredited in the community's eyes, his career in shambles, his reputation shattered.[51]

Exposed, hounded by enemies, tainted by scandal, Buffalo Klan No. 5 struggled to maintain organizational viability in the latter half of 1924. After the burglary at the Calumet Building, the klavern shifted operations to an office on the eighth floor of the Bransom Building, near the intersecton of Main and East Eagle. Within days, however, Lieutenant Roche had ferreted out this new headquarters and the Klan decided to move on. By early October, klavern officers were reduced to holding executive conferences in a quarry at the Buffalo Cement Company.[52]

The activities that the group arranged in this period were primarily social and fraternal in nature. Late in August, Buffalo knights joined hundreds of other western New York Klansmen for an outdoor ceremony north of the town of Clarence, just off Salt Road. One week later, four hundred klavern members and friends traveled to Batavia to participate in a Labor Day picnic and parade sponsored by the Genesee County Klan; more than twenty-five thousand people attended the affair, which concluded with the traditional nighttime initiation and cross-burning.[53] For the remainder of the year, the klavern held regular meetings at a variety of indoor sites; an official Klan message intercepted in

October said that more than a dozen gatherings were scheduled for the next three months. On Christmas Eve, a group of knights in "full regalia" made a rare public appearance at the Protestant Home for Unprotected Children, on Niagara Street; the kluxers distributed woolen sweaters, caps, and mittens to over 150 abandoned and orphaned youngsters.[54]

With George Bryant's challenge to the Walker Law making its way through the courts, and with enemies ready to pounce at a moment's notice, Buffalo Klan No. 5 avoided any form of overt civic activism at this time. This passive stance displeased such moral crusaders as the Reverend L. E. H. Smith, who wanted to continue the reform campaign. Then suddenly, on November 9, Smith fell gravely ill after dining in a downtown restaurant. His physician later informed the press that he suspected that the minister had ingested "black drop," an arsenic-laced compound favored by underworld assassins. Although Smith eventually recovered and resumed some of his activities, he ceased to be an influential force on the local scene. Some months later, after protracted quarreling with George Bryant and other officers, the crusading pastor tendered his formal resignation from the Klan, thus depriving the klavern of one of its few dynamic guiding lights.[55]

As Buffalo Klan No. 5 entered a period of extended decline in the fall of 1924, Mayor Schwab remained vigilant, fearful that the organization might make some type of rash move. After receiving a number of threatening letters, the mayor began carrying a revolver and rarely was seen without a bodyguard.[56] He also continued to receive reports from an undercover investigator, who warned that at one Klan meeting "someone suggested sideswiping the Mayor's car and tarring and feathering him." Late in November, Schwab announced that Klan agents had in fact tried to waylay his car during a trip to the village of Perrysburg, but that he had been able to thwart the assault. In an open letter, Kleagle George Bryant strongly refuted the mayor's accusations, arguing that the klavern "has stood for everything that is clean, decent and commendable in civic affairs." "Nothing," he emphasized, "is more vital to the welfare of the Ku Klux Klan in this state than the personal safety of Francis Xavier Schwab."[57]

After visiting the Niagara Street children's home, the Klan repeated the pattern of earlier years and went into winter seclusion. The *Buffalo Truth*, owned and edited by Klansman Mark H. Hubbell, presented a steady stream of pro-KKK articles concerning activities of the secret order elsewhere in the state and nation, but it carried no news about the local klavern.[58] Then, suddenly, the Klan took on new life in the spring. On the evening of March 31, 1925, the chapter held a large social gathering for both men and women at an undisclosed site inside the city, an event that featured music by a Klan band from Batavia. Five weeks later, Buffalo knights and their Erie County brethren conducted an initiation at "Austin Field" (named in honor of the slain Klan investigator), a fifty-acre plot of farmland between Lancaster and Elma that the order had recently purchased. "Candidates first were assembled in a gully behind a large barn," noted an invited newspaper reporter. "Electric torches, red flares and a cold moon lighted up the vicinity. Two young women collected $10 bills and checks from the candidates, while the Imperial night hawk credited new Klansmen with their donations. A bomb exploded in the 'charmed circle' as the signal for the candidates' advance." A subsequent oath-taking and cross-burning completed the ritual.[59]

This new Klan activity worried Mayor Schwab, who implored Governor Smith to enforce the Walker Law strictly throughout the state.[60] In addition to concerns over his personal safety, Schwab no doubt feared that a successful recruiting drive might encourage the Buffalo klavern to play an active role in the forthcoming city elections. Although the Invisible Empire did not command a sizable bloc of votes, it might do something to exacerbate simmering religious and ethnic resentments and thereby complicate the mayor's reelection plans. As things turned out, however, Buffalo Klan No. 5 decided to take no action; indeed, by the summer of 1925 it was fast dwindling into utter insignificance.

Although the local Klan would soon fade out of existence, many of the attitudes and assumptions that had motivated its members and supporters remained quite viable. Protestant-Catholic tensions had by no means fully subsided, ensuring that many voters would oppose Schwab's reelection on religious grounds; other residents, including some Catholics, had been appalled by his perceived indifference to vigorous enforcement of the vice and

liquor laws and by the continual controversy that had characterized his first four years in office. Increasingly, many of these Buffalonians focused their hopes on the mayoral candidacy of City
Commissioner Ross Graves, a strong prohibition advocate who
had established himself as one of the mayor's chief rivals.[61]

The campaign began quite peacefully, with Mayor Schwab and
Graves emerging as the top two vote-getters in the nonpartisan
primary held in mid-October. The Klan, suffering from serious
internal problems, apparently could not muster the wherewithal
to help oppose the candidacy of its most bitter enemy. The klavern
ordered a few buttons that simply said "Beat Schwab," but evidently this was the extent of its efforts.[62] After the primary, however, Ross Graves launched a hard-hitting campaign that would
have done any Klansman proud. He openly exploited the race
issue, claiming that "Schwabism poses as the only genuine uplift
movement in the city while it licenses all-night joints where white
girls of tender age are lured to hectic dances with black men." He
asserted that lax law enforcement had attracted "underworld riff
raff to Buffalo, thus branding the city with the notorious reputation of affording safe haven for crooks, panderers, and gunmen."
He also tried to capitalize on religious tensions, accusing the
Schwab campaign of sending "its emissaries from house to house
whispering slander and appealing to religious prejudice in a malicious effort to array brother against brother, neighbor against
neighbor." In sum, the Graves campaign centered on many of the
same community concerns that the Invisible Empire had tried to
exploit for the past four years.[63]

The mayor's supporters, as might have been expected, responded vigorously to the commissioner's assertions. "Back of the
mud and slime of the Graves campaign," one political ad stated,
"are the snarling, sneaking hordes who crawl along doorsteps in
the dead and dark of night." Generally, however, Schwab partisans avoided doing anything that might reopen the wounds of the
previous year. The mayor himself made no mention of his role in
the assault on the Klan; in fact, he never mentioned the KKK at
all. Given the positions taken by his opponent, Schwab realized
that Buffalo's large Catholic and ethnic vote was his for the taking,
so it was best to avoid unnecessary controversy. This proved to be

an astute approach. On November 3, he trounced Graves by a tally of 77,697 to 55,413. The results, proclaimed the *Courier*, "stamp Frank X. Schwab as the most popular mayor Buffalo [has] ever had."[64]

The mayor's landslide victory was only the last in a series of setbacks in 1925 that contributed to the precipitous decline of the Ku Klux Klan in western New York. In May, the appellate division of the New York Supreme Court upheld the Walker Law by a vote of four to one, a concurring justice comparing the Klan to "the Carbonari, the Nihilists, the Fenians, the Tugenbund, and the Molly Maguires." The KKK appealed the decision to the New York Court of Appeals, the highest tribunal in the state, but with little hope of ultimate vindication.[65] A few weeks later, an internal dispute threatened to wreck the Niagara County Klan after Imperial officials removed three local officers who were allegedly using the organization to advance their political careers; eventually the incident resulted in mass defections.[66] At the same time, Buffalo Klan No. 5 lost a number of its most stalwart members, including the Reverends George A. Fowler, who moved to Oklahoma, and L. E. H. Smith. The Reverend Smith apparently had learned some important lessons through his involvement with the Invisible Empire, as he observed during a final speech to fellow knights: "I am loyal to the Klan. I fought its battle. I suffered for it. But I tell you, in this country there's no place for a monarchial government. This kleagle and titan business never did appeal to me but the idealism is here." He went on to urge that Klansmen "clean up their own robes" and remember that "in this country, which was raised up to be an asylum for the oppressed and down-trodden of the earth, there is no place for religious hatred or bigotry."[67]

By September 1925, the few remaining local Klansmen had become similarly discouraged, and a number of them threatened to secede and affiliate with the new Independent Klan of America. Trouble was also brewing in the vicinity of Batavia, where Genesee County knights accused George Bryant of having pocketed thousands of dollars in robe-deposit fees. Bryant tried to defend himself at a special meeting arranged by King Kleagle E. D. Smith, but the Buffalo Klansman was shouted down and barely avoided "bodily injury." Soon after returning home, Bryant decided that he had had enough, that the Klan was no longer a "good business proposition." On November 1, he relinquished his joint titles of Grand Kleagle of Western New York and Great Titan of New York Province No. 8 and moved to Florida, hoping to take advantage of the ongoing real estate boom in that state.[68]

Shortly afterward, Atlanta officials appointed the Reverend D. G. Bacon as the new kleagle of Buffalo Klan No. 5. Nearly seventy years old, an outsider unacquainted with the community, Bacon quickly learned that there was little local interest in keeping the klavern going. Early in December 1925, he left on a trip to Ohio and never came back. Meanwhile, the Buffalo Klan quietly died.[69]

Conclusion

On January 12, 1926, the New York Court of Appeals unanimously upheld the constitutionality of the Walker Law, and shortly afterward George Bryant's legal representatives appealed his case to the United States Supreme Court. Briefs were submitted on October 10, 1927, and thirteen months later the nation's highest tribunal rendered its decision. In a majority opinion written by Associate Justice Willis Van Devanter, the court ruled that because it could be reasonably concluded that the Ku Klux Klan stimulated "hurtful religious and race prejudices," aspired to political power, and engaged in violent vigilantism, state governments could regulate the organization "within limits which are consistent with the rights of others and the public welfare"; the Walker Law, in the view of the court, met all pertinent legal tests and was therefore constitutional.[1] The decision meant that Bryant, who had returned to the Buffalo area in 1927 and now operated a meat market in Kenmore, would at last have to face the long-pending charge of having violated New York's anti-Klan law. Late in December 1928, the former Grand Kleagle of Buffalo Klan No. 5 appeared in city court, entered a plea of guilty, and was fined one hundred dollars; after paying the fine, he returned to his butcher block and resumed a life of welcome anonymity.[2] Thus concluded Buffalo's experience with the knights of the Invisible Empire.

A number of important questions about the local KKK episode remain to be answered: What impact did the passage of the Walker Law in the spring of 1923 have upon Klan recruiting and the overall socioeconomic makeup of the Buffalo klavern? Who stole the Klan's records? What groups participated in the war on the KKK? What role did Buffalo women play within the Invisible Empire's organizational life?[3] One hopes that historians will some day discover sources that shed light on these and other unresolved queries. Nonetheless, this study has uncovered a sufficient amount of detailed information concerning Buffalo Klan No. 5 to permit the formulation of several general conclusions.

Numerous factors contributed to the rise of the Ku Klux Klan in Buffalo. Perhaps most importantly, late in 1921, at the very time that the KKK was first organizing in the city, a bitter mayoral election divided the community along ethnic, religious, and class lines, imparting unusual saliency to longstanding social divisions; the controversial style and policies of the subsequent administration of Mayor Frank Schwab helped keep ethnoreligious tensions fully activated, as did political developments at the state level, particularly the efforts of Governor Alfred E. Smith to emasculate prohibition enforcement. At this same time, growing concern over the changing behavior of women and young people, violent labor unrest, and a perceived surge in crime seemed to indicate a widespread abandonment of traditional values and a breakdown of respect for established authority. Confronted with these unsettling trends, certain citizens were receptive to the appeals of a growing national organization that seemed to offer a means of checking social dissolution, or at least a means of forcefully expressing anger and frustration over decay.

For the first two and a half years of its existence, Buffalo Klan No. 5 remained a shadowy group on the fringes of community life. The KKK held secret meetings and conducted several outdoor ceremonials in defiance of local authorities, but the order made little effort to cultivate a positive public image and apparently failed to develop a specific social agenda. Gradually, however, the

Klan entered into close association with evangelical activists, who for months had been assailing the Schwab administration for inadequate enforcement of the vice and prohibition laws. In 1924, the klavern for the first time directly involved itself in the ongoing moral reform campaign, issuing warnings to the owners of suspect establishments, conducting undercover investigations, filing official complaints with state and federal authorities, and causing Mayor Schwab a degree of political embarrassment. Yet this proved the klavern's undoing. Schwab and other anti-Klan partisans struck back hard, and within a few months the order lay in ruins, its secrecy shattered and its members exposed to both legal and extralegal harassment. A few stalwart Klansmen tried to hold firm, but this was to no avail; bereft of any meaningful degree of civic utility, the local branch of the Invisible Empire soon withered away.

Klan leaders confronted a very challenging situation in Buffalo as they attempted to develop their organization. The community included large and politically empowered ethnic populations that were intensely anti-Klan, the major newspapers consistently portrayed the KKK in a negative light, the Invisible Empire's enemies commanded the resources of city government, and after May 1923 the Klan existed beyond the pale of the law. Yet, despite these and other problems, the hooded order succeeded in attracting a sizable following among the eligible white male population. Considering the risks posed by Klan membership, the high cost of dues and fees, and the limited privileges of knighthood, the appeal of the Klan in Buffalo seems nothing less than remarkable. Although the KKK was far from an admirable organization, it clearly inspired an impressive amount of commitment, discipline, and solidarity.

No historical task is more difficult than assessing human motivation, an undertaking that is made infinitely more complex when dealing with hundreds of individuals. No one will ever know for certain how the Invisible Empire's rituals and program—an adaptable blend of romantic historical imagery, mystic fraternalism, crusading reformism, and militant ethnocentrism—impacted upon the great majority of the Buffalonians who affiliated with the secret order. Ultimately, the local klavern, like almost any sizable group, has to be evaluated primarily on the basis of its actions and the overall characteristics of its membership.

Without doubt, one major source of the Klan's appeal was the racism and religious bigotry that prevailed within the klavern; indeed, prejudice was interwoven with almost all aspects of the hooded order's organizational life, including its efforts on behalf of civic improvement. Such intolerance, however, never resulted in the Buffalo Klan using physical violence against its enemies. Although many knights surely enjoyed the fear and uncertainty that their order provoked among opponents, they generally kept their baser instincts in check, using the Invisible Empire not as an agency of terror but, rather, as a medium of peaceful civic action. For the most part, the klavern's activism focused on mainstream concerns, particularly the perception that local officials were promoting social dissolution through lax enforcement of the vice and prohibition laws—an issue that had been previously raised by the Anti-Saloon League, prominent Protestant clergymen, and Mayor George Buck during the 1921 city election. Like most of their fellow white Protestants, Klansmen desired a more orderly and law-abiding community, one in which traditional values and standards would continue to prevail. This being the case, it is both ironic and indicative of the level of local frustration that they resorted to an organization that openly violated the law, promoted social discord, and required its members to lie under oath in courts of law.

An examination of the klavern's membership indicates a strong connection with the social mainstream. Klansmen composed a broad and relatively balanced cross section of the white middle-class Protestant community; they resided in all parts of the city and were employed in a wide variety of occupations. For the most part, the hooded knights appear to have been ordinary, well-established citizens, not a collection of disaffected fanatics on the margins of community life. Buffalo Klansmen did, however, possess certain distinctive characteristics. On average, they were younger than their fellow native-born adult white males, enjoyed more prestigious occupations, and were more likely to live in outlying neighborhoods, away from the largest concentrations of African Americans and foreign-born immigrants; although data are incomplete, evangelicals, World War I veterans, and members of fraternal societies may have been particularly disposed to affiliate with the Klan. Perhaps the most significant feature of the secret order's local membership was the overrepresentation of those whose work involved managing, supervising, and coordinating. Men in such occupations—possibly because of their work experiences and/or psychological disposition—may have had a particularly strong desire for a well-ordered and thoroughly regulated community and thus were unusually receptive to the appeal of the Klan, an organization dedicated to the revitalization of American society in accordance with traditional Protestant values. Evidence of any type of authoritarian impulse at the heart of the klavern, however, is sketchy at best. A strong commitment to a well-ordered community was hardly unusual in American society during the early twentieth century, and there is no indication that managerial Klansmen were more active or influential within the klavern than knights in other occupations. Basically, the group seems to have attracted ordinary citizens who were intensely, and understandably, frustrated by the course of local society in the early 1920s.

In its general features, Buffalo Klan No. 5 closely resembled other klaverns across the nation. In nearly every community where it has been extensively studied, the Klan appears to have constituted a form of grass-roots activism that addressed local concerns such as law enforcement, moral reform, and corruption in government; almost everywhere—although there were some notable exceptions in the South—the hooded order refrained from roughshod tactics, tried to work within the existing legal and political systems, and succeeded in attracting a broad cross section of the white Protestant middle class. In fact, klaverns seem to have attracted memberships that were quite similar socioeconomically, as is indicated by an examination of the occupational-status distributions presented in the few case studies that have been able to make use of detailed membership data.[4] These distributions indicate some local variation, but white-collar and skilled blue-collar workers—the heart of the greater American middle class—composed the large majority of Klansmen, while workers in less prestigious occupations formed a distinct minority. The most current research strongly indicates, therefore, that the Klan of the 1920s was, in its essence and in the broadest sense of the term, a middle-class social movement.

A recognition of similarities among klaverns should not be allowed to obscure important differences. Although Buffalo Klan No. 5 represented, like most other KKK chapters, a form of middle-class grass-roots activism, the group was inevitably influenced and shaped by the local social and political environment. Unlike their hooded brethren in places like Indiana, Oregon, and Colorado, Buffalo knights were confronted by large Catholic and ethnic populations that were intensely anti-Klan. This not only made Klan membership particularly risky but also meant that there was virtually no chance of forging the KKK into a powerful political machine, as occurred elsewhere. Because of these problems—as well as the passage of the Walker Law in 1923—the KKK remained a relatively small and noninfluential (albeit troublesome) group on the local scene. Thus the Buffalo Klan experience suggests that racial, ethnic, and religious diversity, although it surely resulted in social tensions, may also have undermined the appeal of the Klan in certain communities. In Buffalo, the Klan was simply too controversial, too disruptive, to serve as an effective means of civic action. Recognizing this, most white native-born Protestants—although they may have agreed with much of what the KKK stood for—steered clear of the Invisible Empire.

In terms of its social and political agenda, the Ku Klux Klan accomplished little in Buffalo. The hooded order's activities on behalf of law enforcement scarcely improved the local crime situation, and the group never devised an effective means of checking the erosion of traditional social standards. Although for a short period in 1924 it appeared that the KKK might succeed in mobilizing the Protestant community against the policies of the Schwab administration, the organization and its controversial methods soon became the focus of debate, a situation which allowed anti-Klan partisans to pose as the true champions of American traditions and values. In the end, the Invisible Empire proved to be an exceedingly counterproductive approach to civic affairs, one that discredited the cause of moral reform, resulted in the public humiliation of the order's entire local membership, and helped insure the landslide reelection of Mayor Schwab in 1925.

Much research on the Ku Klux Klan of the 1920s remains to be conducted, particularly in small towns and rural areas. No doubt, future Klan historians will discover significant local and regional variation among klaverns, but they will probably find an even greater amount of similarity. This study, in association with other recent scholarship on the hooded order, strongly suggests that Klansmen across the nation were ordinary citizens motivated by traditional civic concerns. This is not to say, however, that the KKK's methods were in any way appropriate or justified. In fact—although staunch defenders of the First Amendment may disagree—one suspects that the anti-Klan forces absolutely did the "right thing" when they crushed the klavern. In a religiously and ethnically diverse society, there should be no place for mass movements that heedlessly inflame prejudice and defy the basic standards of civic discourse.

Notes

Notes to Introduction

1. *Buffalo Truth*, Sept. 4, 1924, 1.
2. Charles O. Jackson, "William J. Simmons: A Career in Ku Kluxism," *Georgia Historical Quarterly* 50 (Dec. 1966): 351–58.
3. William G. Shepherd, "Ku Klux Koin," *Collier's* 82 (July 21, 1928): 38–39; Robert L. Duffus, "Salesmen of Hate: The Ku Klux Klan," *World's Work* 46 (May 1923): 33–36; Charles C. Alexander, "Kleagles and Cash: The Ku Klux Klan As a Business Organization, 1915–1930," *Business History Review* 39 (Autumn 1965): 351–53.
4. The extensive variety of sales pitches utilized by kleagles are described throughout the essays in Shawn Lay, ed., *The Invisible Empire in the West: Toward a New Historical Appraisal of the Ku Klux Klan of the 1920s* (Urbana: University of Illinois Press, 1992).
5. Norman D. Brown, *Hood, Bonnet, and Little Brown Jug: Texas State Politics, 1921–1928* (College Station: Texas A & M Press, 1984), 51.
6. Shawn Lay, *War, Revolution, and the Ku Klux Klan: A Study of Intolerance in a Border City* (El Paso: Texas Western Press, 1985), 159; "The Reign of the Tar Bucket," *Literary Digest* 12 (Aug. 27, 1921): 12; Albert De Silver, "The Ku Klux Klan—'The Soul of Chivalry,' " *Nation* 63 (Sept. 14, 1921): 285–86.
7. Most of the popular press's major anti-Klan articles and reports have been cataloged in Lenwood G. Davis and Janet L. Sims-Wood, *The Ku Klux Klan: A Bibliography* (Westport, Conn.: Greenwood Press, 1984).

Both the *World*'s and *Journal-American*'s exposés were carried by Buffalo newspapers in September 1921, the former in the *Buffalo Evening News* and the latter in the *Buffalo Evening Times*.

8. U.S., Congress, House, Committee on Rules, *Hearings on the Ku Klux Klan*, 67th Cong., 1st sess. (Washington, D.C.: Government Printing Office, 1921), 1–184; Wyn Craig Wade, *The Fiery Cross: The Ku Klux Klan in America* (New York: Simon and Schuster, 1987), 164–65.

9. Kenneth T. Jackson, *The Ku Klux Klan in the City, 1915–1930* (New York: Oxford University Press, 1967), 93–126, 161–214.

10. Wade, *The Fiery Cross*, 119–39.

11. *Papers Read at the Meeting of Grand Dragons, Knights of the Ku Klux Klan, at Their First Annual Meeting Held at Asheville, North Carolina, July 1923, Together with Other Articles of Interest to Klansmen* (Atlanta: Knights of the Ku Klux Klan, 1923), 7.

12. See the historiographical essay at the conclusion of this book for a discussion of these case studies. For an insightful comparison of the Klan with other mass movements, see Robert A. Goldberg, *Grassroots Resistance: Social Movements in Twentieth-Century America* (Belmont, Calif.: Wadsworth Publishing Co., 1991).

13. David M. Chalmers, *Hooded Americanism: The History of the Ku Klux Klan*, 3d ed. (Durham: Duke University Press, 1981), 88–89, 126–29, 162–71, 202–15.

14. Lay, *Invisible Empire in the West*, 221; Leonard J. Moore, *Citizen Klansmen: The Ku Klux Klan in Indiana, 1921–1928* (Chapel Hill: University of North Carolina Press), 184–85.

15. For the most influential work making this assessment, see John Moffatt Mecklin, *The Ku Klux Klan: A Study of the American Mind* (New York: Harcourt, Brace, and Co., 1924).

16. Jackson, *Klan in the City;* Chalmers, *Hooded Americanism;* Charles C. Alexander, *The Ku Klux Klan in the Southwest* (Lexington: University of Kentucky Press, 1965).

17. Christopher N. Cocoltchos, "The Invisible Government and the Viable Community: The Ku Klux Klan in Orange County, California, during the 1920s" (Ph.D. dissertation, University of California, Los Angeles, 1979); Robert A. Goldberg, *Hooded Empire: The Ku Klux Klan in Colorado* (Urbana: University of Illinois Press, 1981); Larry R. Gerlach, *Blazing Crosses in Zion: The Ku Klux Klan in Utah* (Logan: Utah State University Press, 1982); Lay, *War, Revolution, and the Ku Klux Klan* and *Invisible Empire in the West*; William D. Jenkins, *Steel Valley Klan: The Ku Klux Klan in Ohio's Mahoning Valley* (Kent, Ohio: Kent State University Press, 1990); Moore, *Citizen Klansmen*; Nancy MacLean, *Behind the Mask of Chivalry: The Making of the Second Ku Klux Klan* (New York: Oxford University Press, 1994).

18. Chalmers, *Hooded Americanism*, 236–37, 243–78.

Notes to Chapter 1

1. *Buffalo City Directory, 1921* (Buffalo: R. L. Polk and Co., 1921), civic section, 6–7, 36, 77, 93, 110; *The Civic Cooperative Movement, 1903–1923* (Buffalo: Mark H. Hubbell, 1923), 20.
2. U.S., Bureau of the Census, *Fourteenth Census of the United States, 1920: New York State Compendium* (Washington, D.C.: Government Printing Office, 1922), 15, 60; John F. Barry and Robert W. Elmes, eds., *Buffalo's Text Book*, 2d ed. (Buffalo: Robert W. Elmes, 1927), 25–26; *Civic Cooperative Movement*, 11.
3. *Fourteenth Census of the United States, 1920: Manufactures* 8: 19; 9: 975, 1025–26.
4. Barry and Elmes, *Buffalo's Text Book*, 85, 92–93, 218; *Civic Cooperative Movement*, 5–6; U.S., Bureau of the Census, *Fifteenth Census of the United States, 1930: Distribution* (Washington, D.C.: Government Printing Office, 1932), 1: part 3, 304–14; 2: 1070.
5. *Fourteenth Census of the United States, 1920: Population* 4: 1068–70; *Fifteenth Census of the United States, 1930: Population* 4: 1127–30.
6. *Fourteenth Census of the United States, 1920: Population* 4: 1068–70.
7. *Fourteenth Census of the United States, 1920: New York State Compendium*, 60–61; New York, Unpublished State Census Reports for 1925, Buffalo, Wards Four, Five, Seventeen, Eighteen, Nineteen, Twenty, Twenty-Two, Twenty-Three, Twenty-Four, and Twenty-Five; Francis R. Kowsky, *Buffalo Architecture: A Guide* (Cambridge, Mass.: MIT Press, 1991), 99–105, 188–93, 248–53.
8. New York, Unpublished State Census Reports for 1925, Buffalo, Wards Two, Three, Six, Seven, Eight, Nine, Ten, Twenty-One, Twenty-Six, and Twenty-Seven; *Buffalo City Directory, 1921*, civic section, 73; *Fourteenth Census of the United States, 1920: New York State Compendium*, 60–61.
9. *Fourteenth Census of the United States, 1920: New York State Compendium*, 60–61; *Fifteenth Census of the United States, 1930: Population* 3: part 2, 298–99.
10. *Fourteenth Census of the United States, 1920: New York State Compendium*, 60–61; Andrew P. Yox, "Decline of the German-American Community in Buffalo, New York, 1855–1925" (Ph.D. dissertation, University of Chicago, 1983), 312.
11. *Fourteenth Census of the United States, 1920: New York State Compendium*, 60–61; Mark Goldman, *High Hopes: The Rise and Decline of Buffalo, New York* (Albany: State University of New York Press, 1983), 208.
12. *Fourteenth Census of the United States, 1920: Population* 4: 1068–70; *Fifteenth Census of the United States, 1930: Population* 4: 1127–30. For the activities of the NAACP in Buffalo, see issues of the *Buffalo Ameri-*

can. Marcus Garvey's Universal Negro Improvement Association was also active locally, Garvey himself visiting the city on numerous occasions. See *Express,* March 1, 1922, 8; April 15, 1922, 5; May 26, 1922, 4; May 29, 1922, 12; and *Courier,* Jan. 30, 1923, 5.

13. U.S., Bureau of the Census, *Census of Religious Bodies: 1926* (Washington, D.C.: Government Printing Office, 1929), 1: 381–82.
14. John T. Horton, Edward T. Williams, and Harry S. Douglas, *History of Northwestern New York: Erie, Niagara, Wyoming, Genesee, and Orleans Counties* (New York: Lewis Historical Publishing Co., 1947), 1: 359; Roman Catholic Diocese of Buffalo, Annual Parish Reports, 1920–1925; *Express,* March 15, 1922, 5; March 20, 1922, 4; March 22, 1922, 4; *Courier,* Feb. 28, 1923, 12.
15. *Courier,* Dec. 10, 1922, 105; Dec. 9, 1923, 101; *Express,* Dec. 9, 1924, 7.
16. *Courier,* Nov. 3, 1920, 1; Nov. 5, 1924, 1; *Courier-Express,* Nov. 7, 1928, 1.
17. *Courier,* Nov. 6, 1918, 1; Nov. 8, 1922, 1; Nov. 5, 1924, 1; *Courier-Express,* Nov. 3, 1926, 1.
18. Margaret Schwab, "The Administration of Mayor Frank X. Schwab: 1922–1929" (B.A. thesis, D'Youville College, 1968), 1–5; author's interview with Francis X. Schwab IV, April 3, 1992; author's interview with Mary Schwab Murphy, April 10, 1992; *Courier,* Nov. 2, 1925, 5.
19. Frank X. Schwab IV interview.
20. *Catholic Union & Times,* Nov. 16, 1922, 4.
21. Schwab, "Administration of Mayor Schwab," 5–6; *Courier,* Oct. 3, 1921, 12; *Express,* May 11, 1922, 5.
22. *Courier,* Oct. 4, 1921, 5; Oct. 12, 1921, 2; Oct. 13, 1921, 9; Oct. 14, 1921, 5; *Buffalo Evening Times* (hereinafter cited as *Times*), Oct. 12, 1921, 4.
23. *Courier,* Oct. 19, 1921, 1; Oct. 20, 1921, 6; Oct. 30, 1921, 65; *Times,* Oct. 19, 1921, 1, 4; *Buffalo Evening News* (hereinafter cited as *News*), Oct. 19, 1921, 1, 2; "Tabular Statement of the Primary Election Held October 18, 1921," in City of Buffalo, *Proceedings of the Council, 1921* (Buffalo: James D. Warren's Sons Co., 1922), 2100.
24. Schwab, "Administration of Mayor Schwab," 1–6; *Courier,* Oct. 16, 1921, 6; Nov. 2, 1925, 5.
25. *Courier,* Oct. 26, 1921, 2 (first quote); Oct. 28, 1921, 12; Oct. 29, 1921, 10 (third quote); Oct. 30, 1921, 65; Oct. 31, 1921, 12; Nov. 1, 1921, 12 (second quote); Nov. 3, 1921, 12; Nov. 4, 1921, 14; Nov. 5, 1921, 14; Nov. 6, 1921, 53, 57; Nov. 7, 1921, 11; Nov. 8, 1921, 14; *Buffalo Enquirer* (hereinafter cited as *Enquirer*), Nov. 2, 1921, 12; Nov. 3, 1921, 12; *Times,* Nov. 2, 1921, 1, 6; Schwab, "Administration of Mayor Schwab," 7–8.
26. *Courier,* Oct. 25, 1921, 12 (second quote); Oct. 28, 1921, 14 (first quote); *News,* Nov. 2, 1921, 1; *Times,* Nov. 2, 1921, 1, 6.
27. *Courier,* Oct. 25, 1921, 12.

28. *Courier*, Oct. 27, 1921, 14.
29. *Express*, Nov. 7, 1921, 4. Schwab was also openly opposed by the Reverend Dr. Robert J. MacAlpine of the Central Presbyterian Church, the Reverend Charles C. Penfold of Sentinel Methodist Church, the Reverend R. T. Doherty of Woodside Methodist Church, and the Reverend Dr. Roscoe L. Foulke of Trinity Methodist Church. See *News*, Nov. 7, 1921, 26.
30. "Official Canvas for Erie County, 1921," in Erie County, *Proceedings of the Board of Supervisors of Erie County, New York* (Buffalo: Erie County Board of Supervisors, 1921), 1054–55; *Courier*, Nov. 9, 1921, 1; *Enquirer*, Nov. 9, 1921, 1. Data concerning two important variables, the ward-level percentages of Catholics and Protestants are, unfortunately, not available. The federal religious censuses for 1916 and 1926 only present citywide data, and the borders of Buffalo's Catholic parishes did not coincide with ward boundaries. However, because the bulk of the city's Protestants probably were native-born and of native parentage, and because most of the foreign born were probably Catholic, the influence of nativity on the election may have in large part been reflective of Protestant-Catholic ethnocentrism. Yet, it should be recognized that many Irish and German Catholics were native-born and of native parentage, and that the foreign-born population included sizable numbers of non-Catholics, especially Jews. Therefore, unless more precise data can be accumulated, the impact of religion on local politics cannot be fully assessed.
31. *Express*, Nov. 9, 1921, 1.
32. Schwab, "Administration of Mayor Schwab," 8; *Courier*, July 18, 1922, 14.
33. *Courier*, Feb. 2, 1922, 1, 2; Sept. 25, 1922, 6; Feb. 22, 1923, 5; *Express*, March 1, 1922, 1; March 2, 1922, 1; March 3, 1922, 1; March 14, 1922, 4; March 24, 1922, 5; *Times*, March 2, 1922, 3, 19.
34. Buffalo, *Proceedings of the Council, 1922*, 490–93; *Express*, Jan. 1, 1922, sec. 6, 5; Jan. 19, 1922, 5; March 9, 1922, 1, 6; *Times*, March 9, 1922, 3.
35. *Courier*, July 1, 1922, 4 (third, fourth, fifth, and sixth quotes); Sept. 22, 1923, 14 (first quote); *Express*, March 2, 1922, 4; March 28, 1922, 1, 4 (second quote); April 24, 1922, 6.
36. *Express*, May 18, 1922, 1 (quote); *Courier*, Sept. 22, 1923, 14; Oct. 27, 1923, 3; Feb. 21, 1924, 5.
37. *Express*, March 4, 1922, 7; March 5, 1922, sec. 5, 1; April 27, 1922, 5; April 28, 1922, 5 (quotes); April 30, 1922, sec. 5, 1; *Buffalo Commercial* (hereinafter cited as *Commercial*), April 27, 1922, 10; April 28, 1922, 9. After coming to office in 1920, Graves waged a one-man war on the local school board, insisting that the city commission reserved the right to dictate the manner in which school funds would be spent. Because the school board refused to acknowledge such a right, a legal

deadlock developed, resulting in a prolonged construction halt that greatly angered the public. Although Mayor Schwab agreed with Graves that the commission's desires should prevail, the commissioner, who was a Protestant, was by far the leading figure in the struggle with the school board; this meant that the mayor, a Roman Catholic, was largely insulated from charges that he had "designs" on the school system, even when he suggested that he be given a permanent seat on the board. As it turned out, when the Ku Klux Klan became an influence on the local scene, the Buffalo klavern focused almost exclusively on the Schwab administration's shortcomings in regard to law enforcement, never raising the issue of public education—a topic frequently exploited by the KKK elsewhere. An excellent summary of the controversy over the Buffalo schools is presented in the *Courier*, Oct. 13, 1922, 4.

38. *Courier*, Sept. 7, 1923, 16; Sept. 17, 1923, 3; Sept. 28, 1923, 16; Nov. 3, 1923, 16 (Schwab quotes); Nov. 7, 1923, 1; *News*, Nov. 3, 1923, 3; Nov. 7, 1923, 1, 7; "Tabular Statement of the Primary Election Held October 16, 1923," in Buffalo, *Proceedings of the Council, 1923*, 2343; Walter S. Dunn, ed., *History of Erie County, 1870–1970* (Buffalo: Buffalo and Erie County Historical Society, 1972), 259.

39. *Express*, April 20, 1922, 8 (second quote); April 29, 1922, 8 (first quote); *Commercial*, Oct. 26, 1922, 12 (third quote).

40. *Courier*, Oct. 25, 1922, 12.

41. *Express*, March 24, 1922, 8.

42. *Courier*, June 26, 1922, 5.

43. *Courier*, May 22, 1922, 14.

44. *Courier*, Jan. 28, 1924, 5.

45. *Courier*, June 26, 1922, 5.

46. *Express*, Jan. 27, 1922, 8.

47. *Express*, Jan. 16, 1922, 7.

48. *Courier*, June 26, 1922, 5.

49. Dunn, *History of Erie County*, 242–43; Goldman, *High Hopes*, 201–9.

50. *Courier*, June 30, 1922, 1; July 2, 1922, 71; July 3, 1922, 5; July 4, 1922, 1; July 5, 1922, 1; July 12, 1922, 1; July 15, 1922, 1; *Times*, June 30, 1922, 1; July 3, 1922, 1; July 12. 1922, 1, 5; July 14, 1922, 1, 3; July 15, 1922, 3; *Buffalo Labor Journal*, July 6, 1922, 1; July 13, 1922, 1.

51. *Courier*, July 14, 1922, 1.

52. *Express*, July 16, 1922, sec. 5, 3 (Schwab quote); July 19, 1922, 1, 6.

53. *Express*, July 22, 1922, 1 (first quote); July 23, 1922, sec. 5, 1 (second quote), 4; Dunn, *History of Erie County*, 241–42.

54. *Express*, Jan. 2, 1922, 8.

55. *Express*, Jan. 23, 1922, 2; *Courier*, Dec. 31, 1922, 51; "Annual Report of the Department of Public Safety, Police of the City of Buffalo, for the Year Ending December 31, 1924," in Buffalo, *Proceedings of the Council, 1924*, 1286–1314.

56. *Express*, Jan. 7, 1922, 8.

57. *Express*, May 20, 1922, 8.

58. *Express*, Jan. 14, 1922, 10; Jan. 21, 1922, 8 (quote).

59. *Express*, Jan. 27, 1922, 8.

60. *Express*, Jan. 8, 1922, sec. 7, 4; April 11, 1922, 4.

61. *Courier*, Oct. 14, 1922, 16.

62. *Courier*, Nov. 24, 1923, 12.

63. *Express*, Jan. 4, 1922, 1; Jan. 19, 1922, 1; Buffalo, *Proceedings of the Council, 1922*, 77; *Commercial*, Jan. 19, 1922, 10.

64. *Courier*, Aug. 14, 1923, 1; Schwab, "Administration of Mayor Schwab," 2 (quote); Mary Schwab Murphy interview.

65. *Express*, Jan. 1, 1922, sec. 6, 1, 3.

66. *Courier*, Feb. 24, 1922, 15; Sept. 26, 1922, 16; *Express*, Jan. 6, 1922, 4; March 30, 1922, 6; April 14, 1922, 1; April 16, 1922, sec. 5, 1; June 3, 1922, 5; June 6, 1922, 1.

67. *Times*, Oct. 27, 1922, 12; *Courier*, Nov. 9, 1921, 5; June 18, 1923, 14.

68. *Express*, Jan. 7, 1922, 8. Donovan would also later cooperate with the Buffalo Klan, as is related in chapter 3. Although an Irish-American Catholic, he was one of the foremost local proponents of strict prohibition enforcement, earning a reputation for integrity that helped him secure the Republican nomination for lieutenant governor in 1922. Despite his defeat in the general election, Donovan went on to have a remarkable career in federal service, heading the Office of Strategic Services during World War II.

69. *Courier*, Oct. 4, 1921, 5; Sept. 22, 1922, 16; *Express*, March 14, 1922, 4.

70. *Express*, April 6, 1922, 4; May 11, 1922, 10 (quote).

71. *Courier*, June 7, 1922, 5; *Express*, May 30, 1922, 7.

72. *Express*, May 8, 1922, 1, 12 (Anderson quote); *News*, May 8, 1922, 1.

73. *Courier*, July 6, 1922, 18 (quote); *News*, July 6, 1922, 9.

74. *Courier*, Nov. 27, 1922, 6.

75. *Enquirer*, Oct. 30, 1922, 12; *Courier*, Oct. 2, 1922, 14 (quotes); Oct. 9, 1922, 14; Oct. 16, 1922, 12; Dec. 13, 1922, 5; *News*, Oct. 2, 1922, 1; Oct. 9, 1922, 26.

Notes to Chapter 2

1. Jackson, *Klan in the City*, 177; Jay Rubin, *The Ku Klux Klan in Binghamton, New York, 1923–1928* (Binghamton, N.Y.: Broome County Historical Society, 1973), 10; Chalmers, *Hooded Americanism*, 254.

2. *Courier*, Sept. 15, 1921, 1, 3 (quotes); *Enquirer*, Sept. 15, 1921, 12.

3. *Courier*, Sept. 15, 1921, 1 (first and third quotes), 3; Sept. 16, 1921, 5; Sept. 18, 1921, 53 (second and fourth quotes).

4. *Buffalo American* (hereinafter cited as *American*), Sept. 15, 1921, 4 (first and second quotes); Sept. 29, 1921, 4 (third and fourth quotes).

5. *Catholic Union & Times*, Sept. 15, 1921, 4 (first and second quotes); June 1, 1922, 4 (third quote); June 8, 1922, 4 (fourth quote).

6. *Times*, Sept. 18, 1921, 21, 49; Sept. 23, 1921, 18; *Enquirer*, Sept. 17, 1921, 4; *Commercial*, Sept. 17, 1921, 1; Sept. 20, 1921, 1; *Express*, Sept. 19, 1921, 6; Sept. 27, 1921, 8; *News*, Sept. 16, 1921, 1, 2.

7. Unfortunately, copies of the *Buffalo Truth* are missing for certain key periods, including September 1921. As is related in chapter 5, the paper eventually evolved into a spokespiece for the Buffalo Klan. In an editorial on October 6, 1921, the *American* denounced the *Truth*'s stand on the KKK, which apparently was one of neutrality. See *American*, Oct. 6, 1921, 8.

8. *Courier*, Sept. 16, 1921, 5.

9. *Express*, Sept. 26, 1921, 5; *Courier*, Sept. 26, 1921, 10 (quote).

10. *Courier*, Sept. 26, 1921, 10.

11. *Express*, May 23, 1922, 1, 6 (quotes); *News*, May 23, 1922, 38. Mitchell held the position of District Kleagle for the Eastern Domain, which encompassed New York, Massachusetts, Connecticut, New Hampshire, Vermont, and Maine.

12. *Express*, May 23, 1922, 7; May 30, 1922, 1 (first and second quotes); *Courier*, May 31, 1922, 14 (third quote). Webster said that the Klan hoped to recruit five thousand members in Buffalo. See *Times*, May 31, 1922, 3.

13. *Courier*, May 30, 1922, 18 (first and fifth quotes); *Commercial*, June 1, 1922, 1 (second quote); June 2, 1922, 10 (third and fourth quotes). Few of Buffalo's Jewish leaders openly attacked the Klan in the fashion of Rabbi Kopald. The city's major Jewish publication, the *Buffalo Jewish Review*, completely ignored the local klavern, preferring to feature more general articles on anti-Semitism in other parts of the country.

14. *Courier*, June 1, 1922, 16 (quote); June 2, 1922, 5.

15. Chalmers, *Hooded Americanism*, 43–44, 85–89, 175, 236, 254–55; Jackson, *Klan in the City*, 93–103, 170–77.

16. *Courier*, Oct. 26, 1922, 1, 11 (quotes); *Times*, Oct. 26, 1922, 10; *Enquirer*, Oct. 26, 1922, 14; *News*, Oct. 26, 1922, 17. The Klan gathering was held in a meadow off Harlem Road between Main and Genesee streets. Since it took place north of the city limits, the ceremony would have been held in the township of Amherst.

17. *Courier*, Oct. 27, 1922, 6.

18. *Courier*, Nov. 9, 1922, 1, 2.

19. *Commercial*, Nov. 9, 1922, 7 (second quote); *Courier*, Nov. 9, 1922, 1, 2 (first quote); Nov. 10, 1922, 16; Nov. 12, 1922, 88; *News*, Nov. 9, 1922, 3.

20. *Courier*, Nov. 12, 1922, 88; Nov. 16, 1922, 3; Dec. 8, 1922, 3; Dec. 14, 1922, 18 (quotes); *Express*, Nov. 18, 1922, 7; Nov. 27, 1922, 1. The *American* identified one kleagle who operated in Canada as J. P. Martin, who also occasionally visited Buffalo. Recruiting was no

doubt conducted among native-born Americans residing in Canada, but white Protestant Canadians who had become naturalized U.S. citizens were eligible for membership in the Riders of the Red Robe, the KKK's auxiliary for the foreign born. Martin concentrated his efforts on Toronto, which became the primary center of Klan activity in eastern Canada. See *American*, Dec. 14, 1922, 1, and Chalmers, *Hooded Americanism*, 88, 279–80.

21. *Courier*, Sept. 17, 1922, 79.
22. *Courier*, Nov. 13, 1922, 4 (first and second quotes); Nov. 19, 1922, 83 (fourth quote); *American*, Nov. 16, 1922, 1, 4 (third quote); *Times*, Nov. 13, 1922, 3.
23. *Courier*, Nov. 17, 1922, 8 (first quote); Nov. 29, 1922, 4 (second and fourth quotes); Dec. 10, 1922, 91 (third quote); *Express*, Nov. 28, 1922, 7; Dec. 10, 1922, 1; *Enquirer*, Nov. 29, 1922, 1, 14.
24. *Courier*, Dec. 1, 1922, 1 (fourth quote); Dec. 9, 1922, 16 (first and second quotes); Dec. 11, 1922, 5 (third quote); Jan. 29, 1923, 12 (fifth quote); *News*, Dec. 9, 1922, 4; Dec. 11, 1922, 19.
25. *Express*, Dec. 21, 1922, 11; *Courier*, Dec. 21, 1922, 18 (quote). Wild had been employed by the IRC for eleven years and had been out on strike since July. Nineteen Klansmen worked for the IRC, but it is unlikely that this was an authorized threat.
26. *Courier*, Dec. 1, 1922, 1; Dec. 5, 1922, 8; Dec. 11, 1922, 5 (first quote); Dec. 12, 1922, 3; Dec. 13, 1922, 6, 16; Dec. 18, 1922, 5 (second quote); *Express*, Dec. 9, 1922, 5; Dec. 10, 1922, 1; Dec. 11, 1922, 9; *News*, Dec. 11, 1922, 30; *Enquirer*, Dec. 11, 1922, 8.
27. *Courier*, Nov. 27, 1922, 6 (first quote); Dec. 1, 1922, 1 (second quote); Dec. 12, 1922, 3 (third quote); *Express*, Nov. 28, 1922, 7; *News*, Dec. 1, 1922, 2, 8; Dec. 11, 1922, 30; *Times*, Nov. 27, 1922, 1.
28. *Courier*, Dec. 1, 1922, 1 (quote); *News*, Dec. 1, 1922, 2.
29. *Express*, March 26, 1923, 1, 4; *Courier*, March 26, 1923, 1 (quote); *Commercial*, March 26, 1923, 10.
30. *Courier*, March 26, 1923, 1 (first quote); March 28, 1923, 4 (second and third quotes); *Express*, March 31, 1923, 3; June 3, 1923, sec. 6, 1; *News*, March 26, 1923, 30; *Enquirer*, April 2, 1922, 2. The names of three of the church's trustees—Dr. Robert S. Hambleton, Florus G. Turner, and Samuel A. Torrence—appear on the Klan membership list utilized in this study.
31. *Courier*, April 1, 1923, 83. A recruiting meeting was also held in the local Salvation Army hall. See *Enquirer*, April 2, 1922, 7.
32. *Express*, March 27, 1923, 10.
33. *Courier*, April 7, 1923, 4; Jackson, *Klan in the City*, 176–78; Rubin, *Klan in Binghamton*, 10. See *Express*, April 7, 1923, 1, and *Times*, April 7, 1923, 4, for reports of a cross-burning in Niagara Falls at this time.
34. *Express*, May 24, 1923, 1 (first and third quotes); May 26, 1923, 1; *Courier*, May 24, 1923, 1 (second quote); *News*, May 24, 1923, 4.

35. *Courier*, Jan. 15, 1923, 4; Jan. 22, 1923, 1; Jackson, *Klan in the City*, 176–78; Rubin, *Klan in Binghamton*, 10.
36. *New York Times*, Feb. 23, 1923, 4; May 5, 1923, 2; May 24, 1923, 3; *Courier*, Jan. 17, 1923, 1 (quote); Feb. 26, 1923, 4; April 25, 1923, 4; May 24, 1923, 2; Jackson, *Klan in the City*, 177; Rubin, *Klan in Binghamton*, 19–20.
37. New York, *Laws of the State of New York Passed at the 146th Session of the Legislature* (Albany: J. B. Lyon Co., 1923), c. 664, 1110–11. The Walker Law was one of only two comprehensive state measures that targeted the second Klan; the other was passed by the Louisiana legislature in 1924. For the Walker Law's significance in American legal history, see David Fellman, *The Constitutional Right of Association* (Chicago: University of Chicago Press, 1963), 70–72.
38. *Laws of the State of New York* (1923), c. 664, 1111.
39. *Express*, May 28, 1923, 1 (quote); *Courier*, May 28, 1923, 2.
40. *Express*, May 26, 1923, 1; *Courier*, May 26, 1923, 4; *Commercial*, May 26, 1923, 1.
41. *Courier*, May 26, 1923, 4 (quotes); *Express*, May 26, 1923, 1; *Times*, May 26, 1923, 3.
42. *Express*, May 27, 1923, sec. 6, 1 (second quote); May 28, 1923, 5 (first quote).
43. *Express*, May 27, 1923, sec. 6, 1 (first quote); May 28, 1923, 1, 3 (second and third quotes). See *News*, May 28, 1923, 3, for another report of this gathering.
44. *Express*, May 28, 1923, 3.
45. *Express*, May 29, 1923, 5 (first and fourth quotes); *Courier*, June 4, 1923, 4 (second and third quotes); *Times*, June 1, 1923, 17; *Enquirer*, May 28, 1923, 14.
46. *Express*, June 1, 1923, 4; *Courier*, July 20, 1923, 1; Rubin, *Klan in Binghamton*, 20.
47. *Express*, June 1, 1923, 4; June 2, 1923, 1; June 3, 1923, sec. 6, 1; July 24, 1923, 4; July 25, 1923, 1; July 27, 1923, 5; *Courier*, June 2, 1923, 1; July 22, 1923, 60; July 23, 1923, 14; Aug. 15, 1923, 1; Sept. 21, 1923, 3; *Enquirer*, June 1, 1923, 14; June 2, 1923, 8; *Commercial*, June 1, 1923, 2; July 26, 1923, 1, 2; *Times*, July 27, 1923, 1; Rubin, *Klan in Binghamton*, 20.
48. *Courier*, July 29, 1923, 89 (first quote); *Express*, June 3, 1923, sec. 6, 1 (second quote).
49. Rubin, *Klan in Binghamton*, 20.

Notes to Chapter 3

1. *Courier*, June 22, 1923, 10; July 4, 1923, 22; July 5, 1923, 1, 10 (quotes); *Express*, July 3, 1923, 4.

2. *Express*, July 5, 1923, 4 (first and second quotes); *Courier*, July 5, 1923, 1, 10 (third quote); *News*, July 5, 1923, 3.

3. *Courier*, July 26, 1923, 1 (first, second, and third quotes); July 28, 1923, 1; Aug. 27, 1923, 14 (fourth and fifth quotes); *Express*, July 27, 1923, 5; *Times*, July 28, 1923, 9.

4. *Courier*, Oct. 9, 1923, 1; Oct. 21, 1923, 81.

5. *Courier*, Oct. 19, 1923, 1 (quotes); Oct. 20, 1923, 14; Nov. 10, 1923, 5; *Express*, Oct. 20, 1922, 5; *Enquirer*, Oct. 19, 1923, 1.

6. *Courier*, June 3, 1923, 83. As is related later in this chapter, the Klan decided to throw its support to William F. Schwartz, a decision it ultimately regretted.

7. As far as can be determined, State Assemblyman Henry W. Hutt was the only major state or county officeholder to belong to the Buffalo Klan.

8. *Courier*, May 31, 1923, 5.

9. *Express*, Aug. 10, 1923, 4; *Courier*, Aug. 10, 1923, 11; Aug. 18, 1923, 1, 3; Sept. 2, 1923, 81; *News*, Aug. 10, 1923, 3; Aug. 18, 1923, 3.

10. *Courier*, Nov. 18, 1923, 89; Nov. 22, 1923, 1; *Commercial*, Nov. 23, 1923, 1.

11. *Express*, June 2, 1923, 1; *Laws of the State of New York* (1923), c. 871, 1690. Smith carried Buffalo by 60,380 to 43,956 over Nathan Miller in November 1922. Statistical analysis of the Smith vote indicates a very strong and positive correlation (.946) with the 1921 vote for Mayor Schwab, the correlation being statistically significant at .001, one-tailed test. Thus the political following of the two men, at least at this time, seems to have been quite similar.

12. *Courier*, Jan. 31, 1923, 1; March 14, 1923, 2; Jan. 21, 1924, 1; Jan. 25, 1924, 1; Jan. 30, 1924, 1; Jan. 31, 1924, 4; Feb. 9, 1924, 1; *Express*, July 21, 1923, 1; July 26, 1923, 1; *News*, July 20, 1923, 1.

13. Buffalo Klan membership list, located in the archives of the Buffalo and Erie County Historical Society.

14. *Courier*, Sept. 17, 1924, 5.

15. *Courier*, July 26, 1923, 3; Aug. 10, 1923, 11; *Express*, Aug. 10, 1923, 4; *News*, Aug. 10, 1923, 3.

16. *Courier*, July 26, 1923, 1; Nov. 5, 1923, 8 (quotes).

17. *Courier*, Nov. 19, 1923, 3 (quotes); *Express*, Nov. 19, 1923, 1, 4; *Enquirer*, Nov. 19, 1923, 8.

18. *Courier*, April 20, 1924, 88.

19. *Courier*, March 13, 1924, 5 (first quote); March 18, 1924, 16 (second and third quotes); *Express*, March 18, 1924, 9; *Commercial*, March 13, 1924, 12; March 17, 1924, 1, 10.

20. *Courier*, March 13, 1924, 5 (first quote); March 19, 1924, 3 (second and third quotes); *Express*, March 18, 1924, 9; March 19, 1924, 5; *Commercial*, March 18, 1924, 1. Rumors had been circulating of pending Klan raids. See *Courier*, March 8, 1924, 10, and March 13, 1924, 4.

21. *Courier*, March 18, 1924, 16 (third quote); March 20, 1924, 14 (first and second quotes); *News*, March 18, 1924, 36.
22. *Courier*, March 23, 1924, 85 (quotes); *Express*, March 23, sec. 1, 1; *Commercial*, March 24, 1924, 1.
23. *Courier*, March 24, 1924, 1 (quote); March 25, 1924, 14; *Express*, March 24, 1924, 4; March 25, 1924, 14; *Enquirer*, March 24, 1924, 1; *News*, March 24, 1924, 1; *Times*, March 25, 1924, 1.
24. *Courier*, March 26, 1924, 3 (quote); *Express*, March 26, 1924, 4.
25. The undercover reports, hereinafter cited as Klan reports, are located in the archives of the Buffalo and Erie County Historical Society.
26. *Courier*, March 18, 1924, 16; March 24, 1924, 1; *Express*, March 18, 1924, 9; *Times*, March 18, 1924, 13.
27. *Courier*, March 30, 1924, 89; March 31, 1924, 14; April 2, 1924, 16; April 6, 1924, 89; April 11, 1924, 4; July 2, 1924, 10; July 4, 1924, 18; *Express*, March 30, 1924, sec. 6, 1; March 31, 1924, 12; April 1, 1924, 5; April 6, 1924, sec. 8, 1; April 9, 1924, 9; July 2, 1924, 16; *Commercial*, March 31, 1924, 12; April 7, 1924, 9; *Times*, April 8, 1924, 1. Some of these raids took place in nearby Niagara Falls, but all were organized by Smith and Mayne in association with the KKK.
28. *Courier*, March 31, 1924, 14 (first quote); April 1, 1924, 16 (third quote); April 3, 1924, 4 (second quote); *Express*, April 1, 1924, 5; April 3, 1924, 5; *Commercial*, April 2, 1924, 1, 10; *News*, April 1, 1924, 1.
29. *Courier*, April 7, 1924, 11 (quotes); *Express*, April 7, 1924, 4; *News*, April 7, 1924, 3; *Commercial*, April 7, 1924, 9.
30. *Courier*, April 8, 1924, 10 (quote); *Express*, April 8, 1924, 4.
31. *Courier*, April 13, 1924, 91 (quotes); April 15, 1924, 18; *Express*, April 13, 1924, sec. 6, 1; April 15, 1924, 18; *News*, April 14, 1924, 6.
32. *Courier*, April 7, 1924, 11 (first quote); April 14, 1924, 16 (second quote); *Express*, March 31, 1924, 4; April 14, 1924, 1; *News*, April 14, 1924, 6.
33. *Courier*, April 10, 1924, 18 (quote); *Express*, April 10, 1924, 5; *Times*, April 10, 1924, 1.
34. *Courier*, April 14, 1924, 16; May 27, 1924, 4; *Express*, April 14, 1924, 5. Probably at Smith's request, the Klan released a letter claiming that the minister was not a KKK member. As is related in chapter 5, Smith later confessed that he indeed belonged to the hooded order. For the text of the letter, see *Times*, April 14, 1924, 1, 3.
35. Klan reports, July 14, 1924.
36. Obertean reports, May 19, 1924; June 16, 1924; *Courier*, Sept. 1, 1924, 9; Sept. 2, 1924, 16; *Express*, Sept. 1, 1924, 4; Sept. 2, 1924, 1. Obertean's reports are located in the archives of the Buffalo and Erie County Historical Society.
37. Klan reports, June 26, 1924 (first quote); Obertean reports, June 25, 1924 (second and third quotes).

38. See, for example, Klan reports, April 5, 1924; April 27, 1924; May 3, 1924; May 24, 1924; May 31, 1924; June 4, 1924; June 7, 1924; Aug. 10, 1924; Aug. 18, 1924. Even the distinctly German-American Mayor Schwab was on one occasion referred to as a "dirty low down mick." See Klan reports, June 28, 1924.

39. Obertean reports, June 25, 1924 (first quote); Klan reports, May 3, 1924; May 11, 1924; May 24, 1924; June 26, 1924; June 28, 1924 (second quote).

40. Klan reports, May 11, 1924 (first quote); May 14, 1924 (second quote); May 24, 1924 (third quote).

41. Klan reports, April 5, 1924.

42. Klan reports, April 5, 1924 (second and third quotes); April 7, 1924; April 10, 1924 (first quote); May 11, 1924.

43. Klan reports, April 6, 1924 (second quote); May 11, 1924 (first quote). The Klan also suspected that the mayor was connected with illegal gambling. See Klan reports, April 7, 1924.

44. Klan reports, May 11, 1924 (second and third quotes); May 24, 1924 (first quote); May 31, 1924.

45. Klan reports, April 7, 1924 (first, second, and third quotes); May 11, 1924 (fourth quote).

46. Klan reports, April 10, 1924; April 27, 1924; May 3, 1924; May 11, 1924 (first and second quotes); July 27, 1924; *Courier*, April 2, 1924, 16 (third quote).

47. Klan reports, April 5, 1924 (first and second quotes); April 6, 1924; April 7, 1924; April 10, 1924 (Smith quote); April 13, 1924; April 27, 1924; May 11, 1924; May 14, 1924; May 24, 1924; July 27, 1924.

48. Klan reports, April 10, 1924 (first quote); April 13, 1924 (second and third quotes); May 17, 1924; July 29, 1924.

49. Klan reports, April 5, 1924 (second quote); April 6, 1924 (first quote). Because the New York state Klan was never formally chartered as a "realm" of the Invisible Empire (in part, because of the legal complications presented by the Walker Law), all local Klans in the state had only provisional status and were run by appointed officers, usually a kleagle (Klan recruiter). When a klavern received its formal charter, as usually occurred in other states, it was allowed to elect its officers, the highest ranking of whom was the Exalted Cyclops (chapter president). The four provisional leaders of Buffalo Klan No. 5 held the title of Grand Kleagle of Western New York because they not only directed recruiting and other activities inside the city but throughout Erie and neighboring counties. For a useful chart that lays out the KKK's complicated chain of command, see Wade, *The Fiery Cross*, 158.

50. Klan reports, April 5, 1924; April 6, 1924; July 14, 1924; Aug. 18, 1924 (quotes).

Notes to Chapter 4

1. The membership list is located in the archives of the Buffalo and Erie County Historical Society; the public was first given access to this document in 1990.

2. *Courier*, July 2, 1923, 8.

3. Robert A. Goldberg, *Hooded Empire: The Ku Klux Klan in Colorado* (Urbana: University of Illinois Press, 1981), 183–86.

4. The directory is located in the archives of the Buffalo and Erie County Historical Society.

5. These calculations are based on information from *Thirteenth Census of the United States, 1910: Population* 4: 542, and *Fourteenth Census of the United States: Population* 4: 1068–70.

6. By the 1890s, most of Buffalo's major trade unions had federated within the United Trades and Labor Council (UTLC). Possessing a largely Anglo, Irish, and German membership, the UTLC took a strong stand against unrestricted immigration and immigrant labor, protesting, among other things, the use of nonunion Polish and Italian workers on city construction projects. See Goldman, *High Hopes*, 154–55. Union membership records in the 1920s were maintained by local chapters, the great majority of which are no longer in existence or have not kept their older files. For example, the oldest machinists' local still operating (No. 330 of the International Association of Machinists and Aerospace Workers) has regularly discarded its records as members have died or otherwise ceased affiliation; the local has no records as far back as 1924. However, one older electricians' local (No. 41, International Brotherhood of Electrical Workers) does retain records from the 1920s; according to these documents, out of fifty-six Klan-affiliated electricians in the city, only two ever belonged to the local, and one of these joined in 1929, long after the Buffalo klavern had expired.

7. *Fourteenth Census of the United States, 1920: Population* 2: 708–9; New York, Unpublished State Census Reports for 1925, Buffalo Wards Eleven and Twenty-One. Only 55.8 percent of the Klansmen listing addresses in Wards Eleven and Twenty-One were detected by the state census in 1925. Many Klansmen had probably moved since filling out their KKK application forms, and the state census was conducted in a less-than-thorough fashion, missing entire streets at times. For a concise compilation of state census data, see New York, Secretary of State, *Population Figures for the Cities, Incorporated Villages, Towns, and Counties of New York State According to the Census of June 1, 1925* (Albany: J. B. Lyon Co., 1926).

8. One study, Andrew P. Yox's, "Decline of the German-American Community in Buffalo, New York, 1855–1925" (Ph.D. dissertation, Univer-

sity of Chicago), 312, presents ward-level population percentages for several major ethnic (foreign- and native-born together) groups in 1915. How accurately Yox's figures suggest the ethnic composition of wards circa the early 1920s is difficult to ascertain, but one suspects that they provide a fairly reliable approximation. Statistical analysis utilizing this data reveals only a slight correlation between the percentage of Klansmen and the percentage of Germans (.167), Italians (−.164), and Poles (−.237). The correlation with the percentage of Irish is stronger (.380), but this is probably more reflective of the movement of middle-class Irish to outlying areas than of any type of ongoing residential conflict. Overall, Yox's data lends strength to the conclusion that proximity to ethnic populations probably only played a minor role in determining Klan membership.

9. The names on the Klan membership list were evaluated by my research assistant at the State University of New York at Buffalo, Alan C. Nothnagle, a talented graduate student who is a native German-speaker.

10. The occupational distribution of German-surnamed Klansmen is: high nonmanual (3.7 percent), middle nonmanual (19.4), low nonmanual (26.6), skilled (31.3), semiskilled and service (18.0), and unskilled (.6). The non-German-surnamed distribution is: high nonmanual (7.3), middle nonmanual (18.0), low nonmanual (28.2), skilled (30.3), semiskilled and service (15.5), and unskilled (.4).

11. Nine hundred and seventy-eight Klansmen residing inside the city have been located in the unpublished 1925 state census reports (56 percent of city residents on the Klan membership list). Of these, 30.1 percent were single with no children (although some had other types of dependents), .4 percent were single with children (possibly widowers), 16.0 percent were married with no children currently residing at home, and 53.4 percent were married with children at home.

12. Daniel J. Sweeney, ed., *History of Buffalo and Erie County in the World War, 1914–1919* (Buffalo: Committee of One Hundred, 1919), 509–679; Klan membership list.

13. *Fourteenth Census of the United States, 1920: Population* 2: 290; Klan membership list. The only other detailed evaluation of Klan recruiting among veterans is in Goldberg, *Hooded Empire*, 40–41, which reports that a large majority of the Denver klavern never served in the military.

14. *Courier*, Sept. 16, 1921, 5; June 25, 1922, 77; May 1, 1923, 5; Aug. 24, 1924, 77; *Express*, June 3, 1923, sec. 6, 1.

15. *Buffalo City Directory, 1922*, 71–79; *Masonic Directory for Buffalo, N.Y. and Erie County (1st and 2nd Masonic Districts) and Grand Bodies of the State of New York, 1922* (Buffalo: Masonic Life Association, 1922), 6–43; Klan membership list. For an excellent recent study of fraternal societies in the late nineteenth and early twentieth centuries, see

Mary Ann Clawson, *Constructing Brotherhood: Class, Gender, and Fraternalism* (Princeton; Princeton University Press, 1989). Clawson discovered that most fraternal groups, like the Klan, attracted balanced proportions of white- and blue-collar members. Among other sources, she utilizes a comprehensive membership list of the Knights of Pythias in Buffalo in 1891; the list indicates that 6.3 percent of the Knights were upper white-collar, 44 percent lower white-collar, 28.3 percent skilled, 16.6 percent semiskilled, and 4.9 percent unskilled. As can be seen, this is an occupational distribution not dissimilar from that of Buffalo Klan No. 5 thirty years later. See 98 and 105 of Clawson's study. Although it focuses on an even earlier period, many valuable insights concerning men's secret societies can also be found in Mark C. Carnes, *Secret Ritual and Manhood in Victorian America* (New Haven: Yale University Press, 1989).

16. *Express*, June 3, 1923, sec. 6, 1; *Courier*, June 12, 1923, 7; Sept. 1, 1924, 9; March 22, 1925, 10; Klan reports, April 6, 1924 (Klansman quote). Bryant also was a member of the investigation committee of Occidental Lodge No. 766. See *Masonic Directory, 1922*, 45.

17. *Masonic Directory, 1922*, 28.

18. *Masonic Directory*, 44; *Courier*, Oct. 9, 1924, 5.

19. Interestingly, at least two Klansmen were non-Protestants: Benjamin Kershberg and William Michaels were both Jewish. Kershberg indicated this on his KKK application form but was nonetheless admitted to membership. Michaels was a non-practicing Jew married to a Protestant; it is unclear whether he informed the Klan of his ethnoreligious background. *Courier*, Sept. 9, 1924, 3; author's interview with James Michaels, June 29, 1992.

20. For example, during the 1920s there were thirty-two Lutheran churches in Buffalo, but the records of only seven of these bodies are available for inspection, and many of these are of very limited usefulness. If both the Protestant and Klan populations had been evenly distributed throughout the city, one might derive a sample of church members from such records as are available, adjust the sample to conform to Buffalo's overall Protestant denominational distribution, and then determine the percentage of Klansmen in the various denominations represented in the sample. This approach, in fact, has been employed by Leonard Moore in his examination of the KKK in Indianapolis, an overwhelmingly Protestant community where members of denominations were broadly distributed (see *Citizen Klansmen*, 194). In Buffalo, however, religious groups tended to concentrate in various parts of the city, making it much harder to produce a useful sample from the limited membership records that are available—especially considering the relatively small number of Klansmen that one is trying to locate. Accordingly, this study has opted for another sampling method.

21. The survey was conducted by the eighteen members of my History 491 seminar, "The United States during the 1920s and 1930s," at the State University of New York at Buffalo. During the course of the spring 1992 semester, each member of the survey team contacted three hundred local residents with the same surnames as local Klansmen. When a likely respondent was located, his or her relationship to a Klan member was confirmed using the information concerning age, occupation, and residence on the KKK membership list. The denominational data presented in this study are based exclusively on those cases where a respondent was, at the least, fairly certain of a Klansman's religious affiliation.

22. Out of the sixty-five Lutherans in the sample, six were positively identified as evangelical Lutherans, but many respondents indicated that they were uncertain about which type of Lutheran church their Klan-affiliated relative had belonged to.

23. The Klan-affiliated ministers were: O. F. Albert, Presbyterian; Alfred C. Bussingham, Baptist; George A. Fowler, Methodist; H. S. Kissinger, United Brethren in Christ; Charles E. Odell, Methodist; Harry S. Palmeter, Baptist; Charles C. Penfold, Methodist; Littleton E. H. Smith, Presbyterian; Edgar C. Tullar, Methodist; Nicholas Vancassaboom, Methodist; and Joseph G. Wind, Spiritualist. The Klan's business directory also lists J. G. Secord, an Episcopalian minister, but his name does not appear on the klavern roster.

24. *Truth*, Jan. 3, 1924, 1.

Notes to Chapter 5

1. *Courier*, June 4, 1923, 4 (first quote); Dec. 9, 1923, 96 (second quote). Founders of this group included New York Supreme Court Justice Thomas H. Dowd; attorney Charles J. Kennedy; Dr. Francis M. Rich, a physician; realtor Charles Jacobson; businessman Howard S. Edmonds; investment broker Jacob S. Morris; and attorney Henry Stern.

2. *Times*, June 21, 1923, 21; *Courier*, June 21, 1923, 4; July 10, 1923, 5. For the activities of the American Unity League, see Jackson, *Klan in the City*, 103–17.

3. *Courier*, March 24, 1924, 1, 3 (quotes); *Times*, March 24, 1924, 13.

4. *Courier*, March 30, 1924, 89; April 3, 1924, 4 (first and third quotes); April 21, 1924, 8 (second quote); *Express*, April 18, 1924, 1; *Commercial*, April 18, 1924, 1.

5. *Courier*, April 18, 1924, 1 (quote); April 20, 1924, 87; *Express*, April 9, 1924, 1, 4; April 18, 1924, 1, 6; *Commercial*, April 18, 1924, 1. The possibility exists, of course, that Smith and the Klan staged this incident as a means of mobilizing support for the ongoing moral

reform campaign. Indeed, only one month before the bombing, Grand Kleagle George Bryant had written to King Kleagle E. D. Smith, "Keep your ear to the ground and listen to Buffalo. We have a surprise to spring which will be broadcast all over the United States." One suspects, however, that what Bryant was referring to were the Klan's plans to catch Mayor Schwab drinking in violation of the law. Moreover, if L. E. H. Smith wanted to stage an incident, he surely could have chosen to do something less inconvenient—but equally dramatic—than dynamiting his own house. In addition, in March 1925 United States Customs Inspector Orville Preuster, brother of Niagara County Kleagle Lucas Preuster and a close associate of the Reverend Smith, was killed in a similar bombing, indicating that the threat of such attacks was very real. See *Courier*, Sept. 21, 1924, 85 (Bryant quote), and March 2, 1925, 1.

6. *Courier*, April 20, 1924, 87 (quote); May 9, 1924, 16; *Express*, May 9, 1924, 9. The *Express* reported that "The display may have been the prank of boys," producing an angry reaction from the publicity-conscious George Bryant. See Klan reports, May 11, 1924.

7. *Express*, May 21, 1924, 4 (first quote); May 30, 1924, 9; *Courier*, May 21, 1924, 16; May 30, 1924, 5; May 31, 1924, 14 (second quote); *Enquirer*, May 21, 1924, 10. Four of those who were arrested later received ten-dollar fines, while the others received suspended sentences. See *Courier*, June 3, 1924, 18; *Express*, June 3, 1924, 9; and *Enquirer*, June 3, 1924, 3.

8. *Courier*, April 10, 1924, 14, 18; April 11, 1924, 5 (quotes); *Express*, April 10, 1924, 5; April 12, 1924, 5; *Commercial*, April 22, 1924, 1.

9. *Courier*, April 15, 1924, 18; *Express*, April 15, 1924, 4; *News*, April 15, 1924, 38.

10. *Courier*, April 13, 1924, 105 (first quote); April 14, 1924, 16 (second quote); June 3, 1924, 2; June 9, 1924, 16; *Express*, April 13, 1924, sec. 6, 1; June 3, 1924, 4; *News*, April 14, 1924, 6. Schwab also had the police investigate the background of Klansman David Mayne, discovering that Mayne had deserted his wife in Watertown, New York, in 1920. See *Courier*, May 17, 1924, 2, and May 18, 1924, 87.

11. *Courier*, May 24, 1924, 16 (first and second quotes); July 18, 1924, 16 (fifth quote); *Express*, May 24, 1924, 16 (third and fourth quotes); *Times*, May 23, 1924, 21.

12. *Courier*, June 1, 1924, 83; Klan reports, May 31, 1924.

13. *Courier*, July 5, 1924, 1 (first quote); July 7, 1924, 5 (second quote); *Express*, July 5, 1924, 5; *Times*, July 5, 1924, 4; Rubin, *Klan in Binghamton*, 24–26.

14. *Courier*, July 8, 1924, 3; *Express*, July 8, 1924, 16; *Times*, July 8, 1924, 13; *Commercial*, July 8, 1924, 1, 8. Mayor Schwab and the police had been aware of the location of Klan headquarters since early April 1925. See Klan reports, April 5, 1924. Michael Desmond, whose fam-

ily was involved in fighting the Klan, says that it was rumored that William J. Conners, the Roman Catholic owner of the *Buffalo Daily Courier*, hired a burglar to steal the Klan's files. Author's interview with Michael Desmond, July 22, 1992.

15. *Courier*, July 8, 1924, 3 (quotes); *Express*, July 8, 1924, 16; *Times*, July 8, 1924, 13; July 9, 1924, 1.

16. *Express*, July 7, 1924, 4; *Courier*, July 16, 1924, 6; *Vigilance*, July 26, 1924, 6.

17. *Courier*, July 26, 1924, 14 (quotes); July 27, 1924, 69; *Express*, July 26, 1924, 4; July 27, 1924, sec. 6, 2; *News*, July 25, 1924, 1.

18. *Courier*, Aug. 2, 1924, 14 (quotes); *Express*, Aug. 2, 1924, 14; *News*, Aug. 1, 1924, 24.

19. *Courier*, Aug. 4, 1924, 16 (quote); *News*, Aug. 4, 1924, 1; *Times*, Aug. 4, 1924, 1.

20. *Courier*, Aug. 5, 1924, 14 (quotes); *News*, Aug. 5, 1924, 3. Schwab conferred closely with his legal advisors before putting the list on display. Andrew Ronan had advised against making the roster public, but the mayor decided to proceed. See *Courier*, Aug. 3, 1924, 77; Aug. 4, 1924, 16; and *Express*, Aug. 4, 1924, 12.

21. *Courier*, Aug. 7, 1924, 3 (first and second quotes); Aug. 9, 1924, 14; Aug. 13, 1924, 14; Aug. 14, 1924, 16 (third quote); *Express*, Aug. 6, 1924, 14; Aug, 9, 1924, 12; Aug. 14, 1924, 14; *Times*, Aug. 7, 1924, 8; Aug. 14, 1924, 1. The police allowed viewing twice a week, on Wednesdays and Fridays.

22. *Courier*, Aug. 6, 1924, 5; Aug. 8, 1924, 8; Aug. 10, 1924, 78 (Penfold quote); *Express*, Aug. 8, 1924, 14. Hutt had been asked about his affiliation just prior to the lists going on display, after being named as a Klansman in the letter offering to sell the Klan list to Mayor Schwab; see *Courier*, July 26, 1924, 14 (Hutt quotes).

23. Klan reports, Aug. 18, 1924 (first quote); *Courier*, Aug. 7, 1924, 1; Aug. 8, 1924, 3 (second quote); *Express*, Aug. 7, 1924, 1; Aug. 8, 1924, 5; *Times*, Aug. 8, 1924, 1.

24. *Catholic Union & Times*, Aug. 14, 1924, 8 (first quote); *Courier*, Aug. 10, 1924, 77; Aug. 11, 1924, 4; Aug. 12, 1924, 3 (second and third quotes); Aug. 15, 1924, 18; *News*, Aug. 13, 1924, 32; Aug. 15, 1924, 3; *Times*, Aug, 13, 1924, 1.

25. *Courier*, Aug. 15, 1924, 18 (second quote); Aug. 16, 1924, 14 (first quote); *Express*, Aug, 15, 1924, 14; *News*, Aug. 15, 1924, 3.

26. *Courier*, Aug. 20, 1924, 14 (quote); *Express*, Aug. 20, 1924, 14; *News*, Aug. 19, 1924, 1; Klan reports, July 14, July 29, 1924. This letter was almost certainly written by the same person who had written the letter sent to the mayor in late July. It is a transcript of the second membership list that informs this study.

27. *Courier*, Aug. 20, 1924, 14; Aug. 21, 1924, 16 (first, second, and third quotes); Aug. 29, 1924, 16; *Express*, Aug. 21, 1924, 12; Aug. 29, 1924,

9; *News*, Aug. 20, 1924, 30. Owing to the legal proceedings described later in this chapter, city authorities ultimately decided not to return the cards.

28. *Courier*, Aug. 21, 1924, 16 (third quote); Aug. 22, 1924, 14 (first and second quotes); *Times*, Aug. 26, 1924, 1, 3.

29. *Courier*, Aug. 24, 1924, 77 (first quote); Aug. 26, 1924, 16 (second, third, and fourth quotes); *Express*, Aug. 24, 1924, sec. 6, 1; Aug. 26, 1924, 1, 5; *Times*, Aug. 26, 1924, 1, 3.

30. *Courier*, Aug. 29, 1924, 16 (quote); Aug. 30, 1924, 14; Sept. 9, 1924, 3; Sept. 11, 1924, 4; Sept. 16, 1924, 16; *Express*, Aug. 29, 1924, 9; Sept. 16, 1924, 4; *Times*, Aug. 29, 1924, 13; New York Supreme Court, Application of Charles S. Desmond for an Order of Mandamus against Frank X. Schwab, as Mayor of the City of Buffalo, N.Y. (granted Sept. 17, 1924); author's interview with Cathy Desmond Hughes, March 28, 1992; author's interview with Michael Desmond, July 22, 1992; author's interview with Thomas Burke, July 20, 1992; audiotape of W. H. Glover's interview with Charles S. Desmond, May 22, 1972, located in the archives of the Buffalo and Erie County Historical Society.

31. *Courier*, Sept. 11, 1924, 4 (first quote); Sept. 13, 1924, 3; Sept. 14, 1924, 83 (second quote); *Express*, Sept. 11, 1924, 4; *Commercial*, Sept. 11, 1924, 10. Copies of the pamphlet can be found in the archives of the Buffalo and Erie County Historical Society and in the Ku Klux Klan file of the archives of the Roman Catholic Diocese of Buffalo.

32. The *Express* reported a rumor that the Klan list had been published by "three Italians," and a local historian has claimed that a certain Frank A. DeFusto published the roster; I have not be able to confirm either of these claims. See *Express*, Sept. 11, 1924, 4, and Geraldine J. Walter, "The Ku Klux Klan in Buffalo during the 1920s" (History seminar paper, State University of New York at Buffalo, 1980), 15. A copy of Walter's paper is located in the archives of the State University of New York at Buffalo.

33. *Courier*, Sept. 11, 1924, 4; Sept. 13, 1924, 3 (quote); *Express*, Sept. 11, 1924, 4; Sept. 12, 1924, 14; *Commercial*, Sept. 11, 1924, 10; author's interview with Richard Fleischman, April 9, 1992.

34. *Courier*, Sept. 6, 1924, 14 (second quote); Sept. 9, 1924, 3 (first quote); *News*, Sept. 16, 1924, 18.

35. *Courier*, Sept. 3, 1924, 1; Sept. 4, 1924, 1, 16; *Express*, Sept. 2, 1924, 9; Sept. 3, 1924, 1; *Enquirer*, Sept. 3, 1924, 1, 12.

36. *Courier*, Sept. 1, 1924, 9; Sept. 4, 1924, 16; *Express*, Sept. 1, 1924, 4; *News*, Sept. 2, 1924, 1; Obertean reports, May 19–June 25, 1924. Obertean was to be paid out of a special police fund; thus he was not on the official city payroll. His reports regularly complain about not being paid on time. Mayor Schwab later expressed surprise that Obertean worked for the police. In actuality, the mayor personally

appointed the special officer. See *Courier*, Sept. 2, 1924, 16; *Express*, Sept. 2, 1924, 1; and Obertean reports, May 19, 1924. Obertean may well have been involved in the break-in at the Calumet Building, but, as this chapter shows, others were almost surely involved, particularly Mayor Schwab's other, and unidentified, undercover informant.

37. *Courier*, Sept. 2, 1924, 1 (quote); *Express*, Sept. 2, 1924, 9.

38. *Courier*, Sept. 1, 1924, 1 (first quote), 9; Sept. 2, 1924, 1 (second quote), 8; *Enquirer*, Sept. 3, 1924, 1, 12. In the wake of this incident, District Attorney Moore considered filing murder charges against Bryant, on the grounds that Bryant, Austin, and other Klansmen had entered into a conspiracy to kill Obertean. After a thorough investigation, however, Moore decided that he lacked adequate evidence with which to seek an indictment. See *Courier*, Sept. 5, 1924, 16; *Express*, Sept. 6, 1924, 5; and *Commercial*, Sept. 6, 1924, 1.

39. *Courier*, Sept. 2, 1924, 1 (first quote), 8; Sept. 3. 1924, 5 (second quote); Sept. 4, 1924, 1 (third and fourth quotes); Sept. 12, 1924, 8; *Express*, Sept. 3, 1924, 4; Sept. 6, 1924, 4; Sept. 12, 1924, 6; *Truth*, Sept. 13, 1924, 2; *News*, Sept. 6, 1924, 18. Rabbi Louis J. Kopald of Temple Beth Zion expressed a willingness to serve on the committee, but suggested that other approaches might be more constructive. See *Express*, Sept. 14, sec. 6, 4.

40. *Courier*, Sept. 9, 1924, 3, 8; Sept. 10, 1924, 3; Sept. 17, 1924, 5; Oct. 2, 1924, 3; Oct. 3, 1924, 3; Oct. 8, 1924, 8 (Hutt quote); *Express*, Sept. 9, 1924, 1, 4; Sept. 14, 1924, sec. 6, 1; Oct. 2, 1924, 4; Oct. 8, 1924, 4; *Commercial*, Sept. 9, 1924, 1; *News*, Sept. 9, 1924, 3; Sept. 10, 1924, 34; Oct. 7, 1924, 1; *Enquirer*, Sept. 6, 1924, 1, 12; Oct. 7, 1924, 1, 14; City Court of Buffalo, Subpoenas Concerning Complaint of Charles S. Desmond against Invisible Government, Knights of the Ku Klux Klan, Sept. 4, 1924–Oct. 3, 1924. The subpoenas are in the possession of Joseph Desmond, grandson of Charles Desmond. The other Klansmen who were called to testify were Albert H. Zink, prominent insurance man and president of the Buffalo Kiwanis; school principal Fenton H. Dimmick; Major E. G. Ziegler, salesman for the Gerber Nott Company; John C. Sturm, brother of Carl Sturm (who was wounded in the Obertean shoot-out) and assistant general manager of the *Buffalo Commercial;* Albert V. Harvey, electrician; Elmer Dietz, machine operator; Benjamin Kershberg, restaurant owner; Andrew Zimmerman, woodworker and nephew of Police Chief Zimmerman; Wilfred A. Carver, foreman at the Pierce Arrow Company; Robert S. Hoole, assistant principal at the Seneca Vocational School; Mark H. Hubbell, owner and editor of the *Buffalo Truth;* Mervin C. Conner, manager at Meng, Shaffer & Held; William S. Thompson, restaurant manager; Edward J. Brumel, barber; William R. Reed, restaurant owner; Earl J. Isaac, tax and title searcher; Fred C. Brechel, superintendent of the Law Exchange; Pascal P. Pratt, stockbroker; Hartley F.

Rogers, stockbroker; William F. Bethman, toolmaker; Irving Bundt, clerk; Fred S. Withey, attorney; Norman Duffield, insurance salesman; Caryl H. Newell, insurance salesman; M. A. Jackson, candymaker; William F. Brace, manager of Brace-McGuire Company; Herbert C. Schoeplin, automobile dealer; Howard Cox, insurance agent; Norman Haas, optician; Augustus W. Hengerer, physician; David Mayne, detective; Frederick W. Rawe, deputy county clerk; Pomeroy Williams, metal grinder; Fred Hamilton, insurance agent; and the Reverend Charles C. Penfold. Two other alleged Klansmen, Ellis H. Champlin and Harry M. Winkelman, neither of whom appears on the Klan list, were also subpoenaed.

41. *Courier*, Sept. 10, 1924, 3 (quote); *Express*, Sept. 10, 1924, 4.
42. *Courier*, Sept. 27, 1924, 16; Sept. 28, 1924, 90; Oct. 2, 1924, 3; Oct. 7, 1924, 5 (quotes); *Express*, Oct. 2, 1924, 4; Oct. 7, 1924, 4; *Enquirer*, Oct. 6, 1924, 12.
43. *Courier*, Nov. 8, 1924, 4 (quotes); Nov. 11, 1924, 18; Nov. 15, 1924, 4; *Express*, Nov. 8, 1924, 4; Nov. 11, 1924, 16.
44. *Courier*, Aug. 10, 1924, 77; Aug. 12, 1924, 3; Sept. 10, 1924, 3; Sept. 14, 1924, 83; *Express*, Aug. 10, 1924, sec. 6, 1; *Commercial*, Sept. 9, 1924, 1. Acker is regularly mentioned in the undercover reports prepared by Edward Obertean and Mayor Schwab's other informant. Acker evidently viewed the Klan as a means of making money, affixing his stationery with stickers that read "All Kinds of Insurance Arranged," in imitation of the Klan acronym AKIA (A Klansman I Am); he also worked as a part-time kleagle, being the main organizer in the nearby village of Akron. George Bryant disliked Acker and refused to help him when he was arrested, commenting: "The Dirty Son of a B—— asking me to go his bond. I'm not going to get my name mixed up with anything like that." Bryant also said that when Acker was released, he intended to "throw [Acker] out of the Clan [*sic*]." See Klan reports, May 3, 1924, and Aug. 10, 1924.
45. *Courier*, Sept. 16, 1924, 2; Sept. 18, 1924, 3; *Express*, Sept. 16, 1924, 16.
46. Newspaper clipping dated November 22, 1924, located in Ku Klux Klan file, Buffalo and Erie County Historical Society.
47. *Courier*, Sept. 20, 1924, 1, 3 (quotes); *Express*, Sept. 20, 1924, 4; *Enquirer*, Sept. 20, 1924, 12.
48. *Courier*, Sept. 20, 1924, 1 (first quote); Sept. 21, 1924, 85 (third quote), 91 (second quote); Sept. 22, 1924, 4 (fourth quote); *Express*, Sept. 21, 1924, sec. 6, 1; Sept. 22, 1924, 12; *Enquirer*, Sept. 22, 1924, 12.
49. *Courier*, Sept. 23, 1924, 1 (quote); Sept. 27, 1924, 1; *Express*, Sept. 24, 1924, 4; Sept. 27, 1924, 1, 4; *News*, Sept. 23, 1924, 1; Sept. 26, 1924, 1. The minister's attempt at deception may not have been as foolish as it seems: Mrs. Lohr reportedly bore a remarkable resemblance to Mrs. Penfold.

50. *Courier*, Sept. 28, 1924, 85 (quote); *Express*, Sept. 28, 1924, sec. 6, 1, 3; Oct. 4, 1924, 14; *News*, Sept. 27, 1924, 1, 3. Those arrested included Thomas J. Wolfe, chauffeur; William F. Ross, chemical worker; Merrit C. Mills, shoemaker; Harold Pfeiffer, furniture shipper; Raymond Goss, steelworker; and Carl Ross, occupation unknown.

51. *Courier*, Oct. 13, 1924, 3 (quote); Oct. 15, 1924, 5; Nov. 19, 1924, 18; Nov. 20, 1924, 5; Nov. 27, 1924, 30; Nov. 29, 1924, 3; *Express*, Nov. 19, 1924, 16; Nov. 27, 1924, 30; Nov. 29, 1924, 16; *Commercial*, Nov. 19, 1924, 1; Nov. 28, 1924, 1. On April 4, 1925, Erie County Judge Thomas H. Noonan overturned Penfold's conviction for "outraging public decency" on the grounds of lack of evidence. "In this case," Noonan observed, "the facts alleged to have been committed were trivial in character, and, if the defendant had been driving through a crowd in the daytime, none of the acts, except the arm around the woman, could have been seen by the public, and no one could have been offended." District Attorney Moore indicated that he would continue to pursue Penfold's perjury charge, but I have found no evidence that he did. Whatever the ultimate disposition of this case, the pastor was finished as a reputable influence in local affairs. See *Courier*, April 5, 1925, 87, 88 (quote), and May 28, 1925, 3.

52. *Courier*, Aug. 10, 1924, 77; Oct. 4, 1924, 16; Klan reports, Aug. 10, 1924.

53. *Courier*, Aug. 26, 1924, 16; Sept. 2, 1924, 3; *Express*, Sept. 2, 1924, 1; *Commercial*, Sept. 2, 1924, 12.

54. *Courier*, Oct. 7, 1924, 5; *Truth*, Dec. 25, 1924, 2.

55. *Courier*, Oct. 13, 1924, 4; Nov. 10, 1924, 16; Sept. 16, 1925, 7.

56. *Courier*, Aug. 28, 1924, 16; Sept. 14, 1924, 83; Nov. 23, 1924, 83; Mary Schwab Murphy interview.

57. *Courier*, Nov. 23, 1924, 83 (first quote); Nov. 24, 1924, 16 (second and third quotes); *Express*, Nov. 23, 1924, sec. 8, 1, 3; *Times*, Nov. 24, 1924, 13.

58. A longtime voice on behalf of prohibition, strict law enforcement, immigration restriction, and other conservative measures, the *Truth* had always stood on common ground with the Klan. Eventually (probably in either late 1923 or early 1924) publisher Mark Hubbell joined the hooded order. It was only after the exposure of the Buffalo klavern, however, that he let his paper become the KKK's local publicity outlet, relaying Klan propaganda and news items from across the country. Hubbell probably hoped to replace the numerous subscriptions that had been lost because of his exposure with new orders from the Klan faithful. Toward the end of 1925, as the KKK withered away, the *Truth* stopped presenting news about the Klan; in 1926, the paper ceased publication altogether. In later years, Hubbell refused to discuss his involvement with the Klan, even with family members. Author's interview with Nelson Hubbell, July 20, 1992.

59. *Truth,* April 11, 1925, 6; May 9, 1925, 6; *Courier,* May 7, 1925, 16 (quotes); *Express,* May 7, 1925, 4; *News,* May 7, 1925, 44.
60. *Courier,* May 14, 1925, 3.
61. *News,* Sept. 2, 1925, 1; *Courier,* Sept. 3, 1925, 18. See chapter 1 for the mayor's difficulties with Graves.
62. *Express,* Oct. 14, 1925, 1, 4; *Courier,* Sept. 17, 1925, 7; Oct. 14, 1925, 1; *News,* Oct. 14, 1925, 1.
63. *Courier,* Oct. 21, 1925, 5 (quotes); Oct. 24, 1925, 10; *Express,* Oct. 21, 1925, 4; *Times,* Oct. 21, 1925, 3.
64. *Courier,* Nov. 1, 1925, 77 (first quote); Nov. 4, 1925, 1 (second quote); *Express,* Nov. 4, 1925, 1; *Times,* Nov. 4, 1925, 1, 3.
65. *Courier,* May 23, 1925, 8 (quote); *Express,* May 23, 1925, 1, 9; *Truth,* May 28, 1925, 1, 2, 10, 11.
66. *Courier,* Aug. 6, 1925, 5; Sept. 13, 1925, 80; Sept. 17, 1925, 18; *Express,* Sept. 13, 1925, sec. 8, 1; *Times,* Sept. 13, 1925, 37.
67. *Courier,* Sept. 16, 1925, 7 (quotes); Oct. 25, 1925, 90; *Express,* Oct. 25, 1925, sec. 8, 1, 3.
68. *Courier,* Sept. 16, 1925, 7; Sept. 17, 1925, 18; Jan. 7, 1926, 1, 7 (quotes); *Times,* Jan. 7, 1926, 1.
69. *Courier,* Jan. 7, 1926, 1; Jan. 14, 1926, 1, 2; *Times,* Jan. 7, 1926, 1. This information was provided by Klan attorney Julius Grass early in 1926.

Notes to Conclusion

1. "The People of the State of New York *ex rel.* George Bryant, Appellant, v. Charles F. Zimmerman" in New York, *Reports of Cases Decided in the Court of Appeals of the State of New York, July 15, 1925, to January 12, 1926* (Albany: J. B. Lyon Co., 1926), 405–13; "New York *ex rel.* Bryant v. Zimmerman et al." in U.S., *Cases Adjudged in the Supreme Court at October Term, 1928* 278 (Washington, D.C.: Government Printing Office, 1929): 63–77 (quotes). United States Supreme Court Justice James C. McReynolds dissented from the majority decision in Bryant v. Zimmerman, claiming that the case involved "no substantial federal question." See U.S., *Cases Adjudged in the Supreme Court at October Term, 1928* 278: 77–84.
2. *Courier-Express,* Nov. 20, 1928, 1, 4; Nov. 30, 1928, 5; Dec. 18, 1928, 9; Walter, "The Ku Klux Klan in Buffalo," 18.
3. Throughout the course of researching this study, I have sought, largely in vain, information concerning Klanswomen in Buffalo. As is indicated in the text, there were local branches of both the Kamelia and the Women of the Ku Klux Klan, but almost nothing is known about these groups' activities and memberships. This is not an unusual situation; in no part of the country have detailed records of the

women's Klan come to light. In her study, *Women of the Klan: Racism and Gender in the 1920s* (Berkeley: University of California Press, 1991), Kathleen M. Blee was only able to identify 125 Klanswomen in Indiana, a state where the membership of the women's movement numbered in the tens of thousands.

4. See Goldberg, *Hooded Empire*, 46; Moore, *Citizen Klansmen*, 63; Christopher N. Cocoltchos, "The Invisible Government and the Viable Community: The Ku Klux Klan in Orange County, California, during the 1920s" (Ph.D. dissertation: University of California, Los Angeles, 1979), 396; William D. Jenkins, *Steel Valley Klan: The Ku Klux Klan in Ohio's Mahoning Valley* (Kent, Ohio: Kent State University Press, 1990), 84; David A. Horowitz, "Order, Solidarity, and Vigilance: The Ku Klux Klan in La Grande, Oregon," in Lay, *The Invisible Empire in the West*, 195; Nancy MacLean, *Behind the Mask of Chivalry: The Making of the Second Ku Klux Klan* (New York: Oxford University Press, 1994), 54.

Historiographical Essay

In 1990, Leonard J. Moore presented a review article entitled "Historical Interpretations of the 1920s Klan: The Traditional View and the Populist Revision" that remains the most important survey of Klan scholarship to date.[1] The purpose of the following essay is to reemphasize, supplement, and challenge some of the major themes in Moore's work.

Considering the great flowering of the social sciences in the 1920s, it is not surprising that sociologists were the first scholars to evaluate the second Klan. In an article first published in 1923, the prominent sociologist Frank Tannenbaum assessed the KKK in the South, concluding that it was essentially a "rural and small-town institution" sustained by fear of the social advancement of African Americans. Confronted with the "new negro [sic]" of the immediate post–World War I period and an end to "static relations between the races," Klansmen, according to Tannenbaum, were engaging in a "deep-rooted social habit—a habit of ready violence in defense of a threatened social status." He also emphasized the adverse psychological impact of the recent war effort, claiming that a residual "passion for abuse, calumny, and physical brutality" now found expression in the KKK and "all similar movements of hate in the world." Lacking "full, interesting, varied lives," trapped in a state of "emotional infanthood," the denizens of the nonurban South had proved easy prey for Klan recruiters.[2]

Another well-known sociologist, Guy B. Johnson, also evaluated the Klan in a 1923 *Journal of Social Forces* article based on his University of Chicago master's thesis. Like Tannenbaum, he believed that postwar social unrest had produced "unusual psychic reactions" among Klansmen, who had organized in order to defend "doctrines, customs, and traditions which they consider to be essential for the security and well-being of the nation." Unspent passions from the war, a surge in racism, fear of foreign immigration, and economic anxiety had all contributed to the Klan's rise. In its essence, Johnson concluded, the Invisible Empire represented a widespread failure to adjust to new conditions "on a rational basis."[3] Sociologist Frank Bohn's 1925 article, "The Ku Klux Klan Interpreted," likewise stressed the themes of postwar disillusionment and status anxiety. Exploiting the apprehensions generated by a declining Anglo-Saxon birthrate and the loss of "old-time cocksureness," the Klan had proved particularly attractive to "the hard-minded, militant, younger element," many of whom were war veterans. Although most of its membership was nonviolent, Bohn warned that the hooded order threatened to evolve into an "American Facisti" that would reject democratic institutions and values.[4]

A more extensive evaluation of the KKK, John Moffatt Mecklin's *The Ku Klux Klan: A Study of the American Mind*, appeared in 1924. A respected sociologist at Dartmouth College, Mecklin utilized government records, Klan literature, newspaper reports, and "several hundred" questionnaires in an attempt to discover the sources of the secret order's appeal and the nature of its membership. Although he agreed with other scholars that Klan growth had been stimulated by "disturbed post-war conditions," Mecklin argued that the Klan primarily drew strength from the longstanding American social traditions of anti-Catholicism and nativism. These traditions were particularly strong among citizens of "old American stock living in the villages and small towns of those sections of the country where this stock has been least disturbed by immigration, on the one hand, and the disruptive effect of industrialism on the other"—places such as Oregon and large parts of the South and Midwest. Characterized by a "beautiful but unreasoning loyalty to orthodox Protestantism" and a "provincial fear of all things foreign," the residents of these regions had joined the KKK because of their "prosaic and unpoetic environment" and also because kleagles had successfully exploited their "stubborn, uncritical mental stereotypes" of Catholics, Jews, and foreigners. A "refuge for mediocre men, if not for weaklings," the Klan served, in Mecklin's opinion, as a "defense mechanism against evils which are often more imaginary than real."[5]

Well-crafted, reflective, and moderate in tone, Mecklin's work affirmed, consolidated, and expanded upon a number of the key points raised by his fellow sociologists, helping forge an enduring school of scholarly opinion concerning the second Klan. At the core of this "Mecklin thesis" was the alleged social threat posed by "the uninformed and unthinking average man," who easily succumbed to irrational movements such as the Klan during stressful times. In retrospect, of course, it can readily be seen that this insensitive appraisal itself constituted an "uncritical mental stereotype," one frequently employed by the intellectual and literary elite of the 1920s.[6] Yet this only meant that Mecklin's thesis was all the more quickly accepted by those sharing his biases and preconceptions. Largely overlooked was the crucial problem of evidence. What type of data had Mecklin and the other sociologists utilized to construct their portrait of the KKK as a nonurban group composed of the ignorant, mediocre, and socially anxious? Tannenbaum's article appears entirely speculative, and Johnson's assessment focused on the rhetoric and ideas presented in national Klan literature; neither evaluation is documented. Frank Bohn derived his appraisal of this nationwide movement from a short visit to Marion County, Ohio, where he talked to a few Klansmen. Mecklin claimed to have used responses from hundreds of representative citizens, but his study lacks notes and most of the responses evidently came from anti-Klan sources. Overall, judged by current academic standards, this body of work seems patently subjective and bereft of scholarly rigor.

Despite these serious shortcomings, the Mecklin thesis remained largely unchallenged for the next four decades. One major reason for this was that a scarcity of official Klan records and other sources resulted in very few detailed studies of the KKK, but probably even more important was the general impression among scholars that Mecklin and his contemporaries had accurately and comprehensively assessed the Invisible Empire. In his lengthy historical survey, *The Great Crusade and After, 1914–1928* (1930), Preston William Slosson drew heavily upon Mecklin in exploring the appeal of the Klan, emphasizing how devious Klan leaders had employed traditional anti-Catholicism to attract "thousands of honest villagers."[7] Journalist-historian Frederick Lewis Allen's extremely popular *Only Yesterday: An Informal History of the Nineteen-Twenties* (1931) likewise stressed how the KKK cynically played upon the "newly inflamed fears of the credulous small-towner" and exploited the "infantile love of hocus-pocus and mummery [that] survives in the adult whose lot is cast in drab places." "Here," Allen smugly observed, "was a chance to dress up the village bigot and let him be a knight of the Invisible Empire."[8] Ten years later, another journalist-historian, Wilbur J. Cash, presented a similar evaluation in *The Mind of the South* (1941). Although he acknowledged that some Southern business and political leaders had joined the Klan, Cash asserted that the secret order primarily thrived upon the common man's "fears and hates," bringing them "into focus with the tradition of the past, and above all with the ancient Southern pattern of high romantic histrionics, violence, and mass coercion of the scapegoat and the heretic."[9]

Intellectual developments in the 1940s and 1950s helped insure the continued acceptance of the Mecklin thesis. During a period when society had experienced the threats presented by Nazism, Stalinism, and McCarthyism, it is not surprising that scholars should begin to equate militant popular movements such as the Klan with social pathology. Particularly influential were the works of psychoanalysts, social philosophers, and sociologists such as Erich Fromm, Eric Hoffer, William Kornhauser, Theodore W. Adorno, and Seymour M. Lipset, all of whom emphasized the role of alienation, inadequacy, social disintegration, and irrationality in sustaining forms of mass activism.[10] This dark view of social movements complemented and informed the work of a new generation of American historians who stressed the themes of national "consensus" and the abiding "liberal tradition" of the United States. From this perspective, the Klan of the 1920s seemed patently aberrant and reactionary, a temporary upsurge by declining elements that denied America's liberal essence.

Because it conformed well with the basic tenets of consensus history, as well as the increasingly popular concept of status anxiety, the Mecklin thesis was readily incorporated into a number of major historical works in the 1950s. In *The Age of Reform: From Bryan to F.D.R.* (1955), Richard Hofstadter, citing Mecklin, claimed that the second KKK was centered in small towns and appealed primarily to "relatively unprosperous and uncultivated native white Protestants." Not legitimate problems but abstract "evils" preoccupied Klansmen, particularly the "growing sense that the code by which rural and small-town Anglo-Saxon America had lived was being ignored and even flouted in the wicked cities."[11] John Higham's *Strangers in the Land: Patterns of American Nativism, 1860–1925* (1955) also depicted the Klan as a rural and small-town movement, a "final effort to preserve the values of the community against change and against external influences." Like the sociologists of the 1920s, Higham emphasized wartime superpatriotism, economic anxieties, and a longstanding tradition of rural nativism as factors promoting Klan growth.[12] William E. Leuchtenburg's *The Perils of Prosperity, 1914–1932* (1958) similarly embraced the Mecklin thesis and the theory of status anxiety, citing the Klan's particular appeal among the "poorer and less educated" residents of small-town America who resented the rise of the city. To a greater extent than most authors, Leuchtenburg emphasized the violent, even inherently sadistic, nature of the Invisible Empire: "Wherever the Klan entered, in its wake came floggings, kidnappings, branding with acid, mutilation, church burnings, and even murders."[13]

During the 1960s, a decade of civil rights activism and renewed Klan terrorism, historians continued to claim that the second KKK had been essentially lawless and violent. Arnold S. Rice, in *The Ku Klux Klan in American Politics* (1962), portrayed the hooded order as a dangerous group that attracted the "dregs" of society and the "lovers of horseplay," and George Brown Tindall, in *The Emergence of the New South, 1913–1945* (1967), character-ized the group as a manifestation of a "savage ideal" sustained by racism and social reaction. One of the most important works in Klan historiography, David M. Chalmers's *Hooded Americanism: The First Century of the Ku Klux Klan, 1865–1965* (1965), also stressed the theme of Klan violence, presenting numerous ac-counts of floggings, brandings, and other outrages. Assuming a disparaging and mocking tone throughout the volume, Chalmers characterized the order as being "emotional rather than rational, defensive rather than constructive," a terrorist group composed of the poorly educated and socially insecure.[14]

This powerful stereotype of the 1920s Klan and its membership continued to influence scholarship in the 1970s. Seymour M. Lip-set's and Earl Raab's *The Politics of Unreason: Right Wing Extrem-ism in America, 1790–1970* (1970) identified status anxiety among lower-class Americans as the main force sustaining the order, while Ellis W. Hawley, in *The Great War and the Search for a Modern Order* (1979), concluded that the national Klan experience was an episode of "temporary emotionalism" within an American tradition of "middle-class rightism." In the 1980s this standard assessment could also be found in major works by Geoffrey Per-rett, Wyn Craig Wade, and David H. Bennett.[15] Presently, al-though it is hard to know for certain, most scholars probably consider the Klans of all eras to have been irrational, prone to violence, and largely composed of marginal elements.

Only very gradually has it been recognized that the second Invisible Empire resists easy stereotyping. The major factor inhib-iting such recognition prior to the 1960s was a dearth of objective analysis, but two studies managed to avoid the general rush to judgment. In *The Ku Klux Klan in Pennsylvania: A Study in Nativ-ism* (1936), Emerson H. Loucks utilized extensive contacts with former Klansmen to derive a sense of why people had been drawn to the secret order. Although characterized by their fair share of prejudice and intolerance, the Klansmen in Loucks's work appear as ordinary citizens reacting to legitimate problems; they are clearly not extremists or neurotics. In addition, as Loucks details, Klansmen in Pennsylvania were far more often the victims of lawlessness than the perpetrators of violence against others.[16]

Nearly twenty years later, Norman F. Weaver arrived at similar conclusions in a doctoral dissertation that examined the Invisible Empire in Wisconsin, Indiana, Ohio, and Michigan. Weaver claimed that the Klan, despite its "ultra-conservative" orientation, fit well within a mainstream Protestant tradition of voluntary associationalism; as had Loucks, he found the group to be essentially nonviolent. He was also convinced that there was "no 'Klan movement' at all, just many local Klans," which had typically inaugurated community-level crusades "against vice, against bootleggers, against Catholics in the field of education, [and] against crooked politicians in the political arena." The best course for future Klan scholarship, Weaver suggested, would be a "series of community studies" examining the Invisible Empire's social foundations at the local level.[17]

In the 1960s, a time of rising general interest in the Klan, historians began to undertake detailed examinations of the KKK in a number of states and communities. One of the first studies was Charles C. Alexander's *Crusade for Conformity: The Ku Klux Klan in Texas, 1920–1930* (1962), which credited the KKK's growth in the Lone Star State not to the devious manipulation of rural bigotry but to "the white Protestant citizen's reaction against the postwar crime wave and the supposed moral breakdown spreading over the state." Although he was influenced by Theodore Adorno's psychosocial concept of "moral authoritarianism," Alexander acknowledged that Klansmen were reacting to very real problems of crime and social disorder. He additionally noted, in contrast to the Mecklin thesis, that the Texas Klan "achieved its greatest strength and its most notable successes in the booming cities"; he likewise rejected Frank Tannenbaum's assessment that the Klan in the South was a response to the "new negro [sic]," demonstrating that the secret order's vigilantism had primarily been directed against fellow whites. While conducting subsequent research, Alexander discovered that this appraisal could be extended to the Klans in Louisiana, Oklahoma, and Arkansas; this resulted in a second major publication, *The Ku Klux Klan in the Southwest* (1965).[18]

Despite its insensitive approach and overemphasis on Klan violence, David Chalmers's *Hooded Americanism* also helped undermine the Mecklin thesis at this time. Broad in scope and richly detailed, the volume revealed the Invisible Empire's strong appeal in a great variety of communities in almost all regions of the country—certainly not just America's declining villages and small towns. In 1967, Kenneth T. Jackson's *The Ku Klux Klan in the City, 1915–1930* went even further in challenging Mecklin, emphasizing the predominant role of urban residents in the Klan movement, both as leaders and as approximately half of the total membership. Jackson was also the first scholar to develop a socioeconomic portrait of the average Klansman based on official klavern rosters and other data, presenting occupational-status distributions for KKK members in five urban communities. Based on this information—which was actually very limited—he concluded that the "greatest source of Klan support came from rank and file non-union, blue-collar employees of large businesses and factories"; the Klan in the city, therefore, was generally a "lower-middle-class movement." Largely nonviolent and rational, these urban Klansmen were nonetheless deeply upset over two distinct migration patterns: the influx of immigrants from southern and eastern Europe, and the movement of African Americans to the cities, particularly those in the North. The typical Klansman, according to Jackson, was

> frightened at the prospect of a Negro or a Pole coming into his block and causing him to sell his house at a low price. Unable to escape and hesitant to act alone, the threatened citizen welcomed the security and respectability of a large group. Seeking to stabilize his world and maintain a neighborhood status quo, he turned to the promise of the Klan. Not a reaction against the rise of the city to dominance in American life, the Invisible Empire was rather a reaction against the aspirations of certain elements within the city.[19]

Jackson's volume constituted a major landmark in Klan historiography. It confirmed Alexander's earlier conclusion that the Klan had been to a large degree an urban phenomenon, and it lent support to the emerging view of Klansmen as rational citizens responding to real problems. Although the work was not without significant flaws—particularly its continued reliance on the idea of status anxiety—it broke away from many of the limiting precepts of the Mecklin thesis and consensus history. Perhaps most importantly, Jackson had, through his city-by-city treatment of the Klan, indicated the importance of the local case study in assessing the hooded order.

For the next few years there was a lull in Klan studies, but in the mid- and late-1970s, as the historical profession became more receptive to social history in general and the case-study approach in particular, scholars began to produce intensive local studies that further challenged traditional thinking about the Klan. In 1974, Robert A. Goldberg published an examination of the hooded order in Madison, Wisconsin, in which he characterized the group as a nonviolent and essentially rational response to local issues, particularly a perceived deterioration in law enforcement.[20] Strongly influenced by the theory of "resource mobilization" that was gaining popularity among a new generation of political sociologists, Goldberg in a 1977 doctoral dissertation went on to examine the Klan stronghold of Colorado, focusing on the city of Denver and four other communities. Although there were notable exceptions, Goldberg discovered that the vast majority of Colorado knights were ordinary, law-abiding citizens motivated by a sincere desire to improve local society. Expanding upon Kenneth Jackson's efforts, he presented comprehensive occupational-status statistics that proved that Klansmen were drawn from a balanced cross section of the white Protestant community. He further observed that the nature of Klan activism varied from community to community, arguing that the Invisible Empire could not be truly understood outside of its numerous local contexts.[21]

By the time that Goldberg's dissertation was published as *Hooded Empire: The Ku Klux Klan in Colorado* (1981), the work of other historians had strongly endorsed his general conclusions. A 1978 article on the klavern in Youngstown, Ohio, by William D. Jenkins, emphasized the role of moral issues and a longstanding tradition of pietistic Protestant activism in mobilizing local Klansmen. Like Goldberg, he found the knights in eastern Ohio to be largely nonviolent and drawn from the socioeconomic mainstream. Jenkins later decided that this overall evaluation could be applied to the entire Mahoning Valley region (which may have had as many as seventeen thousand Klansmen), and he has presented his findings in *Steel Valley Klan: The Ku Klux Klan in Ohio's Mahoning Valley* (1990).[22] In 1980, a statistical study of Klan electoral behavior in Memphis, Tennessee, by Kenneth D. Wald, also demonstrated the group's appeal across the social spectrum.[23]

At this same time, Christopher N. Cocoltchos completed one of the most important studies in Klan historiography: "The Invisible Government and the Viable Community: The Ku Klux Klan in Orange County, California, during the 1920s" (1979). In the mid-1970s, Cocoltchos's doctoral supervisor, Stanley Coben, had begun exploring the connections between the KKK movement and the defense of social Victorianism and had come across a comprehensive Orange County Klan roster while doing research at the Library of Congress. Utilizing the Klan list in association with a rich assortment of government documents, newspaper reports, oral interview sources, and church rolls, Cocoltchos created extremely detailed social profiles of the Klan, non-Klan, and anti-Klan populations of Orange County communities such as Anaheim and Fullerton. The study produced some intriguing findings:

> Klansmen were younger, a bit wealthier, and had slightly more prestigious jobs than did non-Klansmen; however, they could not match the anti-Klan elite's wealth and prestige. Political party preferences, geographical origins, marital status, and length of prior residence in the county did not differentiate Klansmen from non-Klan white Protestants. Compared to white Protestants, Klansmen were not significantly more likely to belong to evangelical or fundamentalist denominations.

As had Goldberg, Cocoltchos concluded that "the way in which the hooded order grew, the activities in which it engaged, and the reasons for its demise were all locally generated." Composed of decent, respectable citizens, the Orange County Klan had represented a form of grass-roots activism that opposed a "booster-oriented view of local affairs, fostered by the anti-Klan elite, that stressed economic growth to the exclusion of moral aspects of community development."[24]

Three major studies completed between 1982 and 1985 helped consolidate the emerging portrait of the average Klansman as a mainstream activist. Larry R. Gerlach's examination of the secret order in Utah detected some KKK-sponsored violence against immigrants, but the organization by and large attracted law-abiding, middle-class residents. The primary cause for the Klan's rise, he argued, was the longstanding resentment among Protestant non-Mormons of the economic and political primacy of the Church of Jesus Christ of Latter-day Saints, especially in the vicinity of Salt Lake City. The KKK held colorful demonstrations and indirectly involved itself in a few municipal elections, but the overt hostility of the Mormon establishment prevented the Invisible Empire from ever becoming a major influence in Utah.[25] Shawn Lay's *War, Revolution, and the Ku Klux Klan: A Study of Intolerance in a Border City* (1985) also looked at the Klan in a socially distinctive locale, the west Texas community of El Paso. While earlier case studies had mostly focused on cities and towns with small minority and Roman Catholic populations, this work examined a municipality that was approximately 60 percent Hispanic and Catholic during the early 1920s; moreover, the city's location on the Mexican border had produced a particularly acute situation in regard to crime and social immorality. If, in fact, the Klan was composed largely of unrestrained racists, bigots, and moral authoritarians, then El Paso would have been one of the most likely places for the order to engage in roughshod tactics. But such was not the case. The El Paso klavern largely ignored the Hispanic majority, never employed violence, and spent most of its time challenging the policies of fellow Anglos who dominated city government, focusing on such issues as better public education, honest elections, and road construction. Overall, the Klan in this unusual border city had constituted a "medium of progressive civic action" and was quite similar to earlier reform efforts in El Paso's history.[26]

Although the case studies of Goldberg, Cocoltchos, Gerlach, and Lay had arrived at very similar conclusions concerning western klaverns, it remained unclear—the articles of Jenkins and Wald notwithstanding—how applicable their findings were for the Klan in other regions. In 1985, Leonard J. Moore completed a doctoral dissertation on the premiere Klan state of Indiana, an examination that has been published as *Citizen Klansmen: The Ku Klux Klan in Indiana, 1921–1928* (1991). Assisted by an unusual abundance of KKK membership records, Moore employed sophisticated quantitative techniques to assess the hooded order's rank and file. As had the other revisionists, he determined that the Klan had drawn recruits from the socioeconomic mainstream and composed a relatively balanced cross section of the white Protestant population, including many nonevangelicals; in addition, the work found almost no connection between the KKK and religious fundamentalism, thereby supplementing the findings of Cocoltchos and refuting the unsubstantiated claims of a number of earlier historians. The Klan's racist and bigoted rhetoric aside, Moore concluded that ethnic and religious tensions were not the main source of the Invisible Empire's incredible success in the Hoosier State. Far more important was widespread disenchantment with the policies of Indiana's established leaders, who appeared in many citizens' eyes to be arrogant, incompetent, and corrupt; another major factor was the impact of industrialization and economic growth, which had undermined much of the traditional cohesiveness of community life. Therefore, the Indiana Klan was essentially a "populist" movement that reflected the growing dissatisfaction that hundreds of thousands of white Protestants felt about the conduct of public affairs and the course of modern society.[27]

By the late 1980s, the number of local Klan studies had clearly reached critical mass, resulting in a new school of Klan scholarship. Based on extensive work in local sources and informed by the techniques of the new social history, this school viewed the great majority of Klansmen in the 1920s not as unreasonable men on the fringes of American life but as mainstream community activists. Because much of the revisionist scholarship had detected a struggle between the hooded order and established elites, Leonard J. Moore suggested in 1990 that this new interpretation be called "the populist revision."[28] Not all Klan revisionists are happy with this label; it is far easier to equate Moore's huge Indiana Klan with populism than, say, the embattled klaverns in Salt Lake City or El Paso, where the great bulk of "common people" were vehemently anti-Klan. Probably a better label would be the "civic activist school," which does not connote widespread public acceptance of the Invisible Empire.

The past few years have been a time of consolidation for the civic activist school. The monographs presenting this new thesis have received overwhelmingly favorable reviews in scholarly journals, and a major anthology distilling the key themes of recent scholarship was published in 1992.[29] Gradually, it appears, this revisionism has achieved a degree of professional acceptance; a recent review essay in the *American Historical Review*, for example, noted that historians of the 1920s Klan have been the "most assiduous exemplars" of an ongoing and sorely needed reexamination of right-wing social movements in twentieth-century America.[30] Meanwhile, new works have utilized fresh approaches to understanding the Klan. Among the most heralded of these is Nancy MacLean's *Behind the Mask of Chivalry: The Making of the Second Ku Klux Klan* (1994), which has innovatively applied feminist and Marxist theory to probe the special appeal that the KKK held for middle-class Americans.[31] Hopefully scholars in future years will follow MacLean's example and continue to develop new means of evaluating the Invisible Empire, for much more work remains to be done. It is very doubtful, however, that the Mecklin thesis will ever be credibly resurrected. Although Klan revisionists may disagree on certain points, they all concur that the KKK was a group that possessed strong and direct links to mainstream American society; indeed, there could be no more striking evidence of the racism and bigotry that pervaded the United States in the 1920s than the Ku Klux Klan's widespread popularity among average citizens.

Notes

1. Leonard J. Moore, "Historical Interpretations of the 1920s Klan: The Traditional View and the Populist Revision," *Journal of Social History* 24 (Winter 1990): 341–57. A slightly different version of this essay later appeared in Shawn Lay, ed., *The Invisible Empire in the West: Toward a New Historical Appraisal of the Ku Klux Klan of the 1920s* (Urbana: University of Illinois Press, 1992), 17–38.
2. Frank Tannenbaum, "The Ku Klux Klan: Its Social Origin in the South," *Century Magazine* 105 (April 1923): 873–82. This article reappeared in Tannenbaum's *Darker Phases of the South* (New York: G. P. Putnam's Sons, 1924).

3. Guy B. Johnson, "A Sociological Interpretation of the New Ku Klux Movement," *Journal of Social Forces* 1 (May 1923): 440–45.

4. Frank Bohn, "The Ku Klux Klan Interpreted," *American Journal of Sociology* 30 (Jan. 1925): 385–407.

5. John Moffatt Mecklin, *The Ku Klux Klan: A Study of the American Mind* (New York: Harcourt, Brace, and Co., 1924), 18–19, 28, 42, 45, 99–101, 109, 116, 132.

6. Mecklin, *The Ku Klux Klan*, 103. During his discussion of the "deadly monotony of small-town life" and the "petty impotence of the small-town mind," Mecklin even refers readers to the work of Sinclair Lewis. See 104–7.

7. Preston William Slosson, *The Great Crusade and After, 1924–1928* (New York: Macmillan, 1930), 308–9.

8. Frederick Lewis Allen, *Only Yesterday: An Informal History of the Nineteen-Twenties* (New York: Harper & Brothers, 1931), 65–69.

9. Wilbur J. Cash, *The Mind of the South* (New York: Alfred A. Knopf, 1941), 335–37.

10. The influence of these writers is discussed in Robert A. Goldberg, *Grassroots Resistance: Social Movements in Twentieth-Century America* (Belmont, Calif.: Wadsworth Publishing Co., 1991), 4–7.

11. Richard Hofstadter, *The Age of Reform: From Bryan to F.D.R.* (New York: Alfred A. Knopf, 1955), 291–92.

12. John Higham, *Strangers in the Land: Patterns of American Nativism, 1860–1925* (New Brunswick, N.J.: Rutgers University Press, 1955), 288, 295–97.

13. William E. Leuchtenburg, *The Perils of Prosperity, 1914–1932* (Chicago: University of Chicago Press, 1958), 209, 211.

14. Arnold S. Rice, *The Ku Klux Klan in American Politics* (Washington, D.C.: Public Affairs Press, 1962), 17; George Brown Tindall, *The Emergence of the New South, 1913–1945* (Baton Rouge: Louisiana State University Press, 1967), 190–96; David M. Chalmers, *Hooded Americanism: The First Century of the Ku Klux Klan, 1865–1965* (Garden City, N.Y.: Doubleday, 1965), 109, 114–15.

15. Seymour M. Lipset and Earl Rabb, *The Politics of Unreason: Right Wing Extremism in America, 1790–1970* (New York: Harper & Row, 1970), 110–49; Ellis W. Hawley, *The Great War and the Search for a Modern Order: A History of the American People and Their Institutions, 1917–1933* (New York: St. Martin's Press, 1979), 128–29; Geoffrey Perrett, *America in the Twenties: A History* (New York: Simon and Schuster, 1982), 72–78; Wyn Craig Wade, *The Fiery Cross: The Ku Klux Klan in America* (New York: Simon and Schuster, 1987), 140–247; David H. Bennett, *The Party of Fear: From Nativist Movements to the New Right in American History* (Chapel Hill: University of North Carolina Press, 1988), 199–237. For an discussion of these works in the context of Klan historiography, see Moore, "Historical Interpreta-

tions of the 1920s Klan," in Lay, *Invisible Empire in the West*, 17–38.

16. Emerson H. Loucks, *The Ku Klux Klan in Pennsylvania: A Study in Nativism* (Harrisburg, Penn.: Telegraph Press, 1936).

17. Norman F. Weaver, "The Knights of the Ku Klux Klan in Wisconsin, Indiana, Ohio, and Michigan" (Ph.D. dissertation, University of Wisconsin, 1954), 295–306.

18. Charles C. Alexander, *Crusade for Conformity: The Ku Klux Klan in Texas, 1920–1930* (Houston: Texas Gulf Coast Historical Association, 1962), 7, 9, and *The Ku Klux Klan in the Southwest* (Lexington: University of Kentucky Press, 1965).

19. Kenneth T. Jackson, *The Ku Klux Klan in the City, 1915–1930* (New York: Oxford University Press, 1967), 62, 108, 119–20, 240–41, 243, 245.

20. Robert A. Goldberg, "The Ku Klux Klan in Madison, 1922–1927," *Wisconsin Magazine of History* 58 (Autumn 1974): 31–44.

21. The dissertation was published as *Hooded Empire: The Ku Klux Klan in Colorado* (Urbana: University of Illinois Press, 1981). For a discussion of resource mobilization theory, see J. Craig Jenkins, "Resource Mobilization Theory and the Study of Social Movements," *Annual Review of Sociology* 9 (1983): 527–53.

22. William D. Jenkins, "The Ku Klux Klan in Youngstown, Ohio: Moral Reform in the Twenties," *Historian* 41 (Nov. 1978): 76–93, and *Steel Valley Klan: The Ku Klux Klan in Ohio's Mahoning Valley* (Kent, Ohio: Kent State University Press, 1990).

23. Kenneth D. Wald, "The Visible Empire: The Ku Klux Klan As an Electoral Movement," *Journal of Interdisciplinary History* 11 (Autumn 1980): 217–34.

24. Christopher N. Cocoltchos, "The Invisible Government and the Viable Community: The Ku Klux Klan in Orange County, California, during the 1920s" (Ph.D. dissertation, University of California, Los Angeles, 1979), ix–xiv, 612, 616, 623, 628.

25. Larry R. Gerlach, *Blazing Crosses in Zion: The Ku Klux Klan in Utah* (Logan: Utah State University Press, 1982).

26. Shawn Lay, *War, Revolution, and the Ku Klux Klan: A Study of Intolerance in a Border City* (El Paso: Texas Western Press, 1985), 158.

27. Leonard J. Moore, *Citizen Klansmen: The Ku Klux Klan in Indiana, 1921–1928* (Chapel Hill: University of North Carolina Press, 1991).

28. Moore, "Historical Interpretations of the 1920s Klan," *Journal of Social History* 24 (Winter 1990): 341–57.

29. Lay, *Invisible Empire in the West*.

30. Michael Kazin, "The Grass-Roots Right: New Histories of U.S. Conservatism in the Twentieth Century," *American Historical Review* 97 (Feb. 1992): 140.

31. Nancy MacLean, *Behind the Mask of Chivalry: The Making of the Second Ku Klux Klan* (New York: Oxford University Press, 1994).

Index